B.C.
49550

ADVANCE PRAISE FOR

The Evolutionary Rhetorical Presidency

"Twenty-five years ago Gary King issued a call to presidency scholars, urging them to collect systematic data about the operation of our chief executive. Many have answered this call. Ryan Lee Teten is the latest to do so with *The Evolutionary Rhetorical Presidency*. He has collected an amazing array of data that tells an important story about the presidency and how the institution has changed. This book is a welcome and valuable addition to the field."

*John Geer, Distinguished Professor and Chair,
Department of Political Science, and Co-Director
of the Center for the Study of Democratic Institutions,
Vanderbilt University, Nashville, Tennessee*

"All the conclusions Ryan Lee Teten draws are based on literally thousands of primary documents; he cites the pertinent scholarship in connection with new findings and then presents convincing arguments for leaving the unnatural divide of traditional/modern presidential rhetoric behind. With this study Teten proves that scholars have in fact worked on presidential rhetoric with a certain set of preconceived notions. The time has surely come to correct this misconception, and there is no doubt that scholars of presidential rhetoric and history will have to revise their traditional views."

*Wolfgang Mieder, Department of German and Russian,
University of Vermont, Burlington, Vermont*

"Are 'modern' presidents really so different from their 'traditional' predecessors regarding rhetoric? In his new book, Ryan Lee Teten argues that they are more similar than conventional wisdom suggests. Clearly written, insightful, and backed by a wealth of data, Teten's *The Evolutionary Rhetorical Presidency* is an important contribution to the body of literature on presidential rhetoric."

*Jeffrey Crouch, Assistant Professor of American Politics,
American University; Author of* The Presidential Pardon Power

The Evolutionary Rhetorical Presidency

PETER LANG
New York • Washington, D.C./Baltimore • Bern
Frankfurt • Berlin • Brussels • Vienna • Oxford

Ryan Lee Teten

The Evolutionary Rhetorical Presidency

Tracing the Changes in Presidential Address and Power

PETER LANG
New York • Washington, D.C./Baltimore • Bern
Frankfurt • Berlin • Brussels • Vienna • Oxford

Library of Congress Cataloging-in-Publication Data

Teten, Ryan Lee.
The evolutionary rhetorical presidency: tracing the changes
in presidential address and power / Ryan Lee Teten.
p. cm.
Includes bibliographical references and index.
1. Presidents—United States—History. 2. Presidents—United States—
Language—History. 3. Presidents—United States—Messages—History.
4. Political oratory—United States—History. 5. Political leadership—
United States—History. 6. Communication in politics—United States—
History. 7. Rhetoric—Political aspects—United States. I. Title.
JK511.T47   352.23'80973—dc22   2011009625
ISBN 978-1-4331-1542-4

Bibliographic information published by **Die Deutsche Nationalbibliothek**.
Die Deutsche Nationalbibliothek lists this publication in the "Deutsche
Nationalbibliografie"; detailed bibliographic data is available
on the Internet at http://dnb.d-nb.de/.

The paper in this book meets the guidelines for permanence and durability
of the Committee on Production Guidelines for Book Longevity
of the Council of Library Resources.

© 2011 Peter Lang Publishing, Inc., New York
29 Broadway, 18th floor, New York, NY 10006
www.peterlang.com

All rights reserved.
Reprint or reproduction, even partially, in all forms such as microfilm,
xerography, microfiche, microcard, and offset strictly prohibited.

Printed in Germany

To Aidan and Seth, who always help me to remember what is important
and
To my incredible wife Tonya, whose support, encouragement, and love made all of this possible.

"In his heart a man plans his course, but the Lord determines his steps."
Proverbs 16:9

TABLE OF CONTENTS

LIST OF FIGURES ix

ACKNOWLEDGMENTS xiii

I. RHETORICAL LEADERSHIP AND PRESIDENTIAL SPEECHMAKING THROUGHOUT HISTORY 1

    Presidential Rhetoric and Policymaking.. 5
    Changes Within the Presidency and Presidential Rhetoric................ 9
    Four Kinds of Presidential Address.. 15
    Defining Rhetoric as Power... 20
    Research Design and Collection of Data... 23
    The Plan of the Book and the Findings of the Study....................... 26

II. SPEAKING TO THE PEOPLE: THE USE OF POPULAR ADDRESS 31

    A "Modern" Rhetorical Presidency?.. 32
    Speaking to the People or to Congress?.. 34
    Different Forms of Rhetoric of Popular Address 37
    Identification Rhetoric... 38
    Authority Rhetoric.. 40
    Directive Rhetoric 41
    The Popular Address Rhetoric of the Declaration of
        Independence 42
    Tracing the Use of Identification Rhetoric 47
    Tracing the Use of Authority Rhetoric 70
    Tracing the Use of Directive Rhetoric.. 86
    Popular Rhetoric and Presidential Address 102

III. EXCAVATING THE BULLY PULPIT: THE FOUNDATION AND EVOLUTION OF POLICY PROPOSAL 107

    The Length of the State of the Union Address 110

The Presidency and Policy Proposition in the State of the Union
Address 114
The Presidency and Policy Proposition in the Inaugural Address........ 126
The Presidency and Policy Proposition in Presidential
Proclamations.. 136
The Presidency and Policy Proposition in Executive Orders 149
Policy and Policymaking in Presidential History 158

IV. THE BIGGER PICTURE: VISIONS FOR THE NATION AND THE WORLD 161

Visionary Speech, Policy Propositions, and Presidential Address 163
Visionary Speech in the State of the Union Address............................ 164
Visionary Speech in the Inaugural Address 171
Visionary Speech in Presidential Proclamations 177
Visionary Speech in Executive Orders 184
Visionary Policy and Presidential Rhetorical History 187

V. BACK TO THE FUTURE: A NEW UNDERSTANDING OF PRESIDENTIAL DEVELOPMENT 191

The Paradigm of the Traditional and the Modern Reconsidered........... 193
A Deeper Look at Presidential Study: Past, Present, and Future.......... 197
Directions for Further Study and Understanding 200

APPENDICES 203

Appendix A: Varying Words/Phrases Considered As Policy
Proposal/Advocacy 203
Appendix B: Examples of Policy Proposal in the State of
the Union Address from Washington to G. W. Bush........................... 205
Appendix C: Specific Words Counted/Variables Tested
in Content Analysis... 216

BIBLIOGRAPHY 217

INDEX... 227

FIGURES

1.1	The Four Different Types of Presidential Address and the Presidents and Number of Speeches Included in the Study	23
2.1	The Percentage of Popular Reference versus Congressional Address in the State of the Union Address	35
2.2	The Percentage of Identification Rhetoric in the State of the Union Address per President	47
2.3	The Average Percentage of Identification Rhetoric in Presidential Inaugurals	54
2.4	The Average Percentage of Identification Rhetoric in Presidential Proclamations	56
2.5	The Average Percentage of Identification Rhetoric in Presidential Executive Orders	57
2.6	The Percentage of Presidential Proclamations that are Holiday or Observance Related	62
2.7	The Holiday or Observance Related Proclamations Issued by George W. Bush in 2007	65
2.8	The Average Percentage of Authority Rhetoric in the State of the Union Address per President	70
2.9	The Average Percentage of Authority Rhetoric in Presidential Inaugural Addresses	74
2.10	The Average Percentage of Authority Rhetoric in Presidential Proclamations	80
2.11	The Average Percentage of Authority Rhetoric in Presidential Executive Orders	80
2.12	The Average Percentage of Directive Rhetoric in the State of the Union Address per President	87

2.13	The Average Percentage of Directive Rhetoric in Presidential Inaugural Addresses	91
2.14	The Average Percentage of Directive Rhetoric in Presidential Proclamations	96
2.15	The Average Percentage of Directive Rhetoric in Presidential Executive Orders	96
3.1	The Number of Words per State of the Union Address per Year	110
3.2	The Average Word Number per State of the Union Address per President	111
3.3	The Average Number of Policies Proposed per State of the Union Address per President	114
3.4	The Average Total Number of Policies Proposed per "Traditional" and "Modern" Period With Wilson as Demarcation Point	122
3.5	The Average Policy Numbers Proposed per 1000 Words per President in the State of the Union Address	124
3.6	The Average Number of Total Policies Proposed in the Inaugural Address per President	127
3.7	The Average Number of Policies Proposed per 1000 Words of the Inaugural Address per President	134
3.8	The Percentage of Policies Proposed in a Non-Holiday or Observance Related Proclamation	137
3.9	The Average Number of Policies Proposed per Presidential Proclamation per President	139
3.10	The Average Number of Policies Proposed per 1000 Words of Presidential Proclamations per President	148
3.11	Average Number of Policies Proposed per Executive Order per President	150
3.12	The Average Number of Policies Proposed per 1000 Words of Executive Orders Per President	156
4.1	The Average Number of Visionary Policies Proposed per State of the Union Address	165

List of Figures

4.2	The Average Number of Visionary Policies Proposed per 1000 Words of the State of the Union Address	169
4.3	The Average Number of Visionary Policies Proposed per Inaugural Address	172
4.4	The Average Number of Visionary Policies Proposed per 1000 Words of the Inaugural Address	176
4.5	The Average Number of Visionary Policies Proposed per Presidential Proclamation	178
4.6	The Average Number of Visionary Policies Proposed per 1000 Words of Presidential Proclamations	183
4.7	The Average Number of Visionary Policies Proposed per Executive Order	184
4.8	The Average Number of Visionary Policies Proposed per 1000 Words of Executive Order	185

ACKNOWLEDGMENTS

I WOULD like to firstly thank God for providing me with patience, guidance, support, and for using me to complete his master plan. Through him all things are possible. This work would not be possible without the support, encouragement, and guidance of different members of the discipline. I am indebted to Dr. John Geer, Dr. Bruce Oppenheimer, Dr. David Woodard, and Dr. Geoff Layman for the critiques and suggestions that they provided not only for the enrichment of the study, but toward the shaping of this project as a work that would stand in our discipline and against the rigors of peer review. I would also like to thank *Presidential Studies Quarterly* and *Political Research Quarterly*, for granting reprint of previously published work.

I am especially grateful for the continuing support from Dr. David Woodard and Dr. John Geer. Dr. Woodard has been a model of a teacher, father, and husband whom I could only hope to emulate some day. He and his wife have been there for my family during times of trial and tribulation with unflagging support. Dr. John Geer provided me with the model of a mentor, teacher, researcher, and friend that stands as testament to his care and consideration. He was infinitely supportive and able to challenge my research and scholarship so that it could rise to new levels. I can never give enough credit here for what he has taught me.

Lastly, I would like to thank my family. They have been the most important support structure in the pursuit of my degree and the completion of this book. I cannot thank my sisters enough for their encouragement and I ask for their forgiveness for missed births and graduations. My parents, Arnold and Carolyn, and my mother-in-law, Ruby Baugus, have also been unfailing in their support. Most importantly, I would like to thank my loving wife Tonya for unending patience, and my two wonderful children Aidan and Seth who never failed to inspire me or keep my priorities straight. They have had patience with my non-stop typing and I look forward to once again becoming the Teten Family.

CHAPTER I

Rhetorical Leadership and Presidential Speechmaking Throughout History

ON THE eve of January 29, 2002, George W. Bush delivered a State of the Union Address in an atmosphere like the nation had not seen in almost sixty years. On the heels of September 11, 2001, and the deaths of nearly 3000 individuals, the president spent over half of the State of the Union Address proposing plans to fight domestic and foreign terrorism. He spoke in abstract terms, telling the nation that, "tens of thousands of trained terrorists are still at large. These enemies view the entire world as a battlefield, and we must pursue them wherever they are." He then spoke concerning terrorism stating, "Our nation will continue to be steadfast and patient and persistent in the pursuit of two great objectives. First, we will shut down terrorist camps, disrupt terrorist plans, and bring terrorists to justice. And, second, we must prevent the terrorists and regimes who seek chemical, biological or nuclear weapons from threatening the United States and the world. But some governments will be timid in the face of terror. And make no mistake about it: If they do not act, America will." He continued with even more rhetoric on specific policies and goals. "We need to replace aging aircraft and make our military more agile, to put our troops anywhere in the world quickly and safely. Our men and women in uniform deserve the best weapons, the best equipment, the best training—and they also deserve another pay raise. My budget includes the largest increase in defense spending in two decades—because while the price of freedom and security is high, it is never too high. Whatever it costs to defend our country, we will pay."

The modern-day State of the Union Address is undeniably one rhetorical tool that presidents today use to convey their thoughts, propose their own programs and policies, communicate with the public, leave their legacies and set the tone for new administrations. The examination above of the State of the Union Address of George W. Bush in 2002 illustrates many different aspects of presidential rhetoric today. The President was able to speak to the people and address issues, both in the abstract and in their most specific sense, and still propose his policy agenda while doing so. He utilized the State of the Union Address to convey his goals and objectives in both large and small terms in order to get the information to the American people and Congress, and to initiate policy on Capitol Hill. In addition, Bush noted his place in American and world history as the leader that presided over the United States on September 11th, 2001, and as the leader who would determine guilt for the crime and administer justice. Finally, Bush also used many rhetorical techniques of address, speaking as a citizen of the United States, as a member of the governing body in America, and as the president of the United States, passing policy recommendations to Congress in order to make his positions known and advocate the policy objectives he sought to be accomplished.

Notably, however, this kind of policy activism and popular address is not often viewed as a tendency of the presidencies of the 18th and 19th centuries, and certainly not as a characteristic of the founding presidents of the nation. Instead, much of the study tends to ascribe, at times, to the tenets of a "traditional/modern" divide: a categorization of the presidents into two eras on the basis of their rhetoric, their political activity, and, also, their seeming value for academic investigation. Those presidents that governed before the early 1900's are largely dismissed as being more rhetorically stagnant and politically less innovative than their twentieth century counterparts. These presidents of old are allegedly bound by the propriety of their position and the constraints placed on them by the constitution. It does not take long, however, to determine that this kind of stereotyping of presidential rhetoric and history is problematic at best. Even though they are often dismissed as less characteristic of modern rhetoric and presidential behavior, even the earliest State of the Union addresses suggest differently. For example, on January 8, 1790, George Washington approached the podium in front of a joint session of Congress to deliver the first State of the Union Address in presidential history. Although some scholars have suggested that this Address simply updated prior congressional policy and informed the Congress on the relations with foreign countries (Campbell and Jamieson, 1990), a close examination of the text illustrates that much more is being presented.

Washington was indeed the country's first and unanimous choice for president. During the struggle of the colonies against the accused tyranny of King George, Washington had been one of the most able generals in the Revolutionary Army and one of the most clever tacticians, as seen in his Christmas Day crossing of the Delaware to defeat the Hessians who were drunk, asleep, and unprepared; this turned the tide of the Revolutionary effort against Britain. Indeed, his presence as presiding officer at the Constitutional Convention, although he was largely silent, gave stability to the proceedings and a feeling to the delegates that they were both in capable hands and that they were civilly following the operations of government-building. "Both at Philadelphia and in the ensuing months, Americans of every viewpoint seemed to have assumed that there was only one man who could and would inaugurate the presidential office: General Washington" (Cunliffe, 1971, 8). Even those suspicious of the new system of government kept their oppositional rumblings to "other features of the constitution, or—like Franklin—on the hazards that would befall America after Washington had gone" (Cunliffe, 1971, 9). Washington himself was hesitant about accepting this post which could seemingly go to no one else. He worried about the neglect of his affairs at Mount Vernon, the distance from his family, the possibility that his reputation and service to the country would be dragged through the mud if challengers arose, and, at 56 years old, that he had already given many years in the service of the United States; however, when the vote was tallied, each of the 69 electors had cast their vote for George Washington.

The first State of the Union Address, however, was not simply an Address by a hesitant president, unsure of his position and worried about his future. Washington did more than simply summarize the state of the colonies; he proposed many policies that succeeding presidents would also advocate and expand upon. Giving the address on the heels of the Revolutionary War, a president who was afraid to act would surely not delve immediately into the necessity of armaments and weapons of war; however, that is exactly what Washington did. He addressed Congress with authority, suggesting,

> "among the many interesting objects which will engage your attention that of providing for the common defense will merit particular regard. To be prepared for war is one of the most effectual means of preserving peace. A free people ought not only to be armed, but disciplined; to which end a uniform and well-digested plan is requisite; and their safety and interest require that they should promote such manufacto-

ries as tend to render them independent of others for essential, particularly military, supplies."

After making this military stand for the necessity of the troops, he continued to propose that, "the proper establishment of the troops which may be deemed indispensable will be entitled to mature consideration. In the arrangements which may be made respecting it will be of importance to conciliate the comfortable support of the officers and soldiers with a due regard to economy. We ought to be prepared to afford protection to those parts of the Union, and, if necessary, to punish aggressors." For many years to come, this propriety of a standing army would be a point of discussion between Congress and the presidency.

As a former General, Washington did not limit his policy proposals to military aspects of the colonies. He proposed that "various considerations also render it expedient that the terms on which foreigners may be admitted to the rights of citizens should be speedily ascertained by a uniform rule of naturalization." In addition he proposed that, "uniformity in the currency, weights, and measures of the United States is an object of great importance, and will, I am persuaded, be duly attended to." Washington boldly touched on the emerging economic, educational, and postal concerns of the nation, directing the Congress towards the subjects that he believed were of greatest import for the fledgling country.

> "The advancement of agriculture, commerce, and manufactures by all proper means will not, I trust, need recommendation; but I can not forbear intimating to you the expediency of giving effectual encouragement as well to the introduction of new and useful inventions from abroad as to the exertions of skill and genius in producing them at home, and of facilitating the intercourse between the distant parts of our country by a due attention to the post-office and post-roads...Nor am I less persuaded that you will agree with me in opinion that there is nothing which can better deserve your patronage than the promotion of science and literature...Whether this desirable object will be best promoted by affording aids to seminaries of learning already established, by the institution of a national university, or by any other expedients will be well worthy of a place in the deliberations of the legislature."

A national university, promotions of sciences and literature, and encouragement of invention were policies that even the very first president saw as indispensable. And, far from simple reports on naval positions or the budgetary situations of the country, Washington's Address included policy advocacy similar to that proposed by presidents almost two hundred years later.

The purpose of this book is twofold. Primarily, the book examines what kind of differences, if any, have emerged throughout the history of the presidency in the ways in which presidential address has been used as well as its function. A part of this larger observation will be an examination of the "traditional/ modern" divide and which of its tenets may indeed be accurate characterizations of any rhetorical shifts that may have taken place in presidential address. In addition, this study examines a larger number of presidential documents than many other examinations; this will enable the book to provide a detailed and discerning look at the evolution of, or innovations in presidential rhetoric, behavior, and political activity. In order to answer these questions, I conducted a line-by-line reading of over nine thousand executive addresses and speeches in order to provide a more nuanced insight. This study contains data and a line-by-line reading and rhetorical examinations of all 226 State of the Union Addresses, all 58 Presidential Inaugural Addresses, 3,857 Executive Orders, and 5,022 Presidential Proclamations through George W. Bush.[1] By utilizing all of these pieces of presidential rhetoric to evaluate the changes in presidential address that have taken place, I am able to provide one of the more complete evaluations of the evolution of presidential rhetoric as well as the differences that may be present from one century to the next.

Presidential Rhetoric and Policymaking

The variety of rhetoric exhibited by George W. Bush in the 2001 State of the Union Address, as well as the appeal to different levels of the audience in order to achieve his goals is no strange shock to the listening ears of the American community. However, that which was demonstrated above by George Washington might be. From "going public" to achieve his plans and goals as described by Samuel Kernell (1997), to bargaining with the public and Congress as observed by Richard Neustadt (1960), the contemporary president uses his rhetorical skills for many different purposes and to many different ends. After all, "a president who wishes to lead a nation rather than

---

[1] These numbers, especially regarding the executive orders and the presidential proclamations, represent the number of presidential addresses that could be obtained and analyzed electronically. The primary source for their collection was the American Presidency Project (www.presidency.ucsb.edu/index.php) begun by John Woolley and Gerhard Peters at the University of California, Santa Barbara. It is currently updated and maintained by Gerhard Peters.

only the executive branch must be a loquacious president...Speeches are the core of the modern presidency" (Gelderman, 1997, 8-9). But to those who may advocate a distinction between a "traditional" presidential era and a "modern" presidential era, it is asserted that this kind of behavior was not always associated with our chief executive. Indeed, it is asserted that in the 19th century, and especially during the time of Washington in the 18th century, presidential policy activism, as well as public appeal in the content of addresses, was not only infrequent, it was discouraged.

One scholar of the traditional/modern divide, Jeffrey Tulis (1987), proposed that "most of the presidents in the 19th century were constrained by settled practices and the doctrine behind them" (79). He characterized this 'doctrine' of the 18th and 19th century presidencies as a *lack* of policy proposal, *lack* of public appeals, and an absence of public speaking in general, or popular rhetoric (viewed as pandering to the masses). This was, in effect, the "traditional" presidency. Tulis stated that "popular rhetoric was proscribed in the 19th century because it could manifest demagoguery, impede deliberation, and subvert the routines of republican governance" (95). Presidents, according to Tulis, could have acted and spoken the way that they do today, but instead obeyed a "common-law" doctrine of governance that separated itself from popular rhetoric and position-taking and adhered itself to the constraints and formality of the Constitution.

On the other hand, beginning with the benchmark presidency of Wilson, Tulis saw the "modern" rhetorical presidency with "three broad 20th century changes: (1) Less rhetoric would be addressed primarily to Congress and more to the people at large; (2) more emphasis would be placed upon oral speeches and less upon written messages; and (3) the above two changes would bring with them a change in structure of argument, with the 20th century sample manifesting structures more appropriate to 'inspirational' and 'policy stand' rhetoric" (138). The "modern" therefore was the antithesis of the "traditional" in that the presidents spoke with vision, advocated many policy positions, and talked to the people. Tulis has viewed the change from the "traditional" to the "modern" as a significant transformation in the institution as opposed to an evolution of the powers and activity of the office.

This distinction between two eras of presidential activity as well as the two classifications with which to measure presidential activity, greatness, and popular leadership have their merits. Changes in technology as well as presidential responsibilities suggest that there are major differences between the presidents of the past and the presidents of today. However, the dichotomy does raise issues of over simplifying the changes that have taken place throughout the presidential past. Unfortunately, the "traditional/modern" divide has become too easy of a way to conceptualize an understanding of the presidency and its officeholders. As example, one examination of the State of the Union Address and its development, by editors Deborah Kalb, Gerhard Peters, and John T. Woolley, is entitled *State of the Union: Presidential rhetoric from Woodrow Wilson to George W. Bush* (December 2006). The problem with the study is that it fails to include any "traditional" presidents in its look at the ways the presidents have appealed to the public.

Even though the paradigm of the traditional versus the modern can be utilized as a shortcut to presidential study, some scholars have asserted that there is a danger that this approach may be too quickly adopted without full evaluation. As suggested by David Nichols (1994), the "traditional/modern" dichotomy resembles a disproven myth to the discipline in one large respect—"it has been accepted largely on faith. There has been little scholarly work devoted to defining and outlining the development of the 'modern presidency.' While many works use the term, few bother to provide a precise definition or account of its origins" (Nichols, 1994, 2).

Taking this lead, other scholars, such as Halford Ryan (1993), Smith and Smith (1985, 1990, 1994), Colin Seymore-Ure (1982), Richard Ellis (1998), Ellis and Kirk (1998), Laracey (2002), Lim (2002), Dorsey (2002), Zarefsky (2002), Lucas (2002), Andrews (2002), Beasley (2004), and Greenstein (2000; 2006) have further examined the rhetorical past of the presidency in order to discover clues about how it began, when it changed, and the implications of this institutional shift for our political process. Drawing evidence from presidential rhetoric, these scholars attempt to trace the evolution of the modern-day president. This effort involves not only identifying trends in the presidency, but also clarifying which presidents, if any, were responsible for these changes.

These numerous previous presidential rhetorical studies have great merits, and this book attempts to build from their findings to provide a more refined and nuanced understanding of the evolution of the contemporary presidency and presidential rhetoric by utilizing several different forms of presidential address that have been delivered consistently from the founding to the present. In particular, I make use of State of the Union Addresses, Presidential Inaugurals, Executive Orders, and Presidential Proclamations from George Washington to George W. Bush to examine format changes, rhetorical shifts, presidential policy-pushing, and changes that might be able to be attributed to one era of presidents or another. Others have made use of presidential address, but not in as systematic or complete of fashion as I propose. Exactly if and when changes took place, and why, therefore remains in dispute (Gamm and Smith 1998; Tulis 1998; Milkis 1998; Kernell 1997). My hope is that a systematic look at the rhetorical behavior of presidents, through several consistent medium can shed more light on these important issues.

The findings detailed herein do not fully support suggestions that a "modern" rhetorical presidency began with Theodore Roosevelt as argued by some (Gamm and Smith 1998; Milkis 1998; Kernell 1997), Franklin Delano Roosevelt, Eisenhower (Smith and Smith 1990; Greenstein 1977, 1978, 1982, 2000), or Woodrow Wilson (Tulis 1987); I do not find a strong empirical basis to such claims. Nor do my findings support the general adoption or use of a "traditional/modern" demarcation (Liebovich, 2001; Pfiffner, 2000; Rozell and Peterson, 1997; Stuckey, 1997; Campbell, 1996; Shaw, 1987; Landy, 1985; Greenstein et al, 1977; Polsby, 1973; McConnell, 1967). Instead, it appears that presidential rhetoric may not be easily categorized as simply "traditional" or "modern" and may not be easily parsed into separate categories. Many of the elements discussed by Tulis in his work, such as policy proposal and the use of popular rhetoric, seem to appear throughout both the "traditional" and "modern" periods; in fact, some "traditional" presidents exhibit more "modern" characteristics in certain forms of address than do those presidents classified as "modern" themselves. Consequently, it is important that assumptions and generalizations set forth by a clear division of the presidents into two separate eras be carefully re-examined and approached cautiously at best.

This book is not an attempt to simply take issue with the "traditional" versus the "modern" presidencies (Greenstein 2000; Bimes and Skowronek 1998) or presidential development of policy and agenda (Hill 1998; Cohen 1995; Ragsdale 1987; Brace and Hinckley 1991; Parry-Giles 2001; Gleiber and Shull 1999)[2]. Instead, this study approaches the presidential rhetorical tradition itself from a wider view and looks at the developments and innova-

---

[2] I do not attempt to comprehensively address or debate such important issues as the changes in campaigns, elections, congressional relations, and political parties as examined by Peabody (2001), Powell (1999), Dahl (1990), Gamm and Smith (1998), Lowi (1985), Skowronek (1997) and Schlesinger (1973) that have had significant impact on our understanding of the institution of the presidency and the operation therein.

tions from the outset of the nation to the present day. The addresses that will guide the examination are the consistent medium of the State of the Union Address, the Inaugural address, the executive order and the presidential proclamation. The availability of each type of presidential rhetoric across nearly all presidents make them sources that can be compared in order to mark changes in rhetoric, behavior, address, and policy proposition.

In this study, I specifically compare such things as number of words, content, specific word usage, policy proposal, and visionary speech across all these forms of executive address in order to gain insight into the political activity of past presidents such as Polk and Arthur, who might have been previously overlooked. I also hope to be better able to fully trace and add understanding to the development of presidential rhetoric by discussing what appears to be a gradual evolution of rhetorical innovations that involves every past officeholder, as opposed to an individual transformation of presidential speech that is the result of an individual president during the twentieth century and his effort at rhetorical change. My collection of addresses, due to its comprehensiveness, provides the opportunity to better test a host of questions about the changing nature of the chief executive. This type of examination can help to broaden our understanding by providing a much more complete overall picture of what we speak of when we reference presidential rhetoric and its eras and evolution.

Changes Within the Presidency and Presidential Rhetoric

It is clear that the American presidency has changed since its inception in 1788. Through congressional cession of authority and administration, the office of the presidency has expanded its original powers. It no longer consists of only a president and his secretary (whom Washington was forced to pay out of his own pocket before budgetary approval from Congress), but is now an institution with extensive executive offices, a huge staff, and many financial and budgetary duties. A new president will make over 3000 appointments and preside over an Executive Office that will encompass over 1600 staff members and have a budget of over 200 million dollars (Edwards and Wayne, 1997, 180). The president today is presented with more media outlets, as well as coverage, than ever before (Laracey 2002; Kumar 2001; Hart et al 1996; Dayan and Katz 1992). The office of the presidency has gained global influence as well. The media has displayed images of presidents from Nixon to George H.W. Bush to Barack Obama touring the third world and speaking at international summits. It has even shown presidents such as Carter and Clinton, attempting intervention in peace processes between war-torn countries, and presidents such as Bush and Clinton coming together to seek relief for Hurricane and Tsunami victims.

To say much has changed in the office of the presidency is beyond denial. The problem arises when scholars attempt to re-examine the presidential rhetorical past for specific individuals who have altered the office to the extent that there can be a clear before and after picture of the executive. Among others, Tulis has claimed that, "since the presidencies of Theodore Roosevelt and Woodrow Wilson, popular or mass rhetoric has become the principle tool of presidential governance" (Tulis, 1987, 4). He also makes the claim that in the "traditional" period, "presidents preferred written communication between the branches of government to oral addresses to 'the people'...Very few were domestic policy speeches of the sort so common now, and attempts to move the nation by moral suasion in the absence of war were almost unknown" (Tulis, 1987, 5-6).

This conception of the presidency is problematic because, although it seeks to provide us with an understanding of the way that things have dramatically changed under a single president, it fails to give consideration to the fact that popular rhetoric might have been used within written Addresses or that presidential address was commonly carried in the medium of newspaper, and would reach the public and have the possibility of popular appeal long before 1900. This approach also, if misunderstood could lead new scholars to the belief that that presidents of the 18th and 19th centuries proposed no policy at all, or that those who did propose policy, did so with different motivations than contemporary presidents. In addition, it could be assumed that these "old" presidents did not speak to the people, or invoke the reasoning of the constituency in policy proposition and advocacy (in other words, utilize popular address rhetoric) as the presidents of the "new" may do.

Before adopting the belief that only presidents since Wilson or other early 20th century presidents truly and accurately represent contributions to the contemporary presidency, a much closer examination in needed to accurately conclude that the presidents before this time were incapable of the same kind of activity and rhetoric. Most significantly, however, the attempt to separate presidents into different categorizations on the basis of their eras of being, does not truly account for the possibility that presidents have always had a motivation to act on the policies and environment that has surrounded them, regardless of their time or place.

Instead, it would behoove scholars, historians, and followers of the presidency to look at the entire history of presidential rhetoric and action to better characterize the actions, behavior, and proclivities of any presidents who came to govern during the past and the trends that appear. This type of general and sweeping study helps to examine the possibility that as the domestic and international demands on the office of the executive have increased since the founding, so each successive president has adapted his Address and behavior to deal with the changing and increasingly pressing contexts.

Many scholars in the field of the presidency have conducted numerous studies in an effort to provide insights into the developments and innovations in presidential address and rhetoric. One of the seminal works in this genre, Jeffrey Tulis' study, *The Rhetorical Presidency,* sees differences that emerge between a "traditional" and a "modern" era of the presidency. Tulis develops this dichotomy on the basis of a sampling of 900 presidential documents from the 19th and 20th centuries. "His account which emphasizes the impact of a new rhetorical norm established by Woodrow Wilson, is fast becoming the conventional wisdom" (Gamm and Smith, 1998, 87). Although he claims that "one purpose of the book is to articulate a series of explicitly systemic perspectives with which to identify and assess change and development in the American presidency" (Tulis, 1987, 9), his work tends to suffer from various methodological weaknesses that lead to questions concerning generalizability and conclusions.

As one example, his sample consists of "a considerable number of documents to be read and coded—just over 900" (1987, 138). This sample derives from a collection of "the entire nineteenth-century corpus of presidential messages and papers, commissioned by Congress and compiled by James D. Richardson…our major source for the twentieth century is the set of public papers extending from Truman through the third year of Carter's term" (1987, 137). He selects a random sample from each of the available documents from each decade; yet, "because my primary sample could produce few examples of two important categories of rhetoric, Inaugural addresses and State of the Union messages, I supplemented it with another, composed of all of Inaugural and State of the Union messages in both centuries" (1987, 137). In addition, Tulis uses each document as the level of analysis for coding according to whether or not the document itself could be classified into one of four categories: developed argument, series of arguments, list of points, and mixed (series and list). On the basis of these methodologies, Tulis concludes that "not only do we have presidential 'speech' today, whereas there was virtually none in the previous century," but also that "none of the nineteenth-century messages...were characterized as 'lists'" (1987, 139; 142).

These findings are indeed consistent with his data, yet the further generalizations concerning the policy activity of the president as well as the innovations of the Wilson presidency on the basis of the conclusions above are weakened due to inconsistencies in data collection. His sample of 20th century presidential documents presents papers from only 7 of the 13 presidents at the time and he also only deals glancing blows to examination of a few 19th century presidents, examining single speeches of only 7 of the 23 presidents preceding Theodore Roosevelt to make his conclusions of the inactivity of the "traditional" presidents. This study hopes to re-examine Tulis' conclusions within the context of a larger collection of consistently delivered presidential addresses to provide depth of analysis concerning the conclusion that Wilson is the father of the "modern rhetorical presidency" and the proposal of different periods in presidential address.

Other scholars have also come to their own conclusions concerning the possible origins of a "modern" presidency as well. Greenstein looks at the "modern" rhetorical presidency beginning only with Franklin Roosevelt (Greenstein, 2000, 12-13); Kernell samples presidents since Hoover (Kernell, 1997, 107-114); and Theodore Lowi's study emphasizes the period subsequent to 1932 (Lowi, 1985). In "Presidents, Parties, and the Public: Evolving Patterns of Interaction, 1877-1929" (1998), Gerald Gamm and Renee Smith take the beneficial step of looking further into the past to study presidential rhetoric, evolution, and change. These scholars reflect on rhetoric both further into the past and dealing with specific audiences in order to gain insight into presidential rhetoric and function.

Some in the field have examined presidential address across all presidents, and patterns and differences between presidential address and address makers. Studies by Beasley (2001a, 2001b), and Benoit (1999) examine presidential Inaugural addresses, local addresses to specific audiences, and nomination acceptance addresses. Jeffrey Cohen's study (1995) does examine a sample of State of the Union Addresses, and looks at policy implications of the Address as opposed to its reflection on the "traditional" or "modern" presidency debate or the overall development of presidential rhetoric and address.

Lim (2002) takes another step forward with a computer content analysis of the body of State of the Union Addresses and presidential Inaugurals to make several characterizations of the contemporary president. However, this type of content analysis which consists of counting the occurrences of individual words may miss implicit elements or meanings within presidential rhetoric. By relying on the repetition of words in an address to symbolize a particular policy or assertion, the study has the possibility of missing the context in which the word is situated. For example, Lim's study suggests that today's presidential rhetoric is more democratic because pronouns of "family" as well as the word "America" occur with more frequency since Wilson and Theodore Roosevelt. The problem is that "democracy" and "family" word repetitions may not indicate democratic speech at all, but simply a greater awareness by the speaker of the audience and their identifications.

In his collection, *The Presidency and Rhetorical Leadership* (2002), Leroy Dorsey and other scholars engage the division of presidential history into different eras and, apart from looking at the important theme of prudential leadership, raise excellent questions regarding the true place of the founders in the rhetorical tradition. Dorsey, as editor, explains that, under the "traditional/modern" divide, "rhetoric has no meaningful place when the president is envisioned primarily as constitutional leader" (6), as is suggested by Tulis and others under the "first constitution" of behavior. One contributor, David Zarefsky, argues that "the 'modern presidency' sometimes is said to have begun with World War II, and presidential scholarship sometimes seems preoccupied with the last eleven presidents to the neglect of the first thirty one" (2002, 23). Another author, Stephen Lucas, examines George Washington specifically and suggests that he "judiciously adopted traditional rhetorical forms to the new occasions and exigencies faced by the world's first modern republican nation…In the process, he not only met the rhetorical needs of the moment, but he created precedents for presidential discourse that endure to this day" (2002, 46). Although they look at singular presidents for the most part, they also have sought information regarding the evolution of presidential rhetoric and the detriments of "rhetorical stereotyping" that can occur with segmenting the history of the presidency.

Mel Laracey's study (2002) also challenges the assertions of a "traditional/modern" division by exposing different mediums by which presidents in the nineteenth century "go public," and in this way attempts to reject both

Kernell (1997) and Tulis' (1987) assertions that only "modern" (twentieth century) presidents "go public." Laracey examines the question of "Why did presidents of old supposedly avoid going public? The only answer even proposed [by Tulis] is that these presidents did not want to express their positions on policy matters" (3). His study finds that "it is important to avoid imposing our current technologically colored conception of public policy rhetoric on the past" and "that the presidency has, virtually from its inception, contained a component of 'going public'"(Laracey, 2002, 8-9). Through a close examination of presidential public communication, Laracey portends that it is not "fair to assert, as Tulis does, that going public is a wholly new development at odds with the original understanding of government expressed in the constitution of 1789" (Laracey, 2002, 162). He looks at newspaper communications between the president and the public, the transmission of presidential rhetoric (such as the State of the Union Address) through the media, as well as the public communication philosophies of various presidents in his work. The conclusion he reaches concerning going public is contrary to such scholars as Tulis (1987), Kernell (1997), and Greenstein (2000), and proposes that "the answer may well be that nineteenth-century policy making was not all that different from our current process, in which public opinion, bargaining, and deliberation play a role."

In *You the People: American National Identity in Presidential Rhetoric* (2004), Vanessa Beasley takes one of the most comprehensive steps, and looks at Inaugurals and State of the Union addresses since 1885 and the ability of presidents to engage and define the identity of the American people, minorities, and women in society. Indeed, she explains that one of her goals "has been to suggest that, in some senses at least, presidential rhetoric may vary little from president to president" (155). She finds, among many important observations, that the rhetorical presidency may be less a transformation originating with an individual president, and more "an institutional response to the United States' increasing diversity" (7). Presidents from the late-nineteenth century to the present, have simply confronted the "problems and policies from their predecessors and in these inheritances establish parameters that, along with constitutional provisions and congressional assistance, dictate much of what a chief executive can or cannot do" (154). In addition, she suggests that "scholars seeking more complete theories of the presidency may want to pay closer attention to these long term patterns" (Beasley, 2004, 155).

I first would like to acknowledge that this book does not claim to be a panacea for the difficulty faced in conducting research on the presidency. As Gary King explains, "the process of reducing real world phenomena to published work involves two phases: the representation of the real world by essentially descriptive quantitative and qualitative data, and the analysis of these data. Both phases are important components of the replication standard. Future scholars, with only your publication and other information you provide, ought to be able to start from the real world and arrive at the same substantive conclusions. In many types of research this is not possible, but it should always be attempted" (King, 1995, 445). The study of the presidency is one of the categories into which collecting complete, systematic samples and producing clear and generalizable results is very difficult.

However, it is of utmost importance to apply the same rigor to the study of the presidency as to all areas of political science. In this way, I have attempted to build on Tulis' and other prior studies by attempting to provide a more consistent and complete picture of presidential rhetoric and behavior. My study examines four types of presidential address (the State of the Union Address, Inaugural Address, executive Order, and Presidential Proclamation)—not just for the keywords that might appear with frequency, or using the whole address as a level of analysis—but instead, by a line by line reading of each, to determine how these words are properly situated and procure a better idea of the message that is trying to be sent by the president. By expanding not only the timeline of some of the studies above, but also conducting a thorough examination of consistently delivered presidential addresses, I here hope to shed more light on the evolutional development of the contemporary rhetorical presidency and the understanding of presidential policy proposal and activity from the founding to the present.

Four Kinds of Presidential Address

The State of the Union Address, the Inaugural Address, Executive Orders, and Presidential Proclamations are particularly good mediums through which to examine presidential communication because they have their origins in the Constitution and the founding, and have been utilized by George Washington and every subsequent president to the present day. For example, the executive branch, as part of accountability to the Congress, and no doubt part of the system of checks and balances established in the constitution, was expected to inform the legislative branch of presidential desires, observations, and general thoughts on a yearly basis. This excerpt in the Constitution became the foundation of the State of the Union Address:

> "Article 2, Section 3. He shall from time to time give to the Congress Information of the State of the Union, and recommend to their Consideration such Measures as he shall judge necessary and expedient; he may, on extraordinary Occasions, convene both Houses, or either of them, and in case of Disagreement between them, with Respect to the Time of Adjournment, he may Adjourn them to such time as he shall think proper; he shall receive Ambassadors and other public Ministers; he shall take Care that the Laws be faithfully executed, and shall Commission all the Officers of the United States."

At the time of Washington's first State of the Union Address, the Address was simply known as the "Annual Message to Congress" (Tulis, 1987, 55). He delivered the address live to both houses of the Congress. John Adams kept with Washington's style of brief address and live delivery throughout his presidency as well.

However, with the swearing in of Thomas Jefferson, the format of delivery of the state of the union would change for almost 113 years (Tulis, 1987, 56). Jefferson, feeling that a delivery of a speech to both houses of Congress likened itself to a king's pronouncement, ended the live delivery of the address and sent it instead in letter format for the legislative branch to read. He felt this move would end a "speech from the throne" and simplify the way the federal government operated (Tulis, 1987, 56). From that time, presidents then continued to send the address in letter form to the Congress. Early presidents also had freedom about when to give the address, or even to give an address at all. There was little following of the short structure of the founding presidents, and the addresses grew drastically in length.

In 1913, Woodrow Wilson, revived the delivery of the Address in person to the Legislative branch. In 1923, Coolidge was the first to utilize new technology in the United States, and used the radio for the public address. In 1934, Franklin Delano Roosevelt officially made the Address a permanent fixture of the presidential duties and set a standard for its yearly-required delivery. These changes to the address culminated in 1945, when the annual communication officially became known as "The State of the Union Address." The Address then saw further technological advance in 1947, as Truman's State of the Union was the first to be televised. Although televised, this Address took place during the day. In 1965, Johnson shifted the Address from midday to evening televised delivery.

Each technological change was an attempt to enable the public to be witness to and obtain more political information from the Address. And although the consumption of that knowledge is debatable—given the decline in current and historical voting turnout—technology has become a new weapon in the arsenal of the politically active president. Widespread media broadcast has become the permanent standard for the Address, and presidents now are able to use the medium of satellite television and even the internet to update the Congress and the world on the state of the nation, as well as to propose programs, legislative action, and address the people of the United States.

As such, the State of the Union Address provides a particularly good foundation from which to examine the development of presidential rhetoric, and the "traditional/ modern" presidential dichotomy. As mentioned above, it is constitutionally mandated in nature, and its consistent audience (Congress and the people), make the address an excellent source from which to analyze content. In addition, from the founding, the State of the Union Address has been widely available and disseminated to the public whether delivered in written or in oral form (Tulis, 1987, 16; Laracey, 2002). For example, the full text of the very first State of the Union Address by George Washington, delivered on January 8, 1790, was published less than two weeks later by the newspaper the *Massachusetts Spy* on January 21, 1790 (http://www.lexrex.com/enlightened/writings/wash1.html). As Charles Beard reflected, "Whatever may be its purport, the message is the one great public document of the United States which is widely read and discussed" (Quoted in Campbell and Jamieson, 1990, 52).

Because of the consistency of delivery as well as context, analysis of the Inaugural address is another way to trace rhetorical and political activity and development of the presidents of the United States. This is true despite the proposal, discussed by Campbell and Jamieson (1985), that Inaugurals present a different style of presidential rhetoric that possesses a more ceremonial tone. "Inaugurals unify the country…discuss shared values and standards rather than divisive issues…establish the president's suitability by noting the awe in which they hold the office, the potential for power excesses, and their personal humility and responsibility in the face of this role…They provide the president with a highly symbolic moment in which to address history as well as a nation" (Smith and Smith, 1990, 238). However, even though the Inaugural is a more ceremonial speech, this book will illustrate that presidents have utilized this form of rhetoric to set policy goals and priorities for the new administration as well as for the country.

In addition to being another rhetorical weapon in the president's arsenal, the Inaugural address is also a constitutionally mandated presidential speech that has been consistently delivered by presidents from Washington to George W. Bush, and that has always played a major role in the rhetorical development and power of the presidency. In Article II, Section I, the constitution states that the president must take the following oath upon entrance to the office: "I do solemnly swear (or affirm) that I will faithfully execute the office of President of the United States, and will to the best of my ability, preserve, protect and defend the Constitution of the United States." On April 30, 1789, George Washington was the first president to take part in the swearing in, and also set precedent followed to this day by adding the words "So help me God" to the oath itself. Every president since that time has followed Washington's lead in this regard.

In addition to George Washington, subsequent presidents made their own alterations to the Inaugural address delivery and format, as well as to the swearing in process of the president. Washington began the precedent of preparing and delivering a formal "address" after the swearing in ceremony; to this day, it is the first act of a new president in office. John Adams' contributed to the legacy of the Inaugural address by having the Chief Justice of the Supreme Court administer the oath and preside over the ceremony. In 1845, the Inaugural address of James K. Polk was the first to be communicated to the general public by telegraph. In 1853, Franklin Pierce began the precedent of placing one hand on the bible when taking the oath of office as opposed to kissing the book. The Inaugural Address of Calvin Coolidge in 1925 was the first to be broadcast over the radio and, in 1949, Harry Truman's address became the first to be televised. And, finally, in 1997, Bill Clinton's Inaugural Address was the first to be broadcast over the internet.

The other two other forms of presidential rhetoric that are analyzed in this study, though not enumerated in the constitution, have played just as important a role in the evolution of presidential power and activity as have the State of the Union Address and the Inaugural Address. Executive Orders and Proclamations are interesting phenomena that provide the president with the ability to dictate policy with the power of law, while circumventing the usual legislative route of lawmaking. Instead of simply mentioning certain issues in the State of the Union Address or the Inaugural, for Congress to take action on or the people to take note of, the proclamation and the executive order are able to have immediate and significant impact when issued with the weight of legislatively approved law. However, for various reasons, "scholars have devoted scant attention to developing a body of theory regarding the president's unilateral powers" (Warber, 2006, 5). Whether due to the difficulty that may be encountered in collecting them, or the difficulty that is faced in trying to differentiate between them, scholars tend to shy away from the analysis of proclamations and executive orders when evaluating the power of the rhetorical presidency.

Executive Orders and Presidential Proclamations have similar origins that are not found in the explicit writings of the constitution (as is the duty of delivering the State of the Union Address), nor in the administrative necessity of the logistics of the office (as is the Inaugural that each succeeding president is expected to give upon entrance into the office). Instead, executive orders and presidential proclamations were partially rhetorical holdovers from the royal government under which the colonists were governed for so many years. The king's ability to issue writs and commands were in no way included in the colonial constitution, yet even George Washington saw the advantage of this form of policymaking and lawmaking, and utilized both as early as 1789. In 1907, the Department of State began to assign identification numbers to proclamations and executive orders. In addition, in 1935, the Federal Register Act required that all executive orders and presidential proclamations be formally entered into the *Federal Register* (Relyea, 2007, 5; 14). Although there have been significant issues with the ability to collect the proclamations and executive orders prior to 1907, as well as in the ability to determine what is and what is not an executive order or proclamation, more of these writings are available today than almost ever before.

Executive orders and Proclamations are by far the least examined of the four forms of presidential address, and little study has utilized them to evaluate the evolution of presidential rhetoric and power. Scholars have weighed in on the significant impact that they may have for a presidency, the legal implications that they might have, and the strategic nature of their directives, and the role that they play in the execution of bureaucratic tasks (Peterson 1990; Krause and Cohen 1997; Light 1999; Mayer 2001; Howell 2003; Warber 2006). Indeed, "many scholars contend that executive orders are attractive policy tools for presidents because they provide alternative avenues for policymaking during times when there is an increase in the amount of uncertainty within the political environment" (Warber, 2006, 29; Mayer, 2001,

90). Unfortunately, however, presidential proclamations and executive orders have been largely omitted from the scholarly re-evaluations of the evolution of the rhetorical presidency. By including them in this analysis with the Inaugurals and the State of the Union Address, I hope to provide a much richer understanding of their role and the changes that they too have seen throughout presidential history.

Defining Rhetoric as Power

At the core of the discussion of this study, and, indeed, any discussion of presidential speech, is the proposition that the president's words have an incredible amount of power. In fact, many scholars have characterized presidential rhetoric as having the power similar to presidential action itself. Smith and Smith (1990) explain "the American presidency is fundamentally a rhetorical role" (236). In dealing with and researching presidential rhetoric, it is of great importance to first clarify what is meant by presidential rhetoric and the framework under which presidential addresses will be considered for this study. A "framework," as expressed by Mary Stuckey, is a necessary component to understanding and adding to the body of political communication scholarship. "The challenge of political communication research is to unite, in a systematic way, theories on information processing and cognition, of social activity, on persuasion, and on political processes and behavior in such a way as to make sense of the communicative aspects of our shared political worlds" (Stuckey (a), 1996, viii).

For the purposes of this study, I define presidential rhetoric from the Machiavellian/ Aristotelian perspectives that all relations are power relations and that linguistic tools (logos, pathos, ethos) are used to express and claim this power—ethos, or appeal to the speaker's authority, being the paramount rhetorical element at work. According to David Lorenzo (1996), this definition of rhetoric "assumes that persuasion depends as much or more on what people say than on how their words reach the eyes or ears of their audience," and study is "primarily concerned with the substance of messages, and their relationships with environments that are structured by symbols rather than mechanisms" (Lorenzo, 1996, 2). Kenneth Hacker also explains that "it can be said that all forms of power for political leaders, whether pharaohs, kings, or presidents, have stemmed from arguments grounded in language that legitimize the rule of the governing and guarantees the consent of the governed... political leaders may give special attention to language as a tool of power" (Hacker, 1996, 28). Presidents cannot be considered different in this respect as language and rhetoric are undoubtedly tools by which they conduct the business and perform the duties of the office.

As such, this study finds parity with that of Neustadt (1960), that the power of the president is the power to persuade. Tulis correctly states that "rhetorical power is a very special case of executive power because simultaneously it is the means by which an executive can defend the use of force and other executive powers and it is a power itself" (Tulis, 1987, 203). I would further suggest, as posited by Mary Stuckey, that rhetoric possesses strong symbolic power (Stuckey (a), 1996, vii). Hence, at base, rhetoric may be defined as the expression or assertion of an individual's power. "It is only in the light of people's speech that we can see and assess the character displayed in their deeds. So the access to presidential character is through presidential speech" (Thurow, 1996, 17). Therefore, presidential rhetoric is the president's attempt to exhibit, claim, or enact powers.

Roderick Hart concludes that presidential "public speech no longer attends the processes of governance—it is governance" and suggests that the "remarks of presidents exert influence not found in the speeches of others" (Hart, 1987, 14; 79). Whenever speaking publicly or issuing a statement, this is, in effect, the president's exertion of his power. Regardless of the outcome of the policies that are proposed in the president's speech, their mention alone is the president's exertion of power. Indeed, Jeffrey Cohen observes, "The more attention presidents give to policy areas in their State of the Union Address, the more concerned the public becomes with those policy areas...Mere presidential mentions of a policy area seem to elicit a public response...The office bestows a credibility onto the speaker, such that the public listens to all that presidents deem important...the public does not necessarily buy their prescriptions about what to do, only the diagnosis that a problem exists" (Cohen, 1995, 102).

Because of his position and his elevated station, everything that the president says, whether written or publicly delivered, holds a significance that in itself is power. A message from the president is given almost unparalleled importance in contrast to other communications. Speeches and addresses of any sort should therefore be read as statements of presidential power; they are all attempts to assert the power of the presidency in some way—either through policy proposal, attempts to move public opinion through appeals to the people, or direct address to specific audiences. Indeed, "a president's power depends not only on his ability to command, but his ability to persuade" (Thurow, 15, 1996).

Under this framework of rhetoric as power, every proposal of policy, every suggestion for inquiry, every recognition of past success in address is a president's invocation of the powers that he holds as well as the powers of the office.[3] Presidential rhetoric is a flexing of executive power in an attempt to achieve some goal or convey some message that is deemed important. In addition, study of the evolution of presidential rhetoric raises important questions as to rhetorical style utilized in each presidential address and its impact on subsequent presidents. Does the president speak as one of the people? Does he issue commands to Congress or the people? Does he set standards for speaking that subsequent presidents follow? Alternatively, does he speak with assumed authority derived from the auspices of the office that he holds? This seating assumes that there is no presidential drivel and that there is no unimportant (or unintentional for that matter) address. This framework is especially important because it gives us a way of understanding and viewing presidential behavior, innovation, and change in exercise of power that is neither reliant on the success of policy proposition nor resonance in Washington or in the general public.

This power-centered view of presidential rhetoric allows an encompassing framework and mindset within which to examine presidential rhetoric and addresses. Each address can be read as an assertion of the presidential voice. "If rhetoric is the principle subject of investigation, then one might well be concerned with the principles of the art and how those principles function to allow the speaker or writer—who might happen to be a U.S. president—to achieve his ends by symbolic means" (Medhurst, 1996, xiv). Tulis explains that "all presidents are rhetorical presidents. All presidents exercise their office through the medium of language, written and spoken" (Tulis, 1996, 3). He further suggests that "from a president's perspective, the only salient rhetorical issue is this: Will my ability to persuade the people at large advance my ability to secure policy objectives?"(Tulis, 1996, 9) And if "the president's own interests and those of the polity as a whole, conjoin"

---

[3] For specific examinations of the formation and evolution of political communication and rhetoric of the presidency, see also Houck (2001); Watts (1997); Crigler (1996); Edwards (1996); Graber (1996); Negrine (1996); Stuckey (1996 (b), 1996 (c)); Valls (1996); McNair (1995); Ryan (1995, 1988); Hart (1994); Zernicke (1994); Dolan and Dumm (1993); Neuman et al (1992); Hinckley (1990); Swanson and Nimmo (1990); Geis (1987); Malone et al (1987); and Thompson, (1987).

(Tulis, 1996, 10), presidential rhetoric is a power expression by the president invested with the voice of the people. "The president's ultimate task is to express the unspoken desires of the people…The skill needed by a president is the rhetorical skill…The president, as head of the embodiment of expertise, the executive branch, can supply what the people lack" (Thurow, 1996, 24).

Research Design and Collection of Data

The central method by which the "traditional/ modern" divide, as well as the evolution of presidential rhetoric will be evaluated is by content analysis of one of the largest collections of the State of the Union Addresses, the Presidential Inaugurals, Presidential Proclamations and Executive Orders to be studied, to date.

Figure 1.1: The Four Different Types of Presidential Address and the Presidents and Number of Speeches Included in the Study

Speech Type	Presidents Included	Years	Number of Speeches	Approximate Pages	Number of Words
State of the Union Address	Washington-GW Bush	1790-2008	226	6,558	1,803,383
Presidential Inaugurals	Washington-GW Bush	1790-2008	58	471	129,609
Presidential Proclamations	Washington-GW Bush	1790-2008	5,247	9,610	2,642,870
Presidential Executive Orders	JQ Adams-GW Bush	1826-2008	3,857	7,343	2,019,319
		total	9,153	23,982	6,595,181

Scholars describe many possible pitfalls in presidential content analysis research such as small sample size, generalizations made from addresses in differing contexts, and comprehensiveness of study (King, 1993; Edwards and Wayne, 1983; Krippendorff, 1980; Carney, 1972). However, I propose that content analysis in this study has many benefits in evaluating the prior arguments concerning presidential rhetoric, as well as providing a valid and reliable study from which to make inferences and generalizations relating to presidential rhetoric. The extensive content analysis that I will conduct is a thorough and cautious line-by-line examination and reading of each State of the Union Address, Inaugural, Executive Order, and Proclamation included in the study, in order to determine policy proposition, word usage, political activity, and context. A simple word count or use of a content analysis program which could detail frequencies or occurrences of specific words not only tends to miss many implicit suggestions for policy, it occurs largely without regard to context of word use and valuation of terms as a result. My line-by-line reading remedies this issue because of the thorough qualification that can be given to each word or policy proposal to assure its proper inclusion and intent.

In addition to looking at specific words that are used in the presidential address, this study also looks at the policies that are proposed or enacted by the president in his speech. Some studies attempt to do similar work in presidential address by coding the sentence, line, paragraph, or document in which a word indicating a policy occurs as only one policy. However, counting a sentence or line of the speech as a policy proposal does not fully identify presidential policy advocacy or proposal within the addresses. For example, In Bush's 2003 State of the Union Address he states, "I am proposing that all income tax reductions be made permanent this year." This sentence could easily be counted as one policy proposal whether coding policy propositions by sentence or even phrase.

However, the importance of looking closely at presidential address and not necessarily coding policy propositions by sentence or paragraph can be seen in Theodore Roosevelt's State of the Union Address in 1902. In this address, he recommends that "1) All future legislation on the subject should be with the view of encouraging the use of such instrumentality as will automatically supply every legitimate demand of productive industries, 2) and of commerce, 3) not only in the amount, 4) but in the character of circulation, 5) and of making all kind of money interchangeable, 6) and at the will of the holder, convertible into the gold standard" (my insertion of numbers). This sentence may have very well been counted as a single policy proposition if the sentence is the unit of analysis. Through a word-byword reading however, I am able to fully realize and account for the six policies proposed in the single sentence. Therefore, to gain an accurate account of presidential policy-making, presidential position taking, and even popular rhetoric usage in the State of the Union Address, a thorough reading of each address provides a wealthier and more complete account of presidential activity. Indeed, "the ability to extract implicit concepts is vital to much research as meaning is lost when only explicit concepts are used...when implicit as well as explicit concepts are coded, it is possible to enact from the text a richer definition of meaning" (Carley, 1993, 86; 88).

Policy proposals and activity are also carefully examined to be sure that a more accurate evaluation of presidential activity can attempt to be observed. For example, if the president directly recommended a policy to the Congress or the people in his State of the Union Address, such as "Tonight I ask Congress and the American people to focus the spirit of service and the resources of government on the needs of some of our most vulnerable citizens—boys and girls trying to grow up without guidance and attention and children who have to go through a prison gate to be hugged by their mom or dad" (Bush 2003), it was counted as a policy. If the president expressed favor in a policy proposal of one of his departments or a member/bill in congress, such as "I have sent you a Healthy Forests Initiative, to help prevent the catastrophic fires that devastate communities, kill wildlife and burn away millions of acres of treasured forest. I urge you to pass these measures, for the good of both our environment and our economy" (Bush 2003), it was counted as well.

In addition, if the president recommended a policy several times or reiterated his position over and over again, each individual incident was included as a policy proposition because, according to the understanding of rhetoric as power laid out above, reiteration of a policy expresses the gravity and importance which the president obviously feels the subject deserves and his repeated desire and stressing of an issue that he would like to see considered. An example of this can be seen when Bush stated that "Some might call this a good record. I call it a good start. Tonight I ask the House and Senate to join me in the next bold steps to serve our fellow citizens. Our first goal is clear: We must have an economy that grows fast enough to employ every man and woman who seeks a job," this was counted as a policy proposal dealing with the economy. When Bush followed up by saying that "I am proposing that all the income tax reductions set for 2004 and 2006 be made permanent and effective this year" (Bush 2003) it would be counted as another policy proposal dealing with the economy. It would actually be counted as two proposals because the first proposal in the last quote is that the income tax reductions be made *permanent* and the second policy proposal is that they be made *effective this year*.

However, presidential predictions on the effects of the initial policy proposal and his estimation of future policies would not be included in the count because the president was specifically asking for only a single policy at the time and therefore any predictions of future action necessarily would hinge on that single policy. Examples of this are such rhetoric as "Lower taxes and greater investment will help this economy expand. More jobs mean more taxpayers and higher revenues to our government" (Bush 2003). This is not proposal of policy, but instead is the reasoning behind the tax breaks and other specific policies that he has proposed. By carefully determining beforehand the guidelines for counting policy proposal and issue advocacy, I was able to avoid inconsistent coding or readings in a process of Presidential Address perusal that took nearly three years to properly conduct.

The Plan of the Book and Findings of the Study

The main argument encompassed within this study is that, although some patterns may emerge to suggest that the modern president is the product of a transformation in power as the result of an individual officeholder, an overall view of the presidency and its rhetoric are better suited by looking at the presidency as an evolution of rhetoric, contributed to by each individual executive. In order to fully illustrate this incremental change, it is necessary that this book, with its collection of presidential rhetoric, examine the changes that have taken place in each of the forms of presidential address as well as test the main tenets of the "traditional/ modern" divide. As such, each of the chapters of this text deals with pillars of the "modern" rhetorical presidency theory and utilizes data from all four types of presidential address to evaluate those claims and trace the changes that have taken place since the founding.

For example, Chapter 2, Speaking to the People: The Use of Popular Address, focuses specifically on the assertion that presidents during the "modern" period are the only ones to have utilized what is known as "popular address rhetoric" in their speeches and behavior. Talking to the people is frequently viewed as a "modern" presidential trait, and Tulis (1987) specifically suggests that this was a rhetorical penchant that was not easily observed in the speech and activity of those presidents of the "traditional" period.

In order to fully evaluate this claim, I not only look at the frequency with which the president address the people versus the Congress, I also break the general subject of "popular address rhetoric" into very specifically used verbiage that can be measured to evaluate the use of "popular address." I look specifically at three different ways in which the president uses language 1) to present a sense of popular identification, 2) to use his station as president as proxy justification for his proposals of policy and activity, and lastly 3) to direct the people or the Congress to act on issues that he views as in the interest of the people or the nation. The chapter concludes that it is extremely difficult to prove that the presidents of contemporary times are solely those responsible for "popular address" in their speeches and writings. Indeed, a significant finding in the chapter is that presidents as early as the founding have demonstrated rhetorical proclivities toward the usage of popular address rhetoric that were not matched until the speeches of recent twenty first century presidents.

A major focus of those looking to study the exertion of presidential power, regards the observation of political activity, or lack thereof, of presidents during different time periods. Perhaps for more than any other reason, presidents use their addresses to propose policies, reinforce the policy priorities of their administration, and issue policy or take positions that they view as exceedingly important to their goals and the direction of the country. Chapter 3, Excavating the Bully Pulpit: The Foundation and Evolution of Policy Proposal, gets to the heart of the issue by providing a line-by-line examination of the State of the Union Address, the Presidential Inaugural Address, Presidential Proclamations and Executive Orders from George Washington to George W. Bush to trace the evolution of presidential policy proposal and activity. I find that, although presidents today do indeed propose significant amounts of policy in succinct statements and addresses, presidents of the 18th and 19th centuries also proposed numerous policies and programs, though they did so in much longer and drawn out formats. The history of presidential policy proposal and activity appears to be a consistent increase across all of the presidents as opposed to a sudden spike that occurs as the result of an individual administration. The contemporary rhetorical presidency appears as the evolution and culmination of the efforts of each and every individual officeholder as opposed to a transformation brought on by just one.

In addition to proposing more policy and being more policy active on basic issues, the modern president, according to Tulis, can be characterized by an innovation, begun by Wilson, of "visionary" speech and policy proposal. Chapter 4, The Bigger Picture: Visions for the Nation and the World, examines the occurrence and proposal of visionary policies in the four different forms of presidential address from the founding to GW Bush. The picture of presidential speech that emerges is one that is, once again, a story of slight and incremental change that occurs over the course of the presidency with each new president building on the possibilities and rhetoric of those who held the office before him. Far from being an innovation of a singular presidency or even a habit which was not seen by presidents in a "traditional" period, visionary speech originates with the very founders of the country and the incipient presidencies of the nation. Although the use of visionary speech does wax and wane, it does so throughout the entirety of presidential history and, to this day, continues to be reflective of the choices and contexts faced by the individual holding office.

The final chapter of the study, Chapter 5, is entitled Back to the Future: A New Understanding of Presidential Development, and looks at what the findings in the previous chapters mean to the study of the presidency, presidential rhetoric, and the division of presidential history into different eras. When looking at the findings that are presented here in their aggregate, Instead seeing the contemporary presidency and the rhetoric used therein as an innovation of a single individual or as the result of a single era or time period of presidential behavior, it appears as the product of slow change and evolutionary activity.

The rhetorical presidency is similar to any leadership position in government or business around the world. When a new CEO takes power in a company, they enter with goals that they would like to accomplish as well as a vision for what they want the company, the company's workers, and the market to be in the future. To accomplish their priorities, they must look back at history, *necessita* for Machiavelli, and survey the past to see what worked, what did not, what weapons for activity are at their disposal, and the different ways that they can speak to those that will enforce their mandates. Although some former CEO's might have changed the office more than others, to dismiss their tenure without learning about their contributions misses important nuance.

The same principles must apply to the study of the presidency and the way in which the presidents of the past are examined. Although we can say with surety that some individuals who have held the office have either diminished its stature and power or added to it, we must look to each as individual variables that brought change to it. Too often, the main casualty of the "traditional/ modern" divide, and clearly not its intent, is the dismissal of almost two-thirds of presidential history because it is not as "valuable" in contemporary study or understanding of the institution. This dismissal of a significant amount of the presidential past should be disconcerting to those who study this position and the individuals who have held the office. By including the "traditional" presidents, as done in this study, we see that more and more, they have striking similarities to the counterparts classified as "modern." Indeed, the forgotten presidents of the eighteenth and nineteenth centuries should be included in presidential study because, when examined closely, they have the potential to contribute more to our understanding of the evolution of the contemporary presidency, the powers that it enjoys, and the rhetorical weapons at its disposal than their omission by use of a categorization might suggest.

CHAPTER II

Speaking to the People: The Use of Popular Address

The President is the people's lobbyist.

—Hubert H. Humphrey

There is but one national voice in the country and that is the voice of the President.

—Woodrow Wilson

SCHOLARS OF both communication and political science have examined the ways that the executive utilizes his position and time as president in order to provide leadership and service to the American people. "Presidents, of course, are not content to sit and passively read and follow public opinion. They are actively engaged in efforts to *lead* public opinion to support them and their policies" (Edwards and Wayne, 1999, 3). The principal way to engage and lead the public comes from rhetorical leadership, or the power of presidential words in making successful political policy. Indeed, it is "with words minds are changed, votes acquired, enemies labeled, alliances secured, unpopular programs made palatable, and the status quo suddenly unveiled as unjust and intolerable" (Rodgers, 1987, 4). It is the "sound of leadership" that originates at the junction of the office of the presidency and the presentation of policy proposal or political communication. Roderick Hart explains that "Presidents exert influence over their environment only by speaking, and it is largely through speaking their environment responds to them" (Hart, 1984, 5). It is not enough to see presidential speech as attempting leadership however. Because of station and authority, when the president speaks, his "public speech no longer attends the process of governance—it is governance" (Hart, 1984, 14).

The conjoining of this use of presidential communication to the end of executive seeking of popular leadership results in Rhetorical Leadership. "Rhetorical Leadership could be defined as the process of discovering, articulating, and sharing the available means of influence in order to motivate human agents in a particular situation…It is leadership exerted through talk or persuasion" (Dorsey, 2002, 9; 3). It is through the address of various audiences that the president is able to illustrate his support for certain programs, his view of what the people should and should not do, as well as the courses of action that he himself would like to see the country or specific policies take. "Whether we talk in Aristotelian terms of rhetoric as persuasion, or more contemporary Burkean terms of rhetoric as identification, both of these concepts have to do with using our *will* in order to make an outcome true" (McGee, 1998, 32).

A "Modern" Rhetorical Presidency?

If the rhetoric of the president is viewed as power in and of itself, and has the ability to move and persuade, is it fair to suggest that this power results from the innovation of a single officeholder and their use of rhetorical leadership? Can it be said conclusively that "founding fathers were concerned not to erect an executive branch that could become overwrought by constant appeals to the national rabble" and that "the founding fathers would be disconcerted to discover how often and in what ways modern presidents speak" (Hart, 1984, 2; 7)? If yes, and contemporary presidential speech really does differ from the founders in significant and important ways, then we must align ourselves with scholars who attempt to identify the demarcation point, like Tulis who suggested that "the Wilsonian view has replaced the founders' as the basic underpinning of presidential self-understanding and public legitimacy" (Tulis, 1987, 173-4).

In effect, this identification of a singular transformation of the presidency suggests that the speech of the founders should be determinedly different from contemporary presidential rhetoric. As Tulis explains of the founding and "traditional" period, "embodying two demands of republicanism, rhetoric to Congress would be *public* (available to all) but not nearly *popular* (fashioned for all)…the more policy oriented the speech, the less likely it was to be given in the nineteenth century" (Tulis, 1987, 46; 67). Accordingly, Andews (2002) explains that "in the twentieth century, as presidents from Theodore Roosevelt and Wilson began to speak more directly to and for the people, they increasingly took up the task of forging community out of the disparate segments of the American population" (132). In contrast, when viewing presidents of the founding such as Washington, "his Inaugural, State of the Union Address, and other addresses were reported in the press, but he did not employ them to advance an overall program" (Greenstein, 2006, 385).

However, because rhetoric by its very nature is diverse and presidents by their very nature will have different goals and necessarily *must* face different contexts and challenges, can rhetorical leadership truly be an innovation singular to and individual president? In addition, does this mean that the best way to understand the way that the president speaks today is through the examination of those presidents beginning in the 20th century? Several communication and political science scholars have suggested that it is extraordinarily difficult to reach such a conclusion summarily. Daniel Rodgers proposes that "the notion that the history of political argument in America can be shoehorned into a massive paradigm shift seems to me no more convincing than the older assumptions of consensus" (1987, 7).

According to tenets of the "traditional/ modern" divide concerning that rhetorical presidency, the initiative to speak to, as one of, and for the people of the United States is usually a 20th century development. "Popular address" and "popular rhetoric" as they have been coined, are used by the president in his addresses to appeal to Congress and the people. Accordingly, those presidents of the "traditional" presidency refrained from, by the reverence of their position or the limited powers directly granted in the Constitution, utilizing popular rhetoric to attempt to speak to or move the greater populous. Indeed, if the presidents were bound by station and propriety, this kind of speech would be seen as pandering to the people in an almost Johnsonian impeachable offense. In his work, Tulis suggested that "since the presidencies of Theodore Roosevelt and Woodrow Wilson, popular or mass rhetoric has become the principle tool of presidential governance" (Tulis, 1987, 4).

In order to fully examine whether or not the use of popular address rhetoric was or was not a function of the "modern" presidency, as well as to trace the changes in popular address that have taken place in the rhetorical presidency itself, this chapter will examine the usage of public address rhetoric within presidential address in order to identify trends and determine whether presidents since the founding of the United States have used popular appeal in their addresses, or whether the introduction of going public is indeed a "modern" development that was little used in the rhetorical past of the presidency. Specifically, I look at instances in which the president attempts to address his audience as one of them, attempts to use his presidential position as justification for his arguments, and those instances in which the president actually makes a command or request in order to weigh these theses.

Speaking to the People or to Congress?

To evaluate whether or not the president did indeed use popular address rhetoric more in the "modern" times than in the "traditional" period, it is important to the tenets proposed by the "traditional/modern" dichotomy itself to clarify our terms. Tulis provides one proposal, that in the twentieth century, and with the innovations of Wilson, "policy rhetoric which had formerly been *written* and addressed *principally* to *Congress*, would now be *spoken* and principally addressed to the *people* at large" (Tulis, 1987, 133). Laracey (2002) conducts similar work by looking to presidential public communications to determine if there truly was a "norm that held that presidential communications on matters of public policy, were addressed principally to Congress, in writing" and whether or not this "old norm against going public withered away in the twentieth century" (4). Vanessa Beasley (2004) also takes issue with the tenet for evaluations of national identity, suggesting that we need to determine if there might be "some perennial occasions during which the U.S. President must speak to the citizens" (7).

To begin examination of the issue at hand, a good first step is to look at the presidents' uses of rhetoric that illustrate that the audience, or the subject of his discussion, is either the people as a whole or the Congress in general within his speech. Specifically, I look for the frequency of presidential mention of words that would indicate reference to the people ("people," "persons," "citizen," and "citizens") versus the frequency of words that indicate Congressional directive ("congress," and "legislature"). Having done a line-by-line reading of each address herein included, I was able to ensure that their use and meaning was not only intentional in its usage, but also consistent in its meaning across time and presidents. When looking at each type of rhetoric and its employment, however, it is important to realize that different presidents speak with different address lengths and propose different num-

Speaking to the People 35

bers of policy. In order to generalize the specific use of certain types of rhetoric and make them comparable across different deliveries and presidencies, address length is controlled for by dividing the number of sought words by the total number of words. This regulation enables the rhetoric to be expressed as a percentage of the overall address, thereby controlling for the differing address lengths and providing a clearer picture of the frequency with which the rhetoric has been incorporated by presidents from the founding to the present.

Figure 2.1

The Percentage of Popular Reference versus Congressional Address in the State of the Union Address

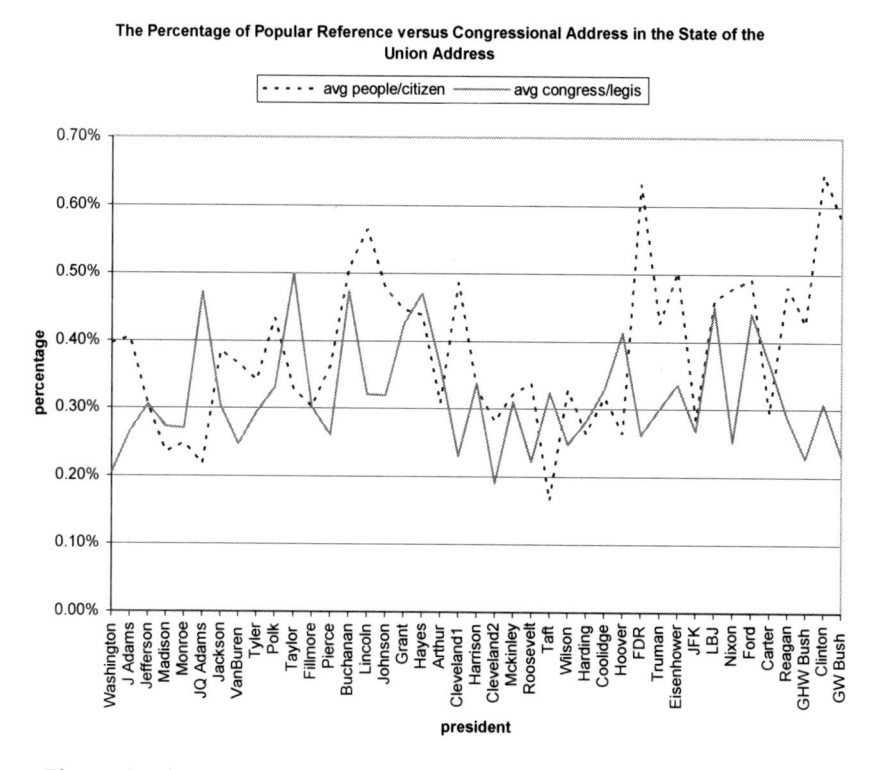

- - - - - avg people/citizen   ——— avg congress/legis

Figure 2.1 is a comparison of the percentages of popular reference words as opposed to Congressional address words per president in the State of the Union Address. If, indeed, the suggestion that the presidents of the twentieth century tend to address and discuss the people more often than the Congress holds true, the Figure above should demonstrate a clear increase in popular address words and a decrease in congressional address rhetoric. However, the results fail to completely support this hypothesis. Instead, the figure illustrates several important things. First of all, there is no clear pattern or shift observable concerning the utilization of congressional address. Instead, there appears to be a consistent use of this form of rhetoric (between .2% and .5% per president) throughout the founding, nineteenth-century, and through the twenty-first century. This indicates that presidents across time have addressed Congress in their Address and are still doing so to dictate policy, indicate course of action, and suggest paths for the country to take. There are variations in the amount of Congressional referrals (the highest points being JQ Adams, Taylor, Buchanan, Hayes, LBJ, and Ford), but they are not dramatic, nor significant enough in their difference to attribute them to a transformation in the way that the president speaks or has spoken. In addition, the presidents who used the highest amounts of Congressional address rhetoric do not easily fall into one time period or another.

The second important observation that can be seen from the figure is the lack of the emergence of a pattern regarding discussion of, and speaking to or about, the people in the State of the Union Address. Although presidents like Franklin Delano Roosevelt and Bill Clinton appear as clear summits of the presidential average, the rest of the twentieth century presidents are largely unremarkable in their incorporation of popular address. In fact, as we look at presidents like Jackson, Polk, and Cleveland (and almost every nineteenth century president from Pierce through Arthur) they utilize the same amount of popular referral as "modern" presidents like Truman, Eisenhower, JFK, Nixon and Reagan (around .45% on the average per president). As with Congressional address, no easy pattern or transformation of presidential speechmaking or referral appears from the data.

Now that the findings above appear to illustrate that presidents during the founding, as well as most of the nineteenth century, did indeed speak to and of the people, with the same regularity as their counterparts during the twentieth century, it is necessary examine how specifically those "people" were addressed. How did the presidents interact with the electorate and what rhetoric was used in this interaction? Did presidents who should be the least likely to use "modern" address, namely the founders (who were allegedly constrained by a precedent of constitutionally appropriate behavior), utilize other forms of popular address in the same way that they spoke generally about the "people?" Further, do the tenets of the "traditional/modern" divide hold true when other language besides congressional and popular address is examined?

Different Forms of Rhetoric of Popular Address

When studying presidential speech and its interaction with the public, it is important to observe the rhetorical shifts that take place in the president's language for varied effect and in order to employ a certain type of power and argument. Although rhetoric by its very nature is diverse, I will classify, and focus on, three types of popular address rhetoric in general, and note their occurrences within presidential address. Specifically, I will look at the instances of popular address when the president attempts to speak as one of the people, identifying himself with them (identification rhetoric), when he attempts to use his station as the President of the United States as justification and authority for what he is asking the people to do (authority rhetoric), and when he is directly asking or telling the listener what should be done (directive rhetoric).

All of these forms of rhetoric can be employed in the simple manipulation of different pronouns. The labels given to the forms of rhetorical address accurately reflect the type of rhetoric and the words that are used in each category. Each label also effectively measures a different attempt of the president to speak as one of the people, to the people, in reference to the people, or as the president, utilizing different pronouns to do so. "Politicians make use of pronouns to good effect: to indicate, accept, deny, or distance themselves from responsibility for political action; to reveal ideological bias; to encourage solidarity; to designate those who are supporters (with "us") as well as those who are enemies (against "us") and to present specific idiosyncratic aspects of the individuals and personality" (Wilson, 1990, 76). In addition, the three typologies of rhetoric above seek to delineate presidential purpose in policy proposal and popular address. "The meanings of selected pronouns shift and change depending on the way in which they are textually employed...selectional choices such as those which operate between exclusive and inclusive 'we' for example, offer politicians ways of directing attention towards or away from their own existential center, i.e. themselves" (Wilson, 1990, 76).

The president uses these variations in his rhetoric to account for the many different interests of his audience as well as different environmental contexts he may face. Wayne Fields remarks that, in presidential speech, the president "must manage to be both apart and included, must be at once particular and universal, present challenges that do not necessarily confront Congressmen or Senators... The job is always, as Washington foresaw, the difficult business of building affection, affection for one another and for the union itself" (Fields, 1996, 16; 228). The president attempts to accomplish this inclusion and unification through a manipulation of the ways in which he speaks to, for, and about his audience using identification rhetoric, authority rhetoric, and directive rhetoric.

The president uses these variations in his rhetoric to account for the many different interests of his audience as well as different environmental contexts he may face. In her study on national identity, Vanessa Beasley observes that "however mythic and outdated, such clear distinctions...between "them" and "us" still persist in presidential talk" (2004, 90). Among many public speakers, the president is not alone in utilizing rhetoric to create and forge different audiences that would be more receptive to his proposals; he is very aware that "a democracy must also have strong and generous words for its common life and common words" (Rodgers, 1987, 222). Wayne Fields remarks that in the presidential address, the president "must manage to be both apart and included, must be at once particular and universal, present challenges that do not necessarily confront Congressmen or Senators... The job is always, as Washington foresaw, the difficult business of building affection, affection for one another and for the union itself" (Fields, 1996, 16; 228). The president attempts to accomplish this inclusion and unification through a manipulation of the ways in which he speaks to, for, and about his audience using identification rhetoric, authority rhetoric, and directive rhetoric.

Identification Rhetoric

The first type of popular address rhetoric that I will look at will be coined "Identification Rhetoric." In Vanessa Beasley's book (2004), much of what she seeks to find in forming a national identity, involves the use of presidential speeches that create a similar identification of president with the people, and they with him. She illustrates that 9/11 brought this very theory to life. "The events of September 11th and their aftermath have demonstrated...how powerful the felt communion of a national 'we' can be" (Beasley, 2004, 4). According to Beasley, presidents use the State of the Union Address to mold the American people into one body that can come together in support or policy and action. "In other words, for there to be an American nation, or an American 'we,' or even an American presidency at all, U.S. presidents must find ways of breathing life into the otherwise abstract notion of American political community" (Beasley, 2004, 8). In order to pass policy and gain support from the electorate, "chief executives clearly had a great interest in making sure that the American people *feel* united, even if citizens' actual demographic, economic, and psychological differences would suggest otherwise...by creating an American identity based on such abstractions, presidents have been able to offer their diverse constituents ways of viewing themselves as a united group" (Beasley, 2004, 46; 63).

It is by the use of certain rhetoric that the president is able to speak to the people and also seek to convince them that he is on their side, on the same page with them, and has the interests of the greater whole in mind. Through the use of identification pronouns (words such as "our," "we," and "us") both presidents and the common man place themselves en masse with the larger group in question. "We are attempting to control our environment in particular ways by promoting an identification with other people or by persuading other people" (McGee, 1997, 127). Under a "traditional" presidency which would suggest that early presidents were actually prevented from speaking to the people through common identification by norms of behavior (he uses Andrew Johnson as an example), precedent, and founders intent (Tulis, 1987), we would expect to find little of this form of rhetoric.

Identification rhetoric is used within State of the Union Addresses in order to make the public, or the listening audience, feel that the president is indeed one of those to whom he speaks. In his 2003 State of the Union Address, George W. Bush proposed that *"We* will not deny, *we* will not ignore, *we* will not pass along our problems to other Congresses, to other presidents, and other generations. *We* will confront them with focus, and clarity, and courage." This was an exercise in the use of identification rhetoric. George W. Bush portrayed himself as one of those in America and in government who would confront the problems of the country and work toward their correction. He continued with this type of identification rhetoric in his attempt to influence the people to support any action that might be taken against the regime in Iraq. "*We* will consult, but let there be no misunderstanding: If Saddam Hussein does not fully disarm, for the safety of *our* people and for the peace of the world, *we* will lead a coalition to disarm him. And if war is forced upon *us, we* will fight with the full force and might of the United States military and *we* will prevail. And as *we* and *our* coalition partners are doing in Afghanistan, *we* will bring to the Iraqi people food and medicines and supplies and freedom." This constant repetition of "we" is the president's attempt to build consensus and agreement by creating identification between the citizens of the United States and himself; if they identify with what he says, he will receive greater support and have the ability to proceed further with policy objectives. This is reminiscent of Roosevelt's "fireside chats" that made the American people feel as though the president really did care, and really was one of them.

Authority Rhetoric

The second rhetorical label that will be used here is that of authority rhetoric. Authority rhetoric is usage of the words "I," "me," and "my" within presidential address. This category is recognized by Tulis, among others, who suggest that "authoritative speech combines the power of command with the power of persuasion (or force of argument)" (1987, 81). By using specific pronouns, the president is attempting to exert the power of his station and the power of the presidency to propose policy and programs. Because of their position, "the spoken remarks of presidents exert influence not found in the speeches of others" (Hart, 1987, 79). In fact, "the speech of presidents is more powerful than most. This power derives in part form the office of the presidency, but it also derives from the attitudes the presidents have toward the speech act itself" (Hart, 1987, 110). It is the president's use of pronouns such as "I," "me," and "my" in his rhetoric that objectify him as commander in chief, and suggest that his speech holds value largely because of that position alone. "It is through the example, the rhetorical leadership, the moral correctness of the leaders of state, and their ability to inspire self-sacrifice, that the power of a state is mobilized" (McGee, 1997, 127).

The State of the Union, for example, is a perfect platform from which to imbue policy suggestions and referrals with added significance because of the reverence with which it is approached and reported. "The State of the Union message gives a chief executive the opportunity to speak as the sole and supreme leader, the symbolic guardian of the public good...Even in those years when the messages were only printed and/or read to Congress by clerks, they had symbolic import that went beyond their constitutional or legislative purposes" (Beasley, 2004, 11). Authority rhetoric offers "the suggestion that leadership stems from a person's formal position...with an officially sanctioned title, the holder of that title can legitimately direct others for the achievement of a goal" (Dorsey, 2002, 4).

We see illustrations of authority rhetoric in the State of the Union Address of 2003, when George W. Bush proposed numerous policies regarding the environment, stating that "*I* have sent you a comprehensive energy plan to promote energy efficiency and conservation, to develop cleaner technology and to produce more energy at home. *I* have sent you Clear Skies legislation that mandates a 70 percent cut in air pollution from power plants over the next 15 years. *I* have sent you a Healthy Forests Initiative, to help prevent the catastrophic fires that devastate communities, kill wildlife and burn away millions of acres of treasured forest. *I* urge you to pass these measures, for the good of both our environment and our economy. Even more, *I* ask you to take a crucial step, and protect our environment in ways that generations before us could not have imagined. Tonight *I* am proposing $1.2 billion in research funding so that America can lead the world in developing clean, hydrogen-powered automobiles." This repetition of the word "I" in the midst of policy proposals sends a message to Congress that the President has been active on certain issues and has certain policies that he would like to see activity on by the Congress. In addition, this use of authority rhetoric reminds the people of the United States that the President is working hard towards many different environmental goals, and that Congress only need approve his plans to get the protection that the President sees as necessary. It is this flexing of the muscle of the power of the presidential position that makes authority rhetoric effective.

Directive Rhetoric

In much the same way that the president uses "I," "me," and "my" to exercise his presidential authority, he can also use his station to give commands and place the need for performance on his audience. This type of rhetorical instruction and popular address can be called "Directive rhetoric" (as the president is effectively directing his remarks towards a certain audience), and will be measured here by the frequency of the words "you," "your," and "yours" which place the need for action on someone other than the president himself. According to Tulis, "rhetoric that was directed primarily to the people at large developed along lines consistent with the case against popular leadership" (1987; 47). This suggests that rhetoric specifically directed at others could be a development of presidents of the twentieth century and might be absent in the founding and nineteenth century. In addition, it would follow that the presidents of the twentieth century, being much more driven by public opinion and being more cognizant of their popular leadership role, should exploit this type of rhetoric more than their predecessors.

The Popular Address Rhetoric of the Declaration of Independence

Although the "modern" rhetorical presidency may propose that popular address rhetoric was completely absent from the speeches, addresses, and presidential directives during the eighteenth and nineteenth centuries, founding documents provide evidence to the contrary. When Thomas Jefferson was drafting the Declaration of Independence, he was forced to walk a very fine rhetorical line in order to address and influence all of the different factions with their differing positions in the American colonies. He created the document under the weight of a divided nation, in which some of the colonists supported action against England, some colonists felt that the colonies should remain loyal to the King of England, and some colonists did not care either way, as they were having enough difficulty trying to establish a life in the new wilderness.

In addition, Jefferson had to create a document in which the founders and those attempting to influence the people of the colonies toward a movement for independence, would not come across as elitist, pretentious, or disdainful of the views and the needs of the common man. As a result of his realization that the colonies were being pulled in so many different directions at once, Jefferson formed a document in which the rhetoric and the object of address was to coax the reader or listener into a feeling of fellowship and identification and then utilize a different rhetoric of authority in order to move the average citizen from simple agreement to action and rebellion. In the Declaration of Independence, Jefferson used "three forms of persuasive appeal: to reason (logos), to emotion (pathos), and to the speaker's authority (ethos)" (Bizzell and Herzberg, 1990, 4).

The first part of the argument in the Declaration of Independence can be interpreted as Jefferson's attempt to set the foundation for the rest of the document, and to convince the reader that this matter deserves attention. He begins by using identification rhetoric, appealing to the logos of the reader or the listener. This is done through the presentation of facts that he establishes as widely accepted and the use of language that identifies those who created the document with those who will read it. "*We* hold these truths to be self evident, that *all* men are created *equal*, that they are endowed by the creator with certain *unalienable Rights*, that among these are Life, Liberty and the pursuit of Happiness...That whenever any Form of Government becomes destructive of these ends, it is the *right of the people* to alter or to abolish it, and to institute new Government" (emphasis added) (Levy, 1988, 81).

The reader or the listener, therefore, existing within the same context and identifying with the same principles, comes to the conclusion that these are logical facts. This appeal to logos is the logical centering that allows Jefferson to continue his argument with every reader exhibiting unity of thought. This method of first focusing the thought of the listener on a subject chosen by the author dates back to classical rhetoricians such as the Sophists, Aristotle, Cicero, and Quintilian. However, it is also reflected in the contemporary writings of such authors as Burke, who would see the argumentational directioning as utilizing a 'teministic screen,' as mentioned above, with which to limit the argument and unify the thought of the audience. Jefferson has established the shared norms and rights of the colonists as well as focused the audience for the second and third sections of the Declaration; he can now move forward with clear purpose and focus.

The second stage of the argument of the Declaration is the establishment of the ethos of Jefferson and the appeal to the pathos of the reader or listener. In this section, Jefferson states the offenses of the King against the colonies in different increasing stages. This method forces the reader to acknowledge that Jefferson has authority and knowledge on the matter and is well acquainted with the offenses (ethos). The appeal to the reader or listener's pathos comes through Jefferson's use of language. He begins by speaking of the King of England subtly and with a distant voice. "He has refused to pass Laws for the accommodation of large districts of people...He has obstructed the Administration of Justice" (Levy, 1988, 82). Most of this first section deals with infractions of the King on matters of government and issues that are at a distance from the people themselves.

This emotional distance and lack of volatile language is then narrowed for stronger expressions of opposition. "He has obstructed the administration of justice...He has made judges dependant on his will alone...He has erected a multitude of New Offices, and sent hither swarms of Officers to harass our people, and eat out their substance" (Levy, 1988, 82). The language used here is stronger than in the primary indictments and begins to take a more personal tone. Instead of simply discussing the state of government and the improprieties that are associated with that relationship with the King, words such as 'obstruct,' 'harass,' and 'eat out the substance' are used to present a stronger point and get a stronger reaction.

In the final section of offenses, however, Jefferson completely closes the distance between the offenses of the King and the lives of the people by the use of identification rhetoric. "For cutting off *our* trade...For imposing Taxes on *us*...For depriving *us* in many cases, of the benefits of Trial by Jury...For transporting *us* beyond seas to be tried for pretended offences...He has plundered *our* seas, ravaged *our* Coasts, burnt *our* towns, and destroyed the lives of *our* people...[he allocates] works of death, desolation, and tyranny, already begun with circumstances of cruelty and perfidy scarcely paralleled in the most barbarous ages " (emphasis added) (Levy, 1988, 82). This use of passionate and pictorially descriptive language attempts to fill the listener or reader with emotion. Gone are Jefferson's descriptions of a government that is taken advantage of by a king. The impropriety of the King is now shown through crimes against mankind in an almost medieval sense, as villages are burned and property is pillaged. The King is suddenly a hated figure who is working to personally attack every member of the colonies. There is little doubt within the audience that they are victims, whether they realize this fact or not, of a tyrannous King inflicting severe and inhumane damage upon them. This appeal to pathos quickens the heartbeat of the audience and prepares them for the next part of the argument which functions as Jefferson's movement toward action.

After stating the common values of the colonies, explaining the offenses against them dealt by the Crown, and stirring up the emotional fervor of the audience, the final part of the argument is a call to arms and action; it employs several manipulations of rhetorical language. Jefferson uses identification rhetoric and gives examples where he and all colonists have tried to cope with the situation and are not rushing into unwarranted problems. "*We* have warned them...*We* have reminded them...*We* have appealed to their native justice...*We* have conjured them by the ties of our common kindred to disavow these usurpations" (emphasis added) (Levy, 1988, 83). Jefferson uses the phrase "We have" over and over to reinforce to the audience that the patience of the colonies has been tried. His use of repetition reiterates to the audience that this is neither rash action by the colonies nor unfounded in its origins.

The conclusion of the Declaration switches voices suddenly, to become that of the representatives of the United States and authority figures to the people. "We, therefore, the Representatives of the United States of America, in General Congress, Assembled, appealing to the Supreme Judge of the world...declare, That these United Colonies are, and of Right ought to be Free and Independent States" (Levy, 1988, 83). The ethos of the Representatives appeals to the pathos of the audience to join with them, under God, in order to move away from the evil of the crown. The declaration of the rights of the colonies, described by the representatives of those colonies, completes the argument that Jefferson constructs. He has declared the rights that are valuable and sacred to all men. He has given examples of how those rights have been trampled on by the King across the sea. He has indicted the King for both offenses against government and the very people themselves. And finally, he has established, as a member of the representative body of the nation, that the single alternative to the infractions is united rebellion and a Declaration of Independence for the colonies.

Jefferson ends the Declaration with a final appeal to the audience and a pledge to uphold the rights of all of the men in the colony who are equal in the rebellion. "We mutually pledge to each other our Lives, our Fortunes and our sacred Honor" (Levy, 1988, 83). Jefferson's final line pleads for the common man to join them in pursuance of freedom and uses language that defines the pure and noble traits accepted by all men.

Though the document is efficient and states the factual information for appealing to the audience and identifying with it, it is Jefferson's style that makes the Declaration of Independence the forceful, rhetorical tool used by the colonies to declare their freedom. First of all, Jefferson has mastered Kairos, as employed by Plato, Socrates, the Sophists, and indeed anyone who wishes to practice successful rhetoric. It is defined as "the immediate social situation in which solutions to philosophical problems must be proposed" (Bizzell and Herzberg, 1990, 56). This, in effect, is the ability to analyze the audience and present appropriately.

Jefferson exhibits his knowledge of Kairos throughout the Declaration. In the beginning, when stating the common laws and the offenses of the King, Jefferson uses identification rhetoric to include himself in the "we" that is used. "We" are the people of the colonies who have been wronged by the King. "We" are those who desire freedom from oppression. The beginning and the middle of the Declaration is an appeal to all men, whether farmer, lawyer, or servant. Jefferson understands that an authoritative tone from the beginning would parallel the forces that the colonies are attempting to reject. The people fear a central government and beginning with "We the

Representatives" would seem to only shift the tyranny from overseas to within the colonies.

However, Jefferson is only able to take the authoritative tone in the latter part of the Declaration because he has already established that he is equal to the common man and that the King has wronged him also. Only then does he assert his standing as a representative of the people. Here, the authority is important because Jefferson switches the focus from what has been done *to* all men to what must be done *by* the leaders of the people. The Representatives have already decided that tyranny must be overthrown; this is the opportunity for the people to voice their agreement. Jefferson appropriately analyzes his audience and he has discovered the appropriate Kairos that is conveyed in the Declaration.

An authoritative document that leads people towards revolution must be extremely delicate and at the same time powerful enough to cause revolt. Through pathos, ethos, logos, and other classical rhetorical tools, the Declaration of Independence establishes itself as an exemplum in presidential popular address rhetoric. Jefferson has mixed emotion, passion, strength, and authority in a document that moved great numbers to throw off the tyranny of the time and find freedom. The Declaration is an argument for the rights of the people and the decisions of their representatives. It accomplishes its goals through style and language that are craftily combined to appeal to the common man and the wealthy citizen.

It is, in fact, this early precedent—illustrated above—which allows for the president and politicians to speak as one of the people or directly on their behalf and that gives gravity and weight to arguments that the president presents to Congress as well as to the people. As examined in Samuel Kernell's *Going Public* (1997), the contemporary presidency uses the ability to speak to the Congress in front of, and on behalf of, the people to both inform the electorate of his plans and policies, and to pressure members of Congress into adopting a favorable disposition towards his policies. Congress grants political levity to the president in fear that he does indeed have the voice of the people and to oppose him would be to ensure the representatives own ousting at the next election. However, the illustration of identification rhetoric, authority rhetoric, and directive rhetoric in the Declaration of Independence, a document that should be constrained by the propriety and hesitance of the "traditional" period, suggests that to fully understand the changes and

Speaking to the People 47

patters of presidential rhetoric and popular address, we need more closely examine presidential documents for a deeper understanding.

Tracing the Use of Identification Rhetoric

In order to determine if identification rhetoric appeared during the founding and nineteenth-century presidential addresses or if it indeed originated with a "modern" period, it is necessary to look at the frequency with which pronouns evoking this kind of identification were utilized. The State of the Union Address provides an excellent starting point for this evaluation.

Figure 2.2

The Percentage of Identification Rhetoric in the State of the Union Address per President

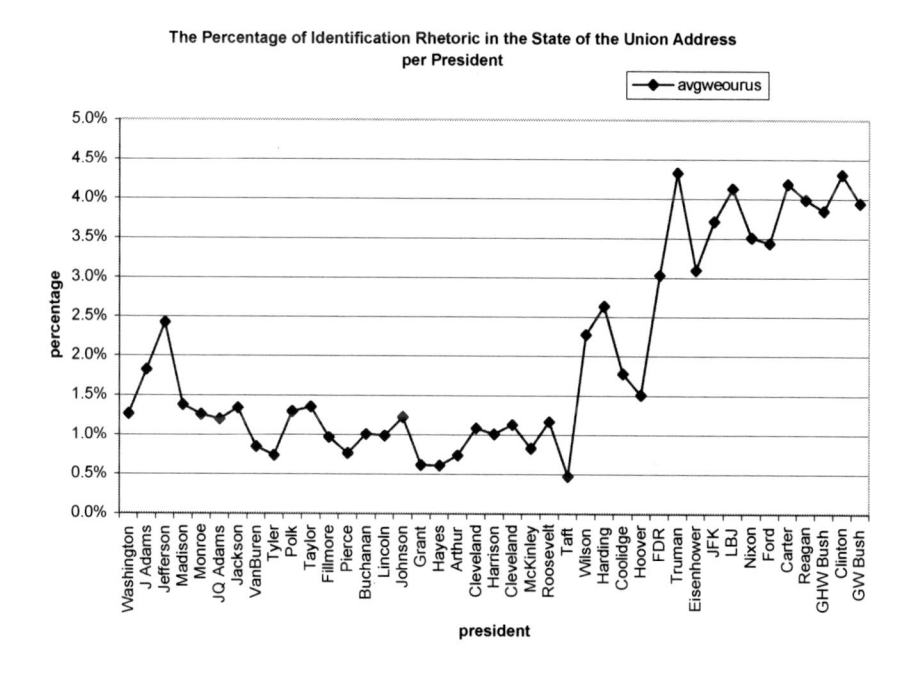

Figure 2.2 is an examination of the average percentage of identification rhetoric used in the average State of the Union Address per president. As discussed above, presidents use these three rhetorical terms ("we," "our," and "us") in order to identify themselves with the listeners (Congress) and the people of the United States. From Figure 2 above, we see that the rhetorical usage of the terms "we," "our," and "us" from Washington until Monroe,

averaged over 1.5% per president. Identification rhetoric then averaged at or just below 1.5% from the late eighteenth century to the early twentieth century. Indeed the high level of identification rhetoric used by Jefferson is not seen again until Wilson's presidency in the twentieth century.

If we consider that the average length of the State of the Union Address from the founding to the present is around 11,000 words, the percentages above suggest that in a address of that length, John Adams and Thomas Jefferson would use the words "we," "our," and "us" almost 275 times. Presidents of the nineteenth and early twentieth centuries would use identification rhetoric 110 times in that 11,000-word State of the Union Address, and presidents of the late twentieth and early 21st centuries would use an estimated 473 identification rhetoric words in a State of the Union Address that averaged 11,000 words. Although the length selected is for illustration purposes (as no orally delivered state of the union address has ever reached that length) the comparison shows that contemporary and founding presidents use "we," "our," and "us" 3 to 5 times more in their State of the Union Address than do their counterparts in the 1800's and early 1900's.

When examined more closely, the high level of incorporation of identification rhetoric in the State of the Union Addresses of the founders becomes more obvious. In the State of the Union Address of 1793, Washington explained that "If *we* desire to avoid insult, *we* must be able to repel it; if *we* desire to secure peace, one of the most powerful instruments of *our* rising prosperity, it must be known that *we* are at all times ready for war" (my emphasis is added for all of the following rhetorical analyses of the State of the Union). The "we" here is the people of the United States, the Congress and the President who are all seemingly behind his proposal for increased defensive measures. In 1798, John Adams also uses this identification rhetoric relating to the defense of the country, "*We* ought without loss of time to lay the foundation for an increase of *our* Navy to a size sufficient to guard *our* coast and protect *our* trade" as well as trade and interaction with France, "Hitherto, therefore, nothing is discoverable in the conduct of France which ought to change or relax *our* measures of defense. On the contrary, to extend and invigorate them is *our* true policy. *We* have no reason to regret that these measures have been thus far adopted and pursued, and in proportion as *we* enlarge *our* view of the portentous and incalculable situation of Europe *we* shall discover new and cogent motives for the full development of *our* energies and resources." The "we" and the "our" are again the Congress, the people and the President of the United States all identifying with the necessary courses of action for the nation.

From the data above, we can say with confidence that contemporary presidents use identification rhetoric in amounts never before seen in the State of the Union Address. This aspect of the findings does indeed seem to support that the "traditional/modern" changes may indeed have bearing. However, we must also importantly recognize that the founding presidents used identification rhetoric percentages that were unmatched during the 1800's and for a large part of the 1900's. They felt identification with the audience to be an essential part of rhetoric, which, in turn, constituted percentages of the State of the Union Address that were similar, if not larger in some cases, to the presidents of the late 20th century and early 21st century.

The possible explanations for this high level of identification rhetoric could be twofold. One explanation may be that Jefferson returned the State of the Union Address from the orally delivered format to the written format, as detailed in previous chapters. This written delivery to Congress may have contributed to a less frequent incorporation of the identification rhetoric that was used in the State of the Union Address as presidents realized that they were no longer on the public platform speaking to a live audience. As seen above, from the point when Jefferson altered the delivery of the State of the Union Address from oral to written, presidents from Madison to Taft included decreasing amounts of identification rhetoric within their addresses. In fact, although Taft delivered the longest average State of the Union Addresses in presidential history (he averaged 22,700 words per address), he included less identification rhetoric in his State of the Union Address than any other president in the history of the United States (0.5%). This would have been only an average of 110 identification rhetoric words per State of the Union Address; this total would be almost exactly half of the 19th and early 20th century averages for identification rhetoric in an Address averaging 11,000 words, as examined above. However, this assumption that written State of the Union Addresses need be less focused on identification rhetoric because of the direct delivery to Congress and bypass of public delivery, cannot be reached with certainty, because, as examined earlier, the methods by which the address was carried to the public prior to the return to oral delivery (newspapers, political mailings, pamphlets) were a significant source by which the message of the president was widely disseminated to the public at large.

A better explanation for the frequent use of identification rhetoric during the founding may lie in the fact that the founders were not only attempting to construct the foundations of the new country, they were also the ones who had designed its rules and governing regulations. Those presidents, through Monroe, were actively involved in the formation of the country and its government. As a result, the increased percentages of identification rhetoric may be present due to the fact that they *actually* identified with the new lawmakers and citizens of the country as opposed to a simple attempt at rhetorical manipulation for policy or support purposes.

The concession that must be made by the "traditional/modern" dichotomy is that, contrary to the claims of its complete absence, presidents in the 19th century *did* use this identification rhetoric within their addresses, although not to the lengths of the founding presidencies. Polk began his second State of the Union Address in 1846 by commenting on the policy of trade in the country and suggesting "In adhering to this wise policy, a preliminary and paramount duty obviously consists in the protection of *our* national interests from encroachment or sacrifice and *our* national honor from reproach. These must be maintained at any hazard. They admit of no compromise or neglect, and must be scrupulously and constantly guarded. From a policy so sacred to humanity and so salutary in its effects upon *our* political system we should never be induced voluntarily to depart." He also uses identification rhetoric in the discussion of Indians—"*Our* laws regulating trade and intercourse with the Indian tribes east of the Rocky Mountains should be extended to the Pacific Ocean; and for the purpose of executing them and preserving friendly relations with the Indian tribes within *our* limits, an additional number of Indian agencies will be required, and should be authorized by law." The use of "we" and "our," is again to detail a universal problem or approach and gain widespread consensus through identification of the listener with the speaker.

Consistent with the findings of Tulis that Wilson had an impact on the rhetoric of the presidency, identification rhetoric experienced a surge in Wilson's address in 1914, in which almost 5% of the State of the Union Address consisted of the words "we," "our," or "us." Wilson reached heights of identification rhetoric unrealized by his predecessors. His average State of the Union Address was just over 4,000 words; this meant that he averaged almost 200 identification rhetoric words per Address. This amount was double the average of his predecessor Taft, and he included twice the number in an address that was 1/6th of the length. Wilson used the rhetoric when speaking of countries embroiled in the European War, proposing, "At any rate, they will need *our* help and *our* manifold services as they have never needed them before; and *we* should be ready, more fit and ready than *we* have ever been. Here are markets which *we* must supply, and *we* must find the means of action." He used the identification rhetoric when speaking of foreign relations with the Philippines, saying, "How better, in this time of anxious questioning and perplexed policy, could *we* show *our* confidence in the principles of liberty, as the source as well as the expression of life, how better could *we* demonstrate *our* own self-possession and steadfastness in the courses of justice and disinterestedness than by thus going calmly forward to fulfill *our* promises to a dependent people, who will now look more anxiously than ever to see whether *we* have indeed the liberality, the unselfishness, the courage, the faith *we* have boasted and professed."

Wilson used identification rhetoric in discussions of domestic policy as well, concerning exploration and mapping, "*We* have not provided adequate vessels or adequate machinery for the survey and charting. *We* have used old vessels that were not big enough or strong enough and which were so nearly unseaworthy that our inspectors would not have allowed private owners to send them to sea. This is a matter which, as I have said, seems small, but is in reality very great. Its importance has only to be looked into to be appreciated," money appropriations, "And, like good stewards, *we* should so account for every dollar of *our* appropriations as to make it perfectly evident what it was spent for and in what way it was spent," and military affairs, "Let *us* remind ourselves, therefore, of the only thing *we* can do or will do. *We* must depend in every time of national peril, in the future as in the past, not upon a standing army, nor yet upon a reserve army, but upon a citizenry trained and accustomed to arms. It will be right enough, right American policy, based upon *our* accustomed principles and practices, to provide a system by which every citizen who will volunteer for the training may be made familiar with the use of modern arms, the rudiments of drill and maneuver, and the maintenance and sanitation of camps. *We* should encourage such training and make it a means of discipline which *our* young men will learn to value. It is right that *we* should provide it not only, but that *we* should make it as attractive as possible, and so induce *our* young men to undergo it at such times as they can command a little freedom and can seek the physical development they need, for mere health's sake, if for nothing more."

After Wilson, the percentage of identification rhetoric in the State of the Union Address never dropped below an average of 1.5% per State of the Union Address per president. Instead, the use of "we," "our," and "us" has shown a steady and permanent increase in its incorporation into the State of the Union Address. As seen in the figure above, presidents today average and surpass almost 4% identification rhetoric per State of the Union Address. Although the address lengths in the 20th century are generally only about 5,000 words, rhetoric in which the president wishes to identify himself as one of his listeners is dramatically increasing.

The 2003 State of the Union Address from George W. Bush at the outset of this chapter gives several examples of his inclusion of identification rhetoric within that address. However, Clinton and Reagan also used large amounts of identification rhetoric their State of the Union Addresses. In speaking on the economic recession in 1983, Reagan stated: "*We* must all do everything in *our* power to bring their ordeal to an end. It has fallen to *us*, in *our* time, to undo damage that was a long time in the making, and to begin the hard but necessary task of building a better future for *ourselves* and *our* children." He addressed Congressional cooperation in the same manner, proposing "So, let *us*, in these next 2 years—men and women of both parties, every political shade—concentrate on the long-range, bipartisan responsibilities of government, not the short-range or short-term temptations of partisan politics." Reagan also used the identification rhetoric speaking of the budget, "The Federal budget is both a symptom and a cause of *our* economic problems. Unless *we* reduce the dangerous growth rate in government spending, *we* could face the prospect of sluggish economic growth into the indefinite future," trade, "*We* must strengthen the organization of *our* trade agencies and make changes in *our* domestic laws and international trade policy to promote free trade and the increased flow of American goods, services, and investments," and education, "*We* must keep that edge, and to do so *we* need to begin renewing the basics—starting with *our* educational system. *We* must join together—parents, teachers, grass roots groups, organized labor, and the business community—to revitalize American education by setting a standard of excellence," to name a few areas of policy.

Clinton frequently presented himself as one of his audience as well. He began his first State of the Union Address in 1993, framing his policy initiatives as common concern from the outset. "When Presidents speak to Congress and the Nation from this podium, typically they comment on the full range and challenges and opportunities that face the United States. But this is not an ordinary time, and for all the many tasks that require *our* attention, I believe tonight one calls on *us* to focus, to unite, and to act. And that is *our* economy." As Reagan did in 1983, Clinton also used identification rhetoric to stress the importance of Congressional Cooperation to achieve his goals. "*We* must now break the habits of both political parties and say there can be no more something for nothing and admit frankly that *we* are all in this together. If *we* have the vision, the will, and the heart to make the changes *we* must, *we* can still enter the 21st century with possibilities *our* parents could not even have imagined and enter it having secured the American dream for *ourselves* and for future generations." In his address, we are almost inundated with the number of policies proposed with identification rhetoric. He spoke of the economy saying "*Our* immediate priority must be to create jobs, create jobs now," and even proposed his own initiatives under the guise that they were policies and proposals of Congress, the president, and even the people themselves, saying "*We* propose a permanent investment tax credit for the smallest firms in this country, with revenues of under $5 million. And *we* propose new rewards for entrepreneurs who take new risks. *We* propose to give small business access to all the new technologies of our time. And *we* propose to attack this credit crunch which has denied small business the credit they need to flourish and prosper." The "we" in question is very unclear as well as seemingly fluid, representing the Congress, the citizenry or the party at various points.

In addition, we see that the *consistent increase* in the percentage of identification rhetoric can be seen as a function of the presidents of the 20th and 21st centuries. Presidents in the 20th and 21st century are escalating the amount of identification rhetoric utilized by .7% over the previous president and by almost 1.2% from the prior State of the Union Address that was delivered. The contemporary president attempts to be in touch with the electorate in ways that no president of the distant past, and very few of the recent past, have imagined. From the internet to e-mail, from 24 hour cable news networks to the permanent campaign, today's president is seemingly always addressing those to whom he can propose initiative, as well as citizens who may be possible voters for his next term in office.

On the other hand, we can see that those presidents who delivered the State of the Union Address in written form consistently decreased the amount of identification rhetoric used, reaching their nadir with the last president to deliver a written address, Taft. We can say with confidence that contemporary presidents use identification rhetoric in amounts never before seen in the State of the Union Address. The president has a larger audience than ever before, and increasingly attempts to portray himself as one of them in order to garner support and further his policy goals.

Figure 2.3

The Average Percentage of Identification Rhetoric in Presidential Inaugurals

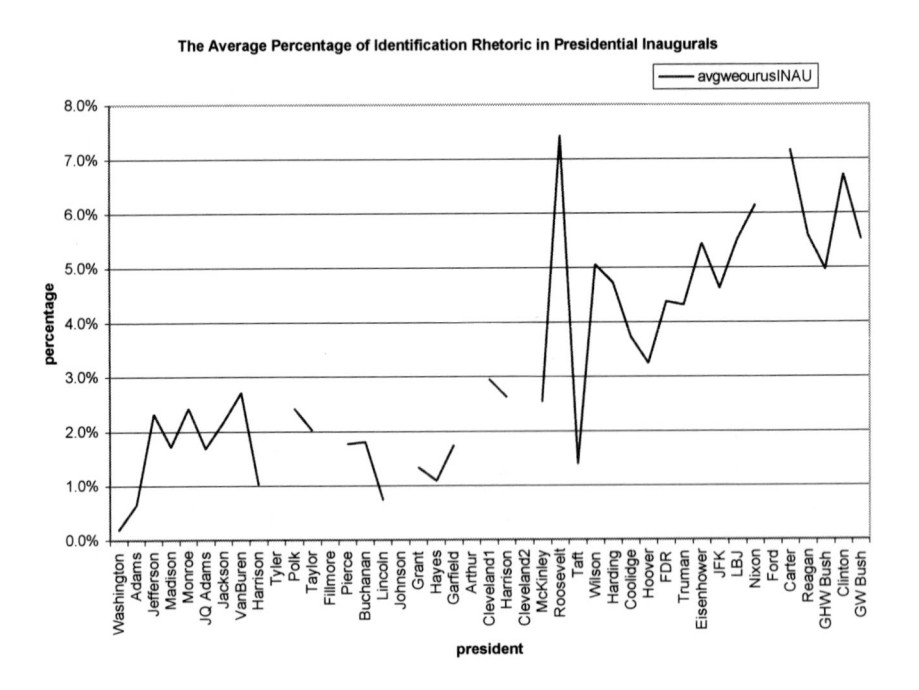

Figure 2.3 is an examination of the average percentage of identification rhetoric used in the Inaugural addresses of each president. In this figure, we are presented with a pattern that is both consistent with the tenets of the "traditional/ modern" divide as well as revealing nuances that it does not account for. The data in Figure 2.3 above suggest two major findings. The first finding is, similar to that above regarding Figure 2.2, that, converse to claim that popular address rhetoric was wholly absent in the speeches of the "traditional" presidents, presidents during the founding and the 1800's utilized anywhere from 1% to 4% of identification rhetoric during their Inaugural address, with Teddy Roosevelt using the highest levels of any president to date with nearly 7.5%.

Indeed, presidents during the founding and the 1800's were no stranger to the use of this type of speech and presidents like Martin Van Buren, Grover Cleveland and William Henry Harrison used almost as much identification rhetoric in their speeches as "modern" presidents like Harding, Coolidge, Hoover, FDR, Truman, and even JFK and GHW Bush. The first Inaugural address of Grover Cleveland can serve as an excellent illustration of the amount of identification rhetoric that was used. In his opening, and discussing the contentious presidential election of 1885, he used nearly 3.0% of identification rhetoric and stated that, "moreover, if from this hour *we* cheerfully and honestly abandon all sectional prejudice and distrust, and determine, with manly confidence in one another, to work out harmoniously the achievements of *our* national destiny, *we* shall deserve to realize all the benefits which our happy form of government can bestow. On this auspicious occasion *we* may well renew the pledge of *our* devotion to the Constitution..."

Cleveland followed up these abstract statements by using identification rhetoric in the targeting of specific policies and issues that he and his administration saw as beneficial to the people. He stated that "A due regard for the interests and prosperity of all the people demands that *our* finances shall be established upon such a sound and sensible basis... and that *our* system of revenue shall be so adjusted as to relieve the people of unnecessary taxation... The conscience of the people demands that the Indians within *our* boundaries shall be fairly and honestly treated as wards of the Government... *Our* duties are practical and call for industrious application, an intelligent perception of the claims of public office, and, above all, a firm determination, by united action, to secure to all the people of the land the full benefits of the best form of government ever vouchsafed to man." His second Inaugural address continues this high level of identification rhetoric inclusion as well.

The second conclusion that can be seen from the above chart is that there has been a gradual increase in the incorporation of identification rhetoric in the Inaugural addresses of the president from the *founding* to the present day. The increase is from about 3% of the Inaugural address during the 1700's and 1800's to around 6% of the Inaugural during the 1900's and early twenty first century. This result suggests that instead of discovering the rhetorical innovations of a single individual who can be credited with the "brand new" use of identification rhetoric in their speech, a picture emerges of presidents who, from the founding, have experimented with its use, included it when necessary, and are continuing to stretch the powers of the office by slowly utilizing more and more of the popular address rhetoric at their disposal. There is no smoothed line that indicates a particularly transformative increase after a single individual or after a certain era of the presidency. Instead, the data illustrate the ups and downs of the office that are occurring, as illustrated in the decline in identification rhetoric seen with Ronald Reagan and GHW Bush, followed by a spike that appears in the speech of Clinton, and then reversed again in GW Bush's addresses. Instead of a significant increase of popular address rhetoric by a single individual, the general trend *since the founding*, not just the early 20th century, is for an increase in the use of identification rhetoric in the Inaugural address of the presidents.

Figure 2.4

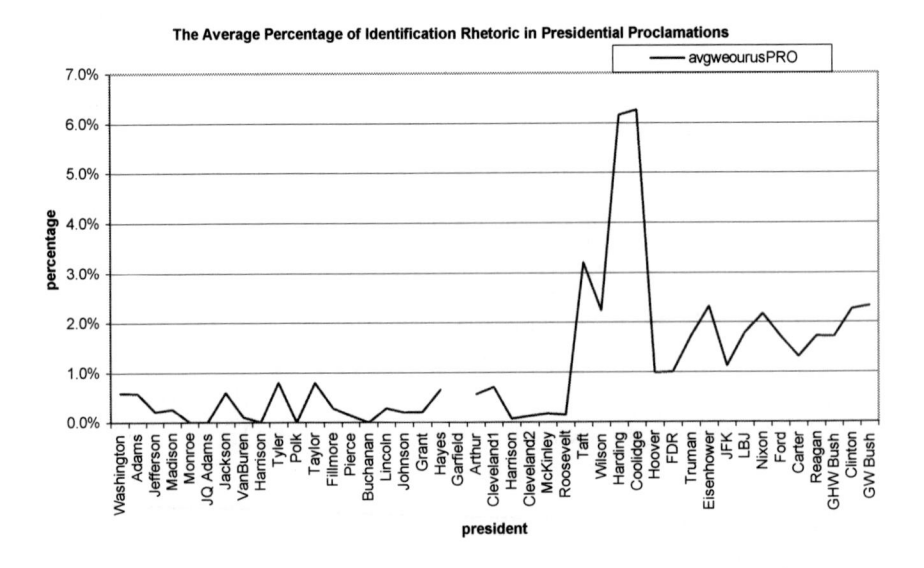

The Average Percentage of Identification Rhetoric in Presidential Proclamations

Figure 2.5

The Average Percentage of Identification Rhetoric in Presidential Executive Orders

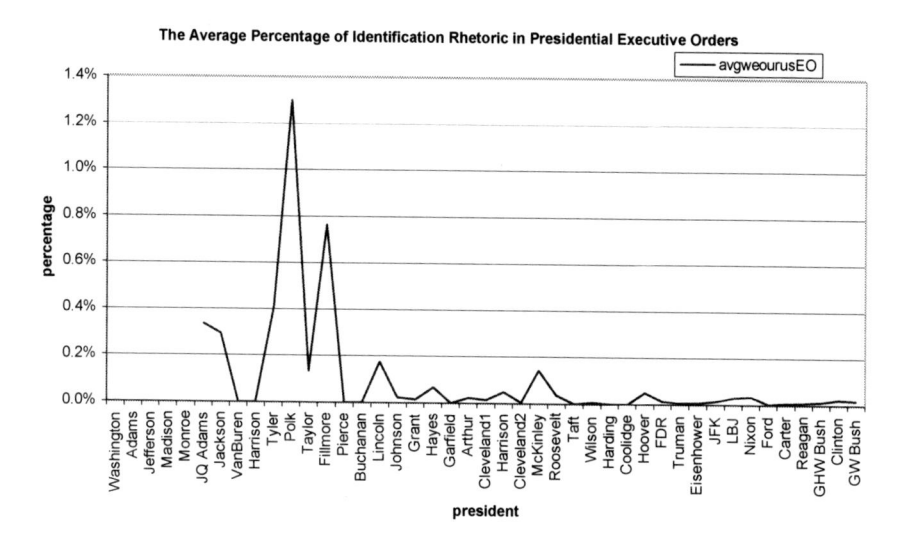

Figure 2.4 is an illustration of the average percentage of identification rhetoric used in the presidential proclamations of each president. Figure 2.5 is an illustration of the average percentage of identification rhetoric used in the executive orders of each president. As opposed to the quantities of identification rhetoric that were found in the State of the Union Addresses or the Inaugural addresses, there is a much lower amount of identification rhetoric used in presidential proclamations and executive orders. However, despite the lower levels in these addresses, they illustrate important points regarding the use of identification rhetoric in the development of presidential address. Namely, in both Figure 2.4 and Figure 2.5, there is no dramatic pattern that emerges that suggests that this form of popular address rhetoric emerged as the result of the "innovation" of a singular presidency.

Instead, what appears in the figures above is a gradual increase in the case of the presidential proclamation, and a gradual decrease in the case of the executive order, in the percentages of identification rhetoric used in these speeches by subsequent presidents. In Figure 2.4, there is a rise in the amount of identification rhetoric used in the presidential proclamations from around .5% during the founding to around 2% at the present day. Executive orders see almost the exact opposite trend in their evolution and show a decline from an average of .3% during the early 1800's to almost 0% during the executive orders of the contemporary presidents. Both speeches illustrate periods that display deviations from the norm, but there is no significant or permanent trend that can be attributed to any individual presidency, nor any specific time period in the speeches' development.

Although Figure 2.4 does not illustrate a clear distinction between a "traditional" presidency and a "modern" one in the development of the presidential proclamation, it does show an interesting spike in use of identification rhetoric during the presidencies of Taft, Harding and Coolidge. When these presidencies, and indeed their proclamations, are examined more closely, their tendency to incorporate higher levels of identification rhetoric in their proclamations than their peers, an average of 5.2% for those three presidents (Taft, Harding, and Coolidge) as opposed to 1% overall for all presidents, becomes more obvious. The answer for this spike lies in the fact that, of the proclamations that were used for this study, those that were collected for these three presidents were proclamations that only celebrated or enumerated the Thanksgiving Holiday.

The Thanksgiving Holiday, a tradition begun by George Washington in 1789, is a public proclamation that is most often transmitted, via any available media, to the people at large. The historical and public nature of this address gives it weight comparable to that of a State of the Union Address or a presidential Inaugural. Indeed, it is a speech talking to the people about the last year that the country as a whole has faced. This type of rhetoric lends itself to be filled with identification rhetoric and popular address. In his Thanksgiving proclamation in 1911, Taft stated that "*Our* industries have thrived far beyond *our* domestic needs; the productions of *our* labor are daily finding enlarged markets abroad. *We* have been free from the curses of pestilence, of famine and of war. *Our* national councils have furthered the cause of peace in other lands, and the spirit of benevolence has brought *us* into closer touch with other peoples." In his thanksgiving address in 1921, Harding explained that "In thankfulness therefore, *we* may well unite in the hope that Providence will vouchsafe approval to the things *we* have done, the aims which have guided *us*, the aspirations which have inspired *us*. *We* shall be prospered as *we* shall deserve prosperity, seeking not alone for the material things but for those of the spirit as well." And, in Calvin Coolidge's 1927 Thanksgiving proclamation, he stated that "*we* should consider the manifold blessings granted to *us*. While in gratitude *we* rejoice, *we* should humbly pray that *we* may be worthy of a continuation of Divine favor."

Because the Thanksgiving proclamation is, in itself, an address to the people, it makes sense that a greater amount of identification rhetoric should appear within that address. Indeed, the thanksgiving address has such a significant impact on the overall average of identification rhetoric in the presidential proclamations, that if we remove Taft, Harding, and Coolidge from the corpus of proclamations, the average amount of identification rhetoric in proclamations for the entire history of the presidency drops from 1.1% to less than .08%. However, Thanksgiving addresses are also present in the proclamations of almost all of the other presidents and the amount of identification rhetoric does not see nearly the jump that it does with these presidents. Although Taft, Harding, and Coolidge could be removed to create a smoother illustration of the trend of slight increase in the use of identification rhetoric in the proclamations, it would be contrary to the thesis of this book and the examination of the propriety of the "traditional/ modern" divide in general. After all, according to that paradigm, there are two clear divisions of presidential behavior and rhetoric in the past. However, the spikes and deviations on the charts, and the ways in which Taft, Harding, and Coolidge choose to address the people, even on Thanksgiving, suggest that such a classification is dangerous at the least, in that, the deviations themselves convey important information about the rhetorical proclivities of the outliers.

In addition, in Figure 2.5, while again not indicating a significant change in the percentage of identification rhetoric used in the executive orders from the founding to the present, we see an increase in the use of identification rhetoric from three presidents yet again: Tyler, Polk, and Pierce. The average percentage of identification rhetoric used in the executive orders by all of the presidents is around .1%. However, if we look at just the executive orders or Tyler (.4%), Polk (1.2%), and Fillmore (.7%), their average use of identification rhetoric is almost 8 times that of the total average at .8%. Indeed, if the three are taken out of the overall presidential average, the percentage of identification rhetoric that is used in executive orders overall drops from .1% to .04%.

A closer look at the executive orders of Tyler, Polk, and Fillmore illustrates the reasoning for the jump in the percentage of identification rhetoric that they utilize. Of the executive orders that were collected for Tyler and Fillmore, almost all of them dealt with the announcement, by executive order, of the death of a notable public figure. The executive order was usually issued to make the public aware of this national tragedy. The president would use the order, as in Fillmore's Executive Order of October 25th, 1852, to direct the military to observe the death with firing of guns and wearing of the badge of mourning. Fillmore, in one executive order, memorialized Daniel Webster, saying "Whilst this irreparable loss brings its natural sorrow to every American heart and will be heard far beyond *our* borders with mournful respect wherever civilization has nurtured men who find in transcendent intellect and faithful, patriotic service a theme for praise, it will visit with still more poignant emotion his colleagues in the Administration, with whom his relations have been so intimate and so cordial." And also that "In these his memory will endure as long as *our* country shall continue to be the home and guardian of freemen" and "The people will share with the Executive Departments in the common grief which bewails his departure from amongst *us*."

Tyler proceeded in a very rhetorically similar fashion when he announced the accidental deaths of the Secretary of State and War due to an explosion aboard the *Princeton* in an executive order on February 29th, 1844. He explained that he had an "announcement of a calamity depriving the country of the public services of two of *our* most accomplished statesmen and popular and deeply esteemed fellow-citizens" and that "Their virtues, talents, and patriotic services will ever be retained in the grateful recollection of their countrymen and perpetuated upon the pages of the history of *our* common country." Although other presidents also utilized the executive order to announce the memorialization of the deaths of notable individuals, Tyler and Fillmore show a significantly higher use of identification rhetoric in their proclamations overall, because most dealt explicitly with the passing of a public figure.

Although Polk's executive orders, the highest of the spikes in Figure 2.5, with a 1.2% percentage of identification rhetoric as opposed to the .1% average, also memorialized the passing of individuals (including the death of Andrew Jackson), the large percentage of popular address inclusion was the result of his dealing with a very different matter in his addresses. The largest percentages of identification rhetoric in Polk's executive orders came in addresses that dealt with the problems of conflict and trade that resulted from the Mexican-American war. In one executive order from March 24, 1847, Polk addressed the cost of the war, saying "I have, on full consideration, determined to order that all the ports or places in Mexico which now are or hereafter may be in the actual possession of *our* land and naval forces by conquest shall be opened while *our* military occupation may continue to the commerce of all neutral nations, as well as *our* own, in articles not contraband of war, upon the payment of prescribed rates of duties." In another executive order from March 30, 1847, Polk used much more identification rhetoric, stating that "It is clear that *we* must either adopt *our* own tariff or that of Mexico, or establish a new system of duties. *Our* own tariff could not be adopted, because the Mexican exports and imports are so different from *our* own that different rates of duties are indispensable in order to collect the largest revenue" and also that "In the meantime it is not just that Mexico, by her obstinate persistence in this contest, should compel *us* to overthrow *our* own financial policy and arrest this great nation in her high and prosperous career. To re-impose high duties would be alike injurious to *ourselves* and to all neutral powers."

The illustrations concerning the outlier presidents in the use of identification rhetoric in the presidential proclamations and executive orders, as well as the shifts towards declined use of popular address rhetoric in one form of speech and an increase in another suggest several things. First of all, the data fail to completely support the assertion that there was a singular presidency that changed the format or the delivery of the proclamation and executive order as it relates to identification rhetoric. Indeed, we don't see a pattern of dramatic increase in the beginning of the twentieth century. Instead, if we are seeking any kind of pattern at all, it is a gradual increase in identification rhetoric in the presidential proclamations and a gradual decrease of the same in the executive orders. It is through a close examination of the context and the text of the presidential proclamations and executive orders that the reason for this shift may be explained.

The gradual decline in the identification rhetoric used in the executive orders as well as the gradual increase that can be seen in the identification rhetoric usage in presidential proclamations stems from their development and function, as opposed to singular innovation or administrative transformation. There has been, over the course of presidential rhetorical history, a redefining of the purposes of the proclamation and the executive order. Although they both began in Washington's tenure as ways in which the president could unilaterally legislate, executive orders have slowly become the rhetorical tool of choice for this power, while the proclamation has evolved into a way for the president to identify with the public. Primarily, when Washington began the precedent of memorializing Thanksgiving with a proclamation, he began an evolution of the address form that would slowly shift it to the realm of almost pure holiday and celebration subject matter that can be seen in the proclamations issued in the contemporary presidency.

To begin the look at the evolution that has taken place in the proclamations, it is first important to examine how they have changed in regard to subject matter from the founding to the present day.

Figure 2.6

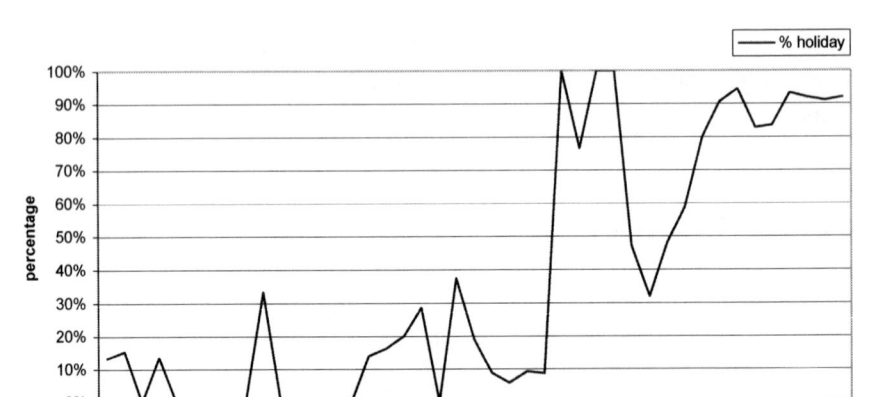

The Percentage of Presidential Proclamations that are Holiday or Observance Related

Figure 2.6 is an illustration of the number of proclamations that were issued from George Washington to George W. Bush that were holiday or observance related in their subject matter. Although this classification is more easily observable with the presidents of the 20th century, where presidential proclamations began to be titled beginning fully with the presidency of Woodrow Wilson, to make this determination consistently across all presidents, I separated all of the presidential proclamations into those whose overall subject matter specifically asked the country to celebrate or observe an accomplishment, event, or individual, and those which dealt with tangible issue of domestic and international affairs, with no mention of the need for the time to be set aside for any purpose.

Apart from several spikes, such as Taft, Harding and Coolidge where all of the sampled proclamations dealt with Thanksgiving, the trend in the Figure appears very similar to Figure 2.4, which examines the use of identification rhetoric in the proclamations. One significant observation is the lack of ceremonial proclamations that are issued during the 18th and 19th centuries, where the presidential proclamation is either not used at all or is used very seldom for holiday purposes. This is truly a time where the proclamations very much resemble their executive order cousins in terms of format, form and function, and in their seeming proclivity to deal only with tangible policy and law.

Beginning during Washington's tenure, we can see the presidential proclamation being used primarily in the same fashion as the executive order. Although proclamations during his administration dealt with varying topics, each had the weight of law and nearly 80% of them were the president's attempt to execute law or direct policy, as opposed to his effort to observe a holiday. Some proclamations during Washington's term dealt with the president's reinforcement of obeying already existing statute, stating "I have therefore thought fit to require, and I do by these presents require, all officers of the United States, as well civil as military, and all other citizens and inhabitants thereof, to govern themselves according to the treaties and act aforesaid, as they will answer the contrary at their peril" (August 26th, 1790).

Others issued by Washington dealt with the construction of the Capitol, explaining that "Now, therefore, in pursuance of the powers to me confided, and after duly examining and weighing the advantages and disadvantages of the several situations within the limits aforesaid, I do hereby declare and make known that the location of one part of the said district of 10 miles square shall be found by running four lines of experiment in the following manner..." (January 24th, 1791). And still other proclamations issued by Washington dealt with foreign affairs and foreign relations, stating that "I have given instructions to those officers to whom it belongs to cause prosecutions to be instituted against all persons who shall, within the cognizance of the courts of the United States, violate the law of nations [between Austria, Prussia, Sardinia, Great Britain, and the United Netherlands of the one part and France on the other] with respect to the powers at war, or any of them" (April 22nd, 1793).

As opposed to this seemingly wide breadth of issue address seen in Washington's proclamations, the presidents of the 21st century appear to have foresworn the tangible in favor of the ceremonial. Another George from the presidential annals, George W. Bush, seems indeed to be a polar opposite of his predecessor. Proclamations that are non-holiday related are few and far between. As an example, in 2007, Bush issued 116 proclamations; of those proclamations, only seven were not holiday related. In addition, when the presidents of the late 20th and early 21st centuries do decide to utilize the proclamation for non-holiday purposes, the directives deal primarily with issues in generally two realms of policy: trade and immigration. During his entire administration, Bush only issued non-holiday proclamations dealing with trade to Vietnam (Proclamation 7446), Jordan (Proclamation 7512), Argentina (Proclamation 7586), Africa (Proclamation 7626), Australia (Proclamation 7857) and Armenia (Proclamation 7860). He has also dealt with items of trade like Lamb (Proclamation 7445), Steel Wire Rod (Proclamation 7505), Line Pipe (Proclamation 7585), and Steel (Proclamation 7741). In each of these instances, the imports from products and countries are altered or amended from prior law.

In regards to the second subject matter, Bush issued proclamations that altered or set-up quotas regarding immigration from specific countries. This use of the proclamation can be traced back as far as Abraham Lincoln who issued a proclamation on April 16, 1863, which dealt with "the immigration of persons of African extraction to a dependency of the Republic of Hayti." Bush used the proclamations in 2007 to speak to immigration quotas and qualifications form the Balkans (Proclamation 7452), Zimbabwe (Proclamation 7524), and Burkina Faso (Proclamation 7853).

Although the previously examined proclamations dealt with issues that were not holiday related, the lion's share of the proclamations by presidents of the late 20th and early 21st centuries have been just that. During George W. Bush's term as president, over 90% of the proclamations that he issued have been holiday and observance related. These proclamations are formatted to mark a national holiday (Thanksgiving), to take note of a significant loss (Supreme Court Justice death), or, more frequently, to create the observance of a day, week, month, year, or even century that will be tied to the observance and information regarding a specific issue. In 2007 alone, George Bush issued, and the United States observed the following:

Figure 2.7: The Holiday or Observance Related Proclamations Issued by George W. Bush in 2007

Date	Proclamation and Observance or Holiday
Jan 11th, 2007	Proclamation 8099 - Martin Luther King, Jr. Day
Jan 11th, 2007	Proclamation 8100 - Religious Freedom Day
Jan 18th, 2007	Proclamation 8101 - National Sanctity of Human Life Day
Jan 25th, 2007	Proclamation 8102 - Fifth Anniversary of USA Freedom Corps
Jan 26th, 2007	Proclamation 8103 - National African American History Month
Feb 1st, 2007	Proclamation 8104 - American Heart Month
Feb 2nd, 2007	Proclamation 8105 - National Consumer Protection Week
Feb 16th, 2007	Proclamation 8106 - 275th Birth of George Washington
Feb 26th, 2007	Proclamation 8107 - Irish-American Heritage Month
Feb 27th, 2007	Proclamation 8108 - American Red Cross Month
Feb 27th, 2007	Proclamation 8109 - Women's History Month
Feb 28th, 2007	Proclamation 8110 - Save Your Vision Week
March 16th, 2007	Proclamation 8113 - National Poison Prevention Week
March 21st, 2007	Proclamation 8115 – Greek Independence Day
March 26th, 2007	Proclamation 8116 - Education and Sharing Day, U.S.A.
March 27th, 2007	Proclamation 8117 - National Child Abuse Prevention Month
March 28th, 2007	Proclamation 8118 - National Donate Life Month
March 29th, 2007	Proclamation 8119 - Cancer Control Month
April 5th, 2007	Proclamation 8120 - Pan American Day and Pan American Week
April 5th, 2007	Proclamation 8121 - Former Prisoner of War Recognition Day
April 6th, 2007	Proclamation 8122 - 400th Anniversary of Jamestown
April 11th, 2007	Proclamation 8123 - National D.A.R.E. Day
April 11th, 2007	Proclamation 8124 - Thomas Jefferson Day
April 11th, 2007	Proclamation 8125 - National Volunteer Week
April 17th, 2007	Proclamation 8126 - Honoring Victims of Virginia Tech Tragedy
April 19th, 2007	Proclamation 8127 - Small Business Week
April 19th, 2007	Proclamation 8128 - Dutch-American Friendship Day
April 20th, 2007	Proclamation 8129 - National Day of Prayer
April 20th, 2007	Proclamation 8130 - National Crime Victims' Rights Week
April 20th, 2007	Proclamation 8131 - National Park Week
April 24th, 2007	Proclamation 8132 - Malaria Awareness Day
April 26th, 2007	Proclamation 8133 - Asian/Pacific American Heritage Month
April 27th, 2007	Proclamation 8134 - National Charter Schools Week
April 27th, 2007	Proclamation 8135 - Law Day, U.S.A.
April 30th, 2007	Proclamation 8136 - Jewish American Heritage Month
April 30th, 2007	Proclamation 8137 - Loyalty Day

(Continued on next page)

(Figure 2.7 Continued)

May 1st, 2007	Proclamation 8138 - National Physical Fitness and Sports Month
May 1st, 2007	Proclamation 8139 - Older Americans Month
May 7th, 2007	Proclamation 8140 - Mother's Day
May 9th, 2007	Proclamation 8141 - Military Spouse Day
May 10th, 2007	Proclamation 8142 - National Defense Transportation Day
May 10th, 2007	Proclamation 8143 - National Safe Boating Week
May 11th, 2007	Proclamation 8144 - Peace Officers Memorial Day/ Police Week
May 15th, 2007	Proclamation 8145 - Prayer for Peace, Memorial Day
May 18th, 2007	Proclamation 8146 - National Hurricane Preparedness Week
May 18th, 2007	Proclamation 8147 - World Trade Week
May 18th, 2007	Proclamation 8148 - National Maritime Day
May 25th, 2007	Proclamation 8149 - Great Outdoors Month
May 30th, 2007	Proclamation 8150 - National Oceans Month
May 31st, 2007	Proclamation 8151 - Black Music Month
May 31st, 2007	Proclamation 8152 - National Child's Day
June 1st, 2007	Proclamation 8153 - Caribbean-American Heritage Month
June 1st, 2007	Proclamation 8154 - National Homeownership Month
June 5th, 2007	Proclamation 8155 - Flag Day and National Flag Week
June 11th, 2007	Proclamation 8156 - Father's Day
July 10th, 2007	Proclamation 8160 - Captive Nations Week
July 12th, 2007	Proclamation 8162 - Death of Lady Bird Johnson
July 12th, 2007	Proclamation 8161 - Parents' Day
July 24th, 2007	Proclamation 8163 – Anniversary -Americans Disabilities Act
August 6th, 2007	Proclamation 8164 - Women's Equality Day
Aug 20th, 2007	Proclamation 8165 - National Ovarian Cancer Awareness Month
Aug 21st, 2007	Proclamation 8166 - National Prostate Cancer Awareness Month
Aug 21st, 2007	Proclamation 8167 - National Alcohol/Drug Recovery Month
Aug 21st, 2007	Proclamation 8168 - Constitution Day/Week, Citizenship Day
Aug 28th, 2007	Proclamation 8169 - Minority Enterprise Development Week
Aug 30th, 2007	Proclamation 8170 - National Preparedness Month
Aug 30th, 2007	Proclamation 8171 - National Support the Guard/Reserve Week
Sept 4th, 2007	Proclamation 8172 - National Historically Black Colleges Week
Sept 4th, 2007	Proclamation 8173 - National Days of Prayer and Remembrance
Sept 4th, 2007	Proclamation 8174 - Patriot Day
Sept 12th, 2007	Proclamation 8175 - National Hispanic Heritage Month
Sept 12th, 2007	Proclamation 8176 - National Farm Safety and Health Week
Sept 20th, 2007	Proclamation 8177 - National POW/MIA Recognition Day
Sept 20th, 2007	Proclamation 8178 - Family Day

(Continued on next page)

(Figure 2.7 Continued)

Sept 21st, 2007	Proclamation 8179 - Gold Star Mother's Day
Sept 28th, 2007	Proclamation 8181 - National Breast Cancer Awareness Month
Sept 28th, 2007	Proclamation 8182 - National Disability Employ/Aware Month
Oct 1st, 2007	Proclamation 8184 - Child Health Day
Oct 1st, 2007	Proclamation 8183 - National Domestic Violence Aware Month
Oct 4th, 2007	Proclamation 8185 - German-American Day
Oct 4th, 2007	Proclamation 8186 - Columbus Day
Oct 4th, 2007	Proclamation 8188 - Fire Prevention Week
Oct 10th, 2007	Proclamation 8189 - General Pulaski Memorial Day
Oct 12th, 2007	Proclamation 8190 - National School Lunch Week
Oct 12th, 2007	Proclamation 8191 - White Cane Safety Day
Oct 19th, 2007	Proclamation 8192 - National Character Counts Week
Oct 19th, 2007	Proclamation 8193 - National Forest Products Week
Oct 23rd, 2007	Proclamation 8194 - United Nations Day
Oct 31st, 2007	Proclamation 8196 - National American Indian Heritage Month
Oct 31st, 2007	Proclamation 8197 - National Family Caregivers Month
Oct 31st, 2007	Proclamation 8198 - National Hospice Month
Oct 31st, 2007	Proclamation 8199 - Veterans Day
Oct 31st, 2007	Proclamation 8200 - National Alzheimer's Disease Aware Month
Oct 31st, 2007	Proclamation 8201 - National Diabetes Month
Oct 31st, 2007	Proclamation 8195 - National Adoption Month
Nov 8th, 2007	Proclamation 8202 - World Freedom Day
Nov 15th, 2007	Proclamation 8203 - America Recycles Day
Nov 15th, 2007	Proclamation 8204 - Thanksgiving Day
Nov 16th, 2007	Proclamation 8205 - National Farm-City Week
Nov 16th, 2007	Proclamation 8206 - National Family Week
Nov 29th, 2007	Proclamation 8207 - World AIDS Day
Nov 30th, 2007	Proclamation 8208 - Drunk/Drugged Driving Prevention Month
Dec. 4th, 2007	Proclamation 8209 - National Pearl Harbor Remembrance Day
Dec 6th, 2007	Proclamation 8210 - Human Rights Day/Week, Bill of Rights Day
Dec 11th, 2007	Proclamation 8211 - Wright Brothers Day
Dec 19th, 2007	Proclamation 8212 - National Mentoring Month

Many different issues, from citizen uprisings and Indian treaties to international affairs occupied a significant portion of George Washington's rhetoric in the presidential proclamations. There seemed to be little focus on special occasions or repose throughout his rhetorical tenure. In fact, out of his proclamations, only two dealt with holidays and observances, and both of these were Thanksgiving. However, during George W. Bush's tenure, as seen above, proclamations were used almost absolutely for holiday proposal, and out of nearly 700 proclamations, only around 52 dealt with issues not surrounding a holiday.

Some of the origins for this evolution of the holiday-related proclamation as opposed to the reliance on the executive order for unilateral lawmaking may be found in the presidencies of Lincoln and other late 19th and early 20th century presidents. The Thanksgiving Day proclamation, which originated with the first presidential proclamation issued by George Washington, was a precedent and a tradition that was followed by every subsequent president to the present day. However, it is with the presidencies of the mid 1800's, and significantly that of Lincoln, that holidays and other observances begin to find their way into the rhetoric of presidential proclamations. In fact, up until the presidency of Lincoln, there were few proclamations that addressed holidays other than Thanksgiving. However, Lincoln put his own stamp on presidential proclamations by observing several other days of his creation. On February 19th, 1862, Lincoln issued a proclamation to honor George Washington, saying "It is recommended to the people of the United States that they assemble in their customary places of meeting for public solemnities on the 22d day of February instant and celebrate the anniversary of the birth of the Father of his Country by causing to be read to them his immortal Farewell Address."

In addition, Lincoln felt free to call for days of thanksgiving and prayer apart from the day usually reserved for that purpose in September. On April 10th, 1862, after Union victories on land and sea, Lincoln asked of "the people of the United States that at their next weekly assemblages in their accustomed places of public worship which shall occur after notice of this proclamation shall have been received they especially acknowledge and render thanks to our Heavenly Father for these inestimable blessings, that they then and there implore spiritual consolation in behalf of all who have been brought into affliction by the casualties and calamities of sedition and civil war, and that they reverently invoke the divine guidance for our national counsels, to the end that they may speedily result in the restoration of peace, harmony, and unity throughout our borders and hasten the establishment of fraternal relations among all the countries of the earth" Further, on March 30th, 1863, he asked the nation for "a day of national humiliation, fasting, and prayer" stating that it "behooves us, then, to humble ourselves before the offended Power, to confess our national sins, and to pray for clemency and forgiveness." He requested another national day of prayer yet again in July of 1864 as well.

Lincoln's use of the presidential proclamation for the observance of holidays, and as an opportunity to bind the country together as a single entity, is of no surprise to rhetoricians or sociologists alike. Rituals and holidays like Thanksgiving are, after all, some of the elements that work to create in the citizens of the United States a common energy and identity. Societies for hundreds of years have used rituals for a sense of shared "sentiments and beliefs or emphasizing common ground where disagreement also exists" (Hermanowicz, 1999, 199). In addition, "Rituals can promote values or behavior among observers. They can be used to claim legitimacy...groups use rituals to define for themselves and their observers what they believe is valuable and right. In doing so, they promote and protect a collective self image" (Hermanowicz, 1999, 199-200).

Presidents, then, like ritualistic leaders of the past, have chosen to seize on holidays, their creation, and recognition, as new ways to both connect the American people as a whole and illustrate their identification with and support for specific interested groups within the country. Holidays like National Ovarian Cancer Awareness Month and National Forest Products Week are attempts by the presidents to reach out to smaller groups within the electorate as a signal that they care about the issue at hand. This is a form of "symbolic quiescence" as described by Edelman (1964) that "provides the spectator with reassurance that his or her values are respected and that his or her goals are being pursued. Such acts have little relation to the 'actual' world of political events" (Gusfield, 1984, 423). In this way, a president can appeal to a specific group through the creation of a holiday that they care about. It is this "group appeal" function of the proclamation that has contributed to the rise in the amount of identification rhetoric used in the presidential proclamation. It is also this evolved use of the proclamation for holiday related purposes that has led to the decline in the use of identification rhetoric in executive orders, as they are now largely legislatively sterile and address changes in law as opposed to people in general.

70   *The Evolutionary Rhetorical Presidency*

Tracing the Use of Authority Rhetoric

In today's political world, when the economy of the country is good, the president most often attempts to take the credit. When it is bad, the voters of America are not shy in attributing to him all of the blame. In times of profit, the president will speak of "my" tax cuts or the plans "I" sent to Congress. But how often does the president actually use this kind of national authority in his addresses? Authority rhetoric here is conceptualized as specific words that are used in presidential rhetoric with which the president attempts to explain his own logic or reasoning on the matter as the basis for policy adoption from the Congress or policy advocacy from the people. In addition, authority rhetoric indicates times when the president attempts to be "The President" and speaks with all of the authority and respect of the office he holds. This can be seen in the frequency of "I," "me," and "my" in each of the four forms of presidential rhetoric observed here.

Figure 2.8

The Average Percentage of Authority Rhetoric in the State of the Union Address per President

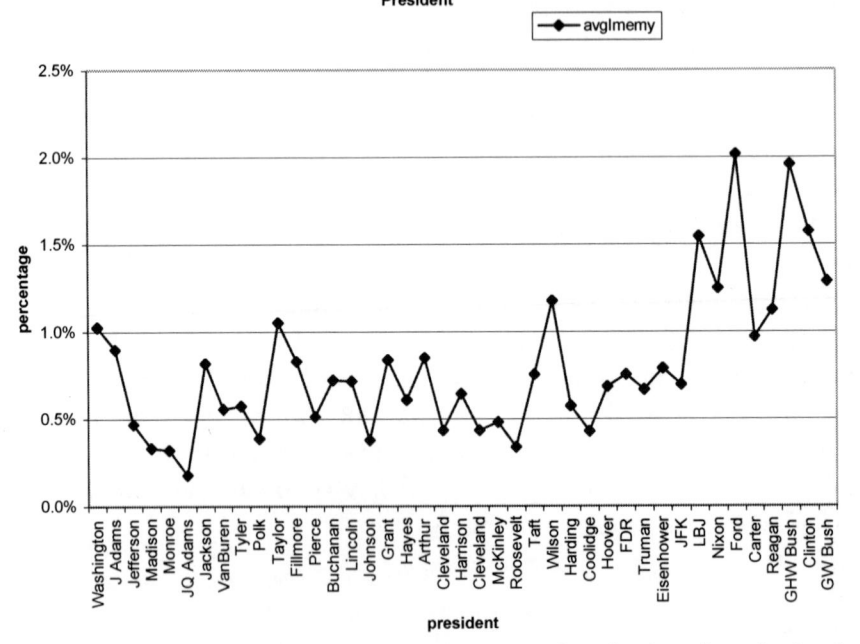

Figure 2.8 shows the average percent use of authority rhetoric in the State of the Union Address per president. From this figure we can see that

authority rhetoric is utilized on a smaller scale in State of the Union Addresses than identification rhetoric. As Figure 2.8 shows, the average percentage of authority rhetoric generally stayed below 1% of the words in the State of the Union Address from the founding until the late 20th century. The most significant changes in the use of authority rhetoric can be seen with the presidencies of Ford and GHW Bush. However, even though authority rhetoric saw spiked increases with these presidencies, it was by no means absent from founding or 19th century State of the Union Addresses. As seen above, presidents such as Washington, Adams, Jackson, Taylor, Grant, and Arthur, all ruling during the time of the "traditional" rhetorical presidency, spoke with levels of authority rhetoric that were not even matched by twentieth century presidents like Harding, Coolidge, Truman, Eisenhower, FDR or JFK. In addition, although LBJ, Ford, and GHW Bush do rise to levels that are unmatched in presidential history, their contemporaries like Nixon, Carter, Reagan, and GW Bush, are not significantly different from the presidents of the founding or nineteenth century.

For example, in 1799, almost 1.3% of John Adams' State of the Union Address consisted of authority rhetoric. This level nearly equals the average level for the entire presidency of LBJ. Adams used much of his address to explain policies that he had initiated as well as policies he wanted commenced during his tenure. As seen in Adams' State of the Union Address in 1798, authority rhetoric appears at the very outset of the address in the initial policy recommendation. "*I* think it my duty to invite the Legislature of the Union to examine the expediency of establishing suitable regulations in aid of the health laws of the respective States." He asserted himself again dealing with trade, "*I* deem it a duty deliberately and solemnly to declare my opinion that whether we negotiate with her or not, vigorous preparations for war will be alike indispensable. These alone will give to us an equal treaty and insure its observance," the budget, "*I* have directed an estimate of the appropriations which will be necessary for the service of the ensuing year to be laid before you, accompanied with a view of the public receipts and expenditures to a recent period," and even in closing the address, "*I* trust that by the temper and wisdom of your proceedings and by a harmony of measures we shall secure to our country that weight and respect to which it is so justly entitled."

In the State of the Union Addresses of LBJ, we can see an increase from the overall average of the authority rhetoric used in the State of the Union Address as well as from that exhibited by Adams. In fact, although his overall average is around 2.0%, Lyndon Johnson's State of the Union Address in

1969 can be seen as a benchmark address that utilized a larger percentage of authority rhetoric (2.8%) than any other State of the Union Address before him and only surpassed by George H.W. Bush in 1992 (2.9%). LBJ used authority rhetoric in his address to propose policy and reinforce the goals of his administration. From social security, "The time has come, *I* think, to make it more adequate. *I* believe we should increase social security benefits, and *I* am so recommending tonight. *I* am suggesting that there should be an overall increase in benefits of at least 13 percent. Those who receive only the minimum of $55 should get $80 a month," to discussion of women and children, "*I* think we should assure decent medical care for every expectant mother and for their children during the first year of their life in the United States of America. *I* think we should protect our children and their families from the costs of catastrophic illness," Johnson felt free to introduce policies with little more rhetorical justification than that he believed the changes necessary.

Johnson further used authority rhetoric to remind Congress to act on previously proposed policies that would stretch far beyond even the next presidency. "This year *I* am proposing that the Congress provide the full $300 million that the Congress last year authorized to do just that....*I* hope the Congress will put the money where the authorization is...*I* believe this is an essential contribution to justice and to public order in the United States. *I* hope these grants can be made to the States and they can be used effectively to reduce the crime rate in this country...Frankly, as *I* leave the Office of the Presidency, one of my greatest disappointments is our failure to secure passage of a licensing and registration act for firearms...*I* think if we had passed that act, it would have reduced the incidence of crime. *I* believe that the Congress should adopt such a law, and *I* hope that it will at a not too distant date. *I* will suggest that Congress appropriate a very small additional allowance for official expenses, so that Members will not be required to use their salary increase for essential official business...In 1967 *I* recommended to the Congress a fair and impartial random selection system for the draft. *I* submit it again tonight for your most respectful consideration."

Although presidents from the founding to almost the 1970's appear to use lower amounts of authority rhetoric in their State of the Union Addresses overall than presidents like LBJ, Ford, and GHW Bush, Adams' example demonstrates that the *individual speeches* themselves may utilize authority rhetoric that rivals even the highest levels of these contemporary presidents.

The overall average for all of the presidents' uses of authority rhetoric is about .6% per State of the Union Address. Ford and GHW Bush are above these averages with 2.0% authority rhetoric in their addresses on the average. However, there are many presidents during the eighteenth, nineteenth, and twentieth centuries that tend to be obscured through an examination of overall averages. Individually, they use levels of authority rhetoric higher than the overall average and similar to each other in their individual addresses. During the 1700's, Both Washington and John Adams used over 1% authority rhetoric in their speeches in 1790, 1792, and 1799. In the 1800's, Jackson (State of the union addresses of 1830, 1831, 1832, 1833), Taylor (1849, 1850), Fillmore (1850), Lincoln (1861), Grant (1870), Hayes (1877), and Arthur (1882) all used levels of authority rhetoric that were exactly the same or similar by hundredths of a percentage point to the speeches by Wilson (1913, 1916, 1920), FDR (1934, 1935, 1936), JFK (1961), LBJ (1965, 1966, 1967, 1968), Nixon (1970, 1972, 1973), Reagan (1983, 1986, 1987, 1988) and Clinton (1993, 1994, 1995, 1996, 1997, 1998, 1999, 2000).

The figure and statistics above illustrate that no singular presidency has significantly impacted the evolution of the use of authority rhetoric. Indeed, if there is any pattern to be found at all, it is the mere suggestion of a slight increase from the founding to the present in the amount of authority rhetoric that is used in the State of the Union Address. However, as demonstrated above, the variation between the individual speeches of the presidents makes even this generalization difficult to conclusively exhibit. In addition, the comparison between the speeches of seven "traditional" presidents with seven "modern" presidents who speak in very similar fashion with this form of popular address suggests that there may be more in common in the rhetoric of presidents of the past than once thought. Further, these commonalities suggest, yet again, that a simple dichotomy based upon eras of presidential history may not be truly indicative of the rhetorical capabilities of each president, nor the nuances that can be gleaned from an in-depth study of each.

Figure 2.9

The Average Percentage of Authority Rhetoric in Presidential Inaugural Addresses

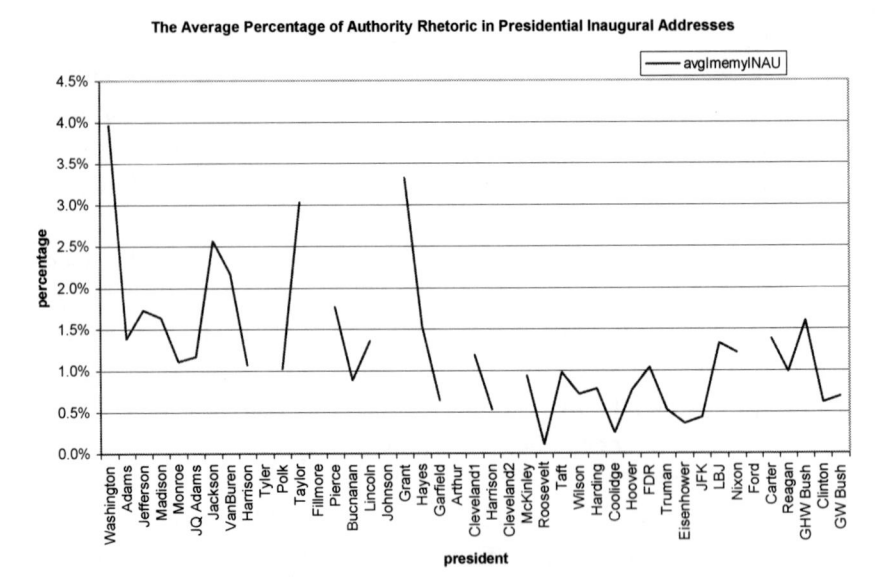

Figure 2.9 shows the average percent use of authority rhetoric in the presidential Inaugural Address per president. An immediate finding is that, similarly to the state of the union address above, presidents, overall, use lower percentages of authority rhetoric in their Inaugurals than they do in the State of the Union Address. The first major finding is that Figure 2.9 illustrates a trend that appears opposite to that of the use of identification rhetoric in the Inaugural address examined in Figure 2.4 above. As opposed to the evolution of identification rhetoric in the Inaugural which illustrated an increase in its use, the use of authority rhetoric in the Inaugural appears to slightly decline over the time of the presidency from an average of around 2% of the address during the 1800's to around 1% of the address today.

This decline and general trend is in contradiction to the "traditional/modern" divide for several reasons. First of all, as discussed in Chapter 1, one of the primary tenets of the paradigm suggests that presidents during the founding as well as the "traditional" period avoided any focus on themselves or used the power of the office towards any of their own ends or for any of their own means. They were, allegedly, bound by the precedent of propriety established by Washington and the constraints of limited power enumerated in the Constitution from actively pursuing their own agenda or proposing policy or activity to be acted upon by Congress. Although the average use of authority rhetoric is 1.2% for all of the presidents, if we follow the classification of "traditional" and "modern" we discover conclusions that contradict the basic premises of the divide. Presidents from the founding through the 1800's utilized an average of 1.6% authority rhetoric in their Inaugural addresses. Presidents during the twentieth and twenty-first centuries, however, only used an average of .8% authority rhetoric in their Inaugural addresses. Not only do the presidents of the "traditional" period exemplify very "modern" behavior in this regard, but the presidents who used the five *highest* levels of authority rhetoric in their Inaugural addresses all governed prior to 1900 (Washington, Jackson, Van Buren, Taylor, and Grant), almost 20 years prior to the suggested "modern" advent of this kind of president-centered speech.

A look at a few of the Inaugural addresses that utilized the highest and lowest levels of authority rhetoric illustrate the evolutionary changes that have taken place regarding this form of address. According to the "traditional/ modern" divide, there should be no early president, either founding or nineteenth century, who should not be bound by precedent and the limitations of the constitution. Yet presidents like Jackson, Van Buren, and the unlikely Taylor and Grant have defied this definition in their Inaugural addresses. Although Washington began Inaugural history as well as presidential rhetorical history with the highest levels of authority rhetoric to date (an average of almost 4% of his Inaugural address), we might expect this from the founder of the country who used his Inaugural to reaffirm his place as simply the political head of the country who would work only towards its unity. He even stated that "I behold the surest pledges that as on one side no local prejudices or attachments, no separate views nor party animosities, will misdirect the comprehensive and equal eye which ought to watch over this great assemblage of communities and interests, so, on another, that the foundation of our national policy will be laid in the pure and immutable principles of private morality, and the preeminence of free government be exemplified by all the attributes which can win the affections of its citizens and command the respect of the world." His large percentage of authority rhetoric was used in stating what he would *not* do to damage the country, as opposed to what he would like to have seen done for the future.

This is hardly the case with the use of authority rhetoric utilized by Jackson and Van Buren in their Inaugural addresses. Jackson asserted his position as president as the main point of logic behind his policies and programs and the new administration almost from the outset of his first Inaugural in 1829. He explained that, as president, he would be faced with several duties and "the principles of action by which *I* shall endeavor to accomplish this circle of duties it is now proper for *me* briefly to explain." He suggested that the economy would be a top priority, and that "This *I* shall aim at the more anxiously both because it will facilitate the extinguishment of the national debt, the unnecessary duration of which is incompatible with real independence." In addition, as a former military man, he immediately requested that "the introduction of progressive improvements in the discipline and science of both branches of our military service are so plainly prescribed by prudence that *I* should be excused for omitting their mention sooner than for enlarging on their importance." He did not stop there, however and used authority rhetoric to address his policy on the Indians, "It will be *my* sincere and constant desire to observe toward the Indian tribes within our limits a just and liberal policy," and on the spoils system and hiring practices, stating that "In the performance of a task thus generally delineated *I* shall endeavor to select men whose diligence and talents will insure in their respective stations able and faithful cooperation." This use of high levels of authority rhetoric is not limited to his first Inaugural, however, and the second speech is of the same tone and tenor, with Jackson asserting his position as justification for action.

Jackson's successor, Martin Van Buren, although a bitter disappointment to Jackson in terms of presidential rule, utilized authority popular address rhetoric to the same effect in his Inaugural address in 1837. Van Buren, much like Jackson, felt that it was his duty, as president of the United States to proscribe the propositions that he viewed in the best interest of the country, and stated that "standing as *I* now do before *my* countrymen, in this high place of honor and of trust, *I* can not refrain from anxiously invoking *my* fellow-citizens never to be deaf to its dictates. Perceiving before *my* election the deep interest this subject was beginning to excite, *I* believed it a solemn duty fully to make known *my* sentiments in regard to it, and now, when every motive for misrepresentation has passed away, *I* trust that they will be candidly weighed and understood." This statement alone contains eight instances of authority rhetoric in the Inaugural, and Van Buren hadn't even addressed the specifics of his policies yet.

Having laid the foundation of his own authority and that of the office, he continued by addressing one of the most troubling issues of the time, slavery, and attempting to quell the unrest on the issue from the beginning of his administration with the authority of his office. After having decided that the government should not intervene in the issue of slavery, he stated that "*I* submitted also to my fellow-citizens, with fullness and frankness, the reasons which led *me* to this determination. The result authorizes *me* to believe that they have been approved and are confided in by a majority of the people of the United States, including those whom they most immediately affect. It now only remains to add that no bill conflicting with these views can ever receive *my* constitutional sanction." Not only did Van Buren exclaim, from the beginning of his presidency, that the country could defer to him and his decisions and reasonings as president, but that the issue of slavery also needed to be a non-issue, because this was his promise should he be elected successfully. This is, in fact, the true essence of authority rhetoric: it is the president's assertion that his programs and policies should be followed because he holds the highest office in the land, and little more explanation is needed.

As other presidents who were above the average, both Taylor and Grant utilized around 3% authority rhetoric in their Inaugural addresses as well. In his address in 1849, Taylor began his Inaugural by utilizing authority rhetoric for abstract claims, stating that "*I* this day renew the declarations *I* have heretofore made and proclaim *my* fixed determination to maintain to the extent of my ability the Government in its original purity and to adopt as the basis of *my* public policy those great republican doctrines which constitute the strength of our national existence." He also grew much more specific with its usage relating to international relations, "In the conduct of our foreign relations *I* shall conform to these views, as *I* believe them essential to the best interests and the true honor of the country," patronage, "*I* shall make honesty, capacity, and fidelity indispensable prerequisites to the bestowal of office," and basic domestic issues, "It shall be *my* study to recommend such constitutional measures to Congress as may be necessary and proper to secure encouragement and protection to the great interests of agriculture, commerce, and manufactures." Grant too used authority rhetoric to set the general tenor for the power of his administration in his Inaugural address of 1869, stating that "*I* will always express *my* views to Congress and urge them according to *my* judgment, and when *I* think it advisable *I* will exercise the constitutional privilege of interposing a veto to defeat measures which *I* oppose." Similarly to Taylor, he then utilized authority rhetoric to enumerate the policy positions of his administration relating to Indians, "*I* will favor any course toward them which tends to their civilization and ultimate citizenship," as well as suffrage, saying that "*I* entertain the hope and express the desire that it may be by the ratification of the fifteenth article of amendment to the Constitution." Contrary to the tenets of the "traditional/ modern" divide, these presidents neither shirked away from asserting the power of their position to the public, nor did they refrain from enumerating their policies with the weight of the executive branch behind them.

The other extreme in the use of authority rhetoric that is illustrated in Figure 2.9 is the significant number of presidents, all of whom governed during the twentieth century, who used the least amount of this kind of popular address rhetoric in their Inaugural addresses. Teddy Roosevelt, Coolidge, Eisenhower, and Clinton all rank the lowest in terms of the use of authority rhetoric in the Inaugural. With these individuals, we see a commitment to refrain from frequent assertion of their position as logic, reasoning, or reinforcement for policy in their Inaugural. Theodore Roosevelt used neither "I," nor "me" throughout his entire Inaugural in 1905, and only used "my" one time to state "My fellow Americans." Coolidge's Inaugural in 1925 was also completely devoid of the use of the word "me," and used "my" only in the salutation and closing. Coolidge did, however, use "I" several times relating to the economy, saying not only that "I favor the policy of economy, not because I wish to save money, but because I wish to save people," but also that "I am opposed to extremely high rates, because they produce little or no revenue, because they are bad for the country, and, finally, because they are wrong."

In the latter half of the twentieth century, both Eisenhower and Clinton used percentages of authority rhetoric in their Inaugural addresses that were below the overall average and some of the least in presidential history. Eisenhower used no authority rhetoric in the context of any policy proposal, and instead, almost all of his inclusion of this type of speech originated from a prayer he proposed in his first Inaugural in 1953, saying, "*My* friends, before *I* begin the expression of those thoughts that *I* deem appropriate to this moment, would you permit *me* the privilege of uttering a little private prayer of *my* own. And *I* ask that you bow your heads." Although it could be weakly argued that Eisenhower was using his office to cow the listener into joining him in a prayer, this is a loose interpretation of authority rhetoric and misplaces the purpose and priority with which it is used. Bill Clinton used almost all of the "my" instances in his Inaugurals to speak to a group under the heading "My fellow_____." He also refrained almost completely from the use of "I" except when he stated that "we must do the work the season demands. To that work *I* now turn with all the authority of my office. *I* ask the Congress to join with me... *I* challenge a new generation of young Americans to a season of service." Instead of using authority rhetoric to communicate his desires, Clinton employed identification rhetoric, as discussed earlier, in very high percentage with the phrase "Let us;" this identification phrase appeared more times than all three words associated with authority rhetoric combined.

Figure 2.9 reiterates, yet again, the difficulty faced with the classification of the "traditional/ modern" divide. By breaking down the ephemeral "popular address" into different ways that the president speaks, we find variation among presidencies and among forms of popular address in the Inaugurals of the presidents. Indeed, even when considering only one form of presidential address, the Inaugural, and the data presented with regard to the use of authority rhetoric, it tells a very different story than that of the use of identification rhetoric. Instead of a clear distinction with consistent ways of utilizing rhetoric and speech, the presidential Inaugural, like the State of the Union Address, shows an evolution with each president toward a certain style of popular address. Again however, the outliers in this graph tell stories that are integral to the understanding of the evolution of the rhetorical presidency. This rich heritage is diminished when both periods of history and presidents are dismissed because of assumptions regarding what they "should" or "should not be" without the careful study to determine if this is really so.

Figure 2.10 is an illustration of the average percentage use of authority rhetoric in the presidential proclamations per president from Washington to GW Bush. Figure 2.11 shows the average percentage use of authority rhetoric in the executive orders from Adams to GW Bush. The levels of authority rhetoric that are used in the presidential proclamations are similar to those levels utilized by the presidents in the State of the Union Addresses as well as the Presidential Inaugurals. The percentage use of authority rhetoric in the executive orders, however, is far below that of any of the other three types of addresses. This difference, again, can be largely attributed to the summaries regarding the evolution of the proclamations and executive orders above. Namely, that the proclamation and its holiday related status is still very much a public address utilizing high levels of popular address rhetoric. Whereas, the executive order has become a rhetorical weapon by which the president makes or tweaks existing policy without the concern for public dissemination seen in the other kids of speech.

80 　　　　　　　　*The Evolutionary Rhetorical Presidency*

Figure 2.10

The Average Percentage of Authority Rhetoric in Presidential Proclamations

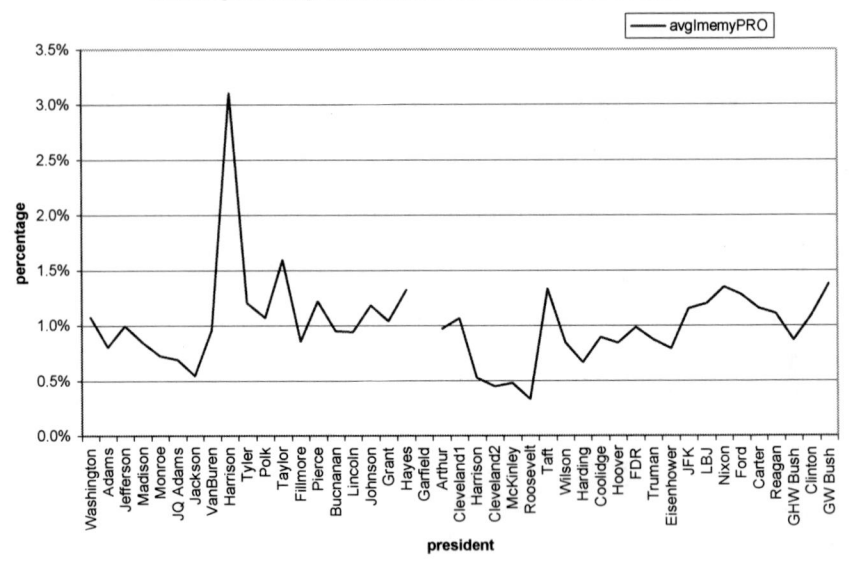

Figure 2.11

The Average Percentage of Authority Rhetoric in Presidential Executive Orders

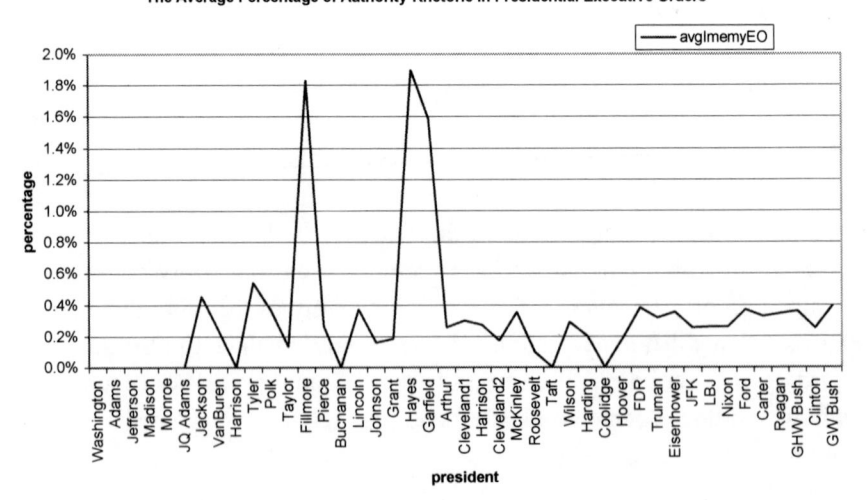

There are other important observations that can be made from the above figures. In figure 2.10, we see the evolution of the use of authority rhetoric in presidential proclamations. On the whole, apart from variation between presidents and a single spike in the use of authority rhetoric with the presidency of William Henry Harrison, there is no significant increase or decrease in the use of that form of popular address rhetoric. In addition, although there are highs, Harrison as an example, and lows, Teddy Roosevelt is the example in that case, presidents during the 1700's, 1800's and 1900's all remain at or extremely close to the overall average of 1.0% use of authority rhetoric in the presidential proclamations. Neither Wilson (0.8%), FDR (0.9%), Reagan (1.1%), Clinton (1.0%), nor any of the presidents that scholars have asserted as being "modern" or "transformative" in their handling or use of popular address rhetoric differ from such "traditional" presidents as Jefferson (0.9%), Van Buren (0.9%), Polk (1.0%), Lincoln (0.9%), or Arthur (0.9%) in their use of authority rhetoric. In fact, even if we look at the periods that are supposed to be indicative of the "traditional" and the "modern" presidencies, pre 1900 and post 1900, we still find that the averages are neither significantly dissimilar nor indicative of a major shift, with averages of 1.0% and .97% respectively.

Although the average use of authority rhetoric may be 1.0% in the presidential history of presidential proclamations, those of William Henry Harrison stand out as utilizing levels of authority rhetoric that are nearly three times that of the presidential average (3.1%). As the president who served the briefest term in the history of presidential tenures, this comes as a serious deviation from the norm. Yet, when we look more closely at his proclamations, the reason for this difference becomes more obvious. Primarily, the reason for this spike is due to the fact that one proclamation included from the Harrison presidency calls Congress into session. As the president is the one who holds the ability to convene an extraordinary session of Congress, the proclamation is heavily imbued with authority rhetoric. Harrison states that "*I* do therefore by this my proclamation convene the two Houses of Congress to meet in the Capitol, at the city of Washington, on the last Monday, being the 31st day, of May next; and *I* require the respective Senators and Representatives then and there to assemble, in order to receive such information respecting the state of the Union as may be given to them and to devise and adopt such measures as the good of the country may seem to them, in the exercise of their wisdom and discretion, to require." Because the proclamation itself is brief and the subject is primarily that Harrison is calling the Congress to hear his address, the result is a high average percentage of authority rhetoric in the proclamation.

A close examination of several of the presidencies from the 1800's and the 1900's illustrate how authority rhetoric is used in the proclamations and why presidents use different quantities of this form of popular address rhetoric in their speech. Zachary Taylor used nearly 1.6% authority rhetoric in his presidential proclamations; this number is slightly above the presidential average. Many of these occurrences of "I," "me," or "my" in his proclamations and many of the other presidents as well, are the result of either the recognition of dignitaries who have not done their jobs. This can be seen in the proclamation of January 4th, 1850, where Taylor stated that "*I* do no longer recognize the said Carlos de Espana as consul of Her Catholic Majesty in any part of the United States, nor permit him to exercise and enjoy any of the functions, powers, or privileges allowed to the consuls of Spain; and *I* do hereby wholly revoke and annul the said exequatur heretofore given, and do declare the same to be absolutely null and void from this day forward."

Presidents, and Taylor specifically, also used authority rhetoric to suggest that the citizens of the United States should obey the laws set forth by Congress and the president, saying in the proclamation of August 11th, 1849 that "*I* exhort all good citizens, as they regard our national reputation, as they respect their own laws and the laws of nations, as they value the blessings of peace and the welfare of their country, to discountenance and prevent by all lawful means any such enterprise; and *I* call upon every officer of this Government, civil or military, to use all efforts in his power to arrest for trial and punishment every such offender against the laws providing for the performance of our sacred obligations to friendly powers."

The proclamations of Richard Nixon also illustrate how presidents continued to use authority rhetoric in presidential proclamations in the 1900's. Nixon's average of 1.35% of authority rhetoric in his presidential proclamations is, as was Taylor's, above the presidential overall average. They exhibit the similarities to the proclamations of the 1800's as well as illustrate the differences that have occurred in the evolution of the use of the proclamation itself. As did many of the presidents of the eighteenth and nineteenth centuries, Nixon used authority rhetoric in proclamations that memorialize or recognize the loss of significant individuals in American life. For example, in Proclamation Number 3907, given on March 28th, 1969, Nixon requested that Americans take the opportunity to remember the life of Eisenhower, who had passed away. He stated that "*I* also do appoint Monday, March 31, 1969 to be a National Day of Mourning throughout the United States. *I* earnestly recommend that the people assemble on that day in their respective places of divine worship, there to bow down in submission to the will of the Almighty God, and to pay their homage of love and reverence to the memory of President Eisenhower. *I* invite the people of the world who share our grief to join us in this day of mourning and rededication." It is in this proclamation that Nixon used his station as president to not only mark the passing of a former president, but to bring the event to the attention of the American people and ask them for solemnity on that occasion.

Nixon's proclamations and use of authority rhetoric also illustrate the change in function of the proclamation from a strict enumeration of unilateral law, to a ceremonial occasion to mark a specific observance or subject related holiday. In Proclamation 3919 that was issued on July 16th 1969, Nixon marked the launch of the Apollo spacecraft and the importance of its mission stating that "*I*, RICHARD NIXON, President of the United States of America, do hereby proclaim Monday, July 21, 1969, to be a National Day of Participation; and *I* invite the Governors of the States and the Commonwealth of Puerto Rico, and officials of other areas subject to the jurisdiction of the United States to issue similar proclamations." In Proclamation 4160, issued on September 30th, 1972 Nixon asked the American people to recognize the diverse society that they had become, saying, "NOW, THEREFORE, *I*, RICHARD NIXON, President of the United States of America, do hereby proclaim Sunday, October 1, 1972, as National Heritage Day. *I* call upon all Americans to reflect upon the composite vitality, enthusiasm and tenacity of the many separate peoples who have built our beloved country." And in Proclamation 4181, on January 26th, 1973, Nixon recognized the end of hostilities in Vietnam by asking for a National Moment of Prayer and Thanksgiving. He explained that "*I* urge all men and women of goodwill to join the prayerful hope that this moment marks not only the end of the war in Vietnam, but the beginning of a new era of world peace and understanding for all mankind. *I* authorize the flying of the American flag at the appointed hour, and *I* call on all the people of the United States to observe this moment with appropriate ceremonies and activities." Nixon's proclamations are indicative of many of the presidents of the late twentieth century and the twenty-first century; they used authority rhetoric in percentages that were not significantly different than the presidents of the nineteenth century, but were seated in the observation of holidays and observances that they, as Presidents of the United States, expected the citizens to recognize and observe.

As opposed to the proclamations, which saw fairly high levels of authority rhetoric used in their delivery, Executive Orders only had an average of .3% authority rhetoric from Adams through GW Bush. There are several presidents who utilize much higher levels of authority rhetoric than the overall average, like Fillmore (1.83%), Hayes (1.9%) and Garfield (1.59%), and there are also several presidents who did not use any authority rhetoric at all in their executive orders, such as Adams, Harrison, Buchanan, Taft, and Coolidge. Regardless however, of the variation illustrated by the aforementioned presidents and their executive orders, things that can not be seen in Figure 2.10 are a clear differentiation between periods of presidential address, nor a single presidency that utilized amounts of authority rhetoric in executive orders that set a new standard that would be followed by all subsequent presidents. In addition, if we were to look for a significant increase in the use of this type of popular address rhetoric with the presidents of a "modern" period, we would find no support for this in the use of authority rhetoric. Instead, the data illustrate that presidents after 1900 use levels of authority rhetoric (0.2%) that are not only below the presidential average of 0.3%, but almost half of that used by presidents before 1900 (0.4%). Although a doubling of the percentage of a form of rhetoric may suggest a significant shift, because of the low levels of authority rhetoric used in the executive orders, the change between the uses of authority rhetoric over any segregated periods of presidential history is minimal at best.

Instead of a significant shift characterized by two periods of presidential rhetoric, the executive orders illustrate the proclivity of individual presidents to use variation in the percentages of authority rhetoric that they use from the nineteenth century to the present. Millard Fillmore, for example, used almost six times the average percentage of authority rhetoric in his executive orders. For example in his executive order of June 29th, 1852, Fillmore observed the death of Henry Clay, stating that "The tolling bells announce the death of the Hon. Henry Clay. Though this event has been long anticipated, yet the painful bereavement could never be fully realized. *I* am sure all hearts are too sad at this moment to attend to business, and *I* therefore respectfully suggest that your Department be closed for the remainder of the day." In the executive order of May17th, 1852, Fillmore addressed the possible riots and rebellions in New York. He explained that "*I* have just issued an authority to Hugh

Maxwell, collector at New York, under the eighth section of the act of April 20, 1818, to arrest any unlawful expedition that may be attempted to be fitted out within his district, and *I* have given him power to call upon any military and naval officers that may be there to aid him in the execution of this duty; and *I* will thank you to issue the necessary instructions to the proper military officer in that district." This shows not only the use of authority rhetoric in executive orders, but of the similarity of proclamations and executive orders of the nineteenth century. In fact, the proclamations examined from the nineteenth century seem to parallel the executive orders during that time in both form and function. As mentioned at the outset of this study, before formal record keeping of proclamations and executive orders was required by law in the early twentieth century, executive orders and proclamations often were used almost interchangeably and toward the same end.

In the twentieth and twenty-first centuries, the use of authority rhetoric in the executive orders takes on a slightly different use. For example, Ronald Reagan utilized 0.3% authority rhetoric in his executive orders; this is exactly in line with the overall presidential average of the use of this form of popular address. At this time in presidential history, however, executive orders have evolved to become rhetorical addresses that neither memorialize significant deaths, nor celebrate holidays. Instead, they have a much more sterile and legislative feel to them. In the case of Reagan's Executive Orders, which are comparable in format to those of contemporary presidents, authority rhetoric is used only when ordering that an action be taken or extending the existing law to cover additional subsections of citizens, related groups, or extend time periods to which a regulation is bound.

An illustration of the first example can be seen in Reagan's Executive Order on Emergency Deficit Control Measures for Fiscal Year 1988 that was delivered on October 20th, 1987. He stated that "I hereby order that the following actions be taken immediately to implement the sequestrations and reductions determined by the Director of the Office of Management and Budget in his report dated October 20, 1987, under section 251 of the Act," and followed that statement with six sections that specifically amended the existing law. The use of authority rhetoric in the extension of existing law can be illustrated by Reagan's Ronald Reagan Executive Order number 12629 that was issued on March 9th, 1988. In that order, Reagan recognized that the end to an existing provision of the Atomic Energy Act of 1954 that was set to expire would "be seriously prejudicial to the achievement of U.S. non-proliferation objectives and would otherwise jeopardize the common defense and security of the United States." Therefore, Reagan stated that "I hereby extend the duration of that period to March 10, 1989." Because the holidays that address the common man are now relegated to presidential proclamations, executive orders have become, in effect, little more than enumerations of legislative alterations and the details that need to be integrated into law as a result.

Regardless of the change in their utility, however, the authority rhetoric that is used in both Presidential proclamations and executive orders from the founding to the present suggests a consistency of use, and challenges the notion of dramatic or transformative change in presidential rhetoric. The use of authority rhetoric in State of the Union Addresses and Presidential Inaugurals also exhibits little, if any, dramatic shift in the ways that the presidents of the past utilized this form of popular address rhetoric in their addresses. Instead, there are two conclusions that this sections can provide. First of all, regardless of time period or form of speech, authority rhetoric, similarly to identification rhetoric, shows extraordinary variation between presidents of the eighteenth, nineteenth, and twentieth centuries. Whereas some presidents incorporate larger amounts of authority rhetoric in their addresses, others utilize almost none at all. This suggests that the use of popular address rhetoric is extraordinarily president-specific and hinges on the personal proclivities of the officeholder. In addition, the second finding that emerges from the look at authority rhetoric is the lack of any "transformation" in the ways that the presidents use this speech. At best, the data illustrate slow evolutions of increase and decrease in the amount of popular address rhetoric that is used in the different kinds of presidential address as the address form itself evolves. There is no presidential "smoking gun" to which we can trace the origins of its use. Instead, we are presented with a picture of presidential adaptation and innovation with each administration, where presidents craft their own personal preferences and look at what has been done before them to determine their contributions to and usages of this form of popular address.

Tracing the Use of Directive Rhetoric

In addition to speaking as one of the people and using the authority of the office to justify programs and policy proposals, the president can also use his station to command the people and the Congress to act as he sees fit and to proceed with legislation on which he would like to see activity. This type of rhetoric, as detailed above, is known as directive rhetoric and is the use of the words "you" and "yours" in presidential address.

Figure 2.12

The Average Percentage of Directive Rhetoric in the State of the Union Address per President

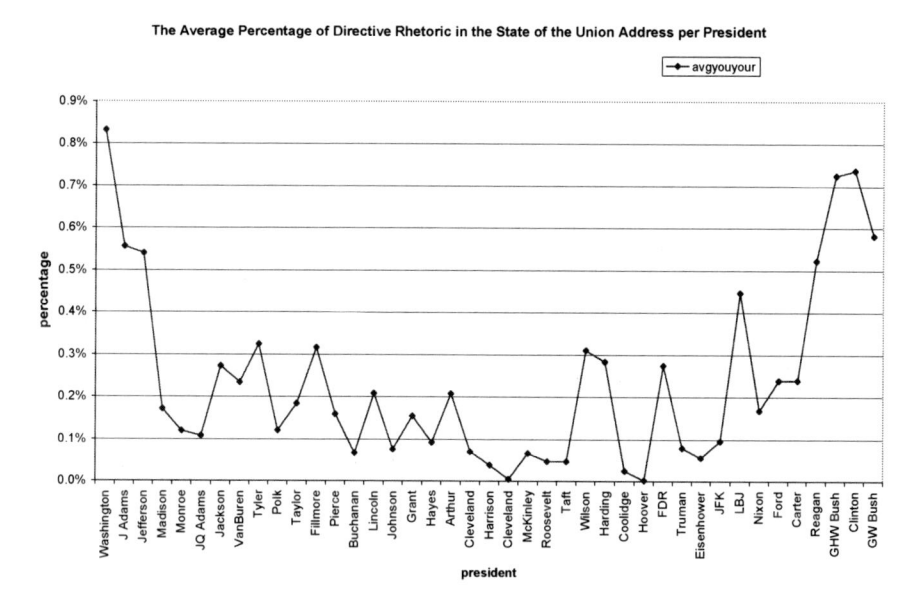

Figure 2.12 illustrates the average percentage of directive rhetoric per president in the State of the Union Address. This graphs show us several things. First of all, the data show that directive rhetoric is used in smaller amounts than either authority rhetoric or identification rhetoric. In fact, presidents are almost five times as likely to use rhetoric that proposes that they are one of the citizenry (identification) and even twice as likely to attempt to use the authority of their position in their addresses (authority), as they are to directly address and command the audience at hand. However, these lower levels do not negate the importance of determining the presence of directive rhetoric in the eighteenth and early nineteenth century.

A significant finding is that the figure above shows no prominent delineation between a period that could be considered "traditional" and one that could be considered modern in the use of directive rhetoric in the State of the Union Address. Instead, the figure presents an image of presidents like Jackson (0.25%), Van Buren (0.23%), Tyler (0.32%), Fillmore (0.30%), Lincoln (0.21%), and Arthur (0.20%) that utilize similar, or higher levels of directive rhetoric than do their "modern" successors like Wilson (0.29%), Harding

(0.28%), FDR (0.24%) and Gerald Ford (0.20%). In addition, the figure shows no support for a separation of presidential eras according to their use of directive rhetoric as popular address rhetoric. Indeed, if we compare the periods that are most often demarcated as "traditional" versus "modern," namely the period before 1900 (0.21%) and the period after 1900 (0.24%), there appears no significant deviation from the overall average percentage use of directive rhetoric throughout presidential history (0.23%).

Another important graphic illustrated in the figure above, and a direct challenge to a "traditional" constraint against using popular address rhetoric, is the similarity with which directive rhetoric is utilized by presidents of the founding period and contemporary presidents. Indeed, presidents of the late twentieth century like LBJ (0.4%), Ronald Reagan (0.5%), George H.W. Bush (0.7%), Bill Clinton (0.7%), and George W. Bush (0.6%) have seemingly returned to the levels of directive rhetoric practiced by George Washington (0.8%), John Adams (0.6%), and Thomas Jefferson (0.5%).

The founding period was a rhetorical time in which the initial presidents spoke with high levels of directive rhetoric to the people and the Congress. George Washington's second State of the Union Address gives a good example of the use of directive rhetoric in the founding. Washington used the words "you," "your," and "yours" frequently in the proposal of policy during his address due largely to the closeness that he may have felt to those who were members of the Congress who had helped to shape the Constitution and the other original institutions of the country. More than a command, it was often a reference to what Congressional attention should be focused upon. Subjects such as state entrance to the colonies, "The liberality and harmony with which it has been conducted will be found to do great honor to both the parties, and the sentiments of warm attachment to the Union and its present Government expressed by our fellow citizens of Kentucky can not fail to add an affectionate concern for their particular welfare to the great national impressions under which *you* will decide on the case submitted to *you*," commerce, "*Your* attention seems to be not less due to that particular branch of our trade which belongs to the Mediterranean," the judicial system, "The laws *you* have already passed for the establishment of a judiciary system have opened the doors of justice to all descriptions of persons. *You* will consider in your wisdom whether improvements in that system may yet be made," and other varying topics, "the establishment of the militia, of a mint, of standards of weights and measures, of the post office and post roads are subjects which I presume *you* will resume of course, and which are abundantly urged by their own importance," were all proposals utilizing directive rhetoric.

This high percentage of directive rhetoric that is reflected in the State of the Union Addresses of Washington, Adams, Jefferson, and Madison, mirrors the directive rhetoric of late twentieth century State of The Union Addresses by LBJ, Reagan, GHW Bush, Clinton and GW Bush. Just as Washington's address above was largely comprised of suggestions for the new duties of a new Congress, GHW Bush used directive rhetoric to directly propose policy recommendations to Congress as well as to pass the policy goals of his administration. In his State of the Union Address of February 9, 1989, he utilized directive rhetoric to ask both the citizens of the country as well as the Congress to aid him in the implementation of his policy goals. At one point he spoke to the youth, saying, "And to the young people of America, who sometimes feel left out, I ask *you* tonight to give us the benefit of *your* talent and energy through a new program called YES, for Youth Entering Service to America." He spoke also to the parents of America, and stated that "And to the parents of America, I ask *you* to get involved in *your* child's schooling." Further, he addressed the Congress, and told them that "I will send to *you* shortly legislation for a new, more effective Clean Air Act... Many of these changes can only be made with the participation of the Congress, and so, I ask for *your* help. We need fewer regulations. We need less bureaucracy. We need multiyear procurement and 2-year budgeting." In Bush's State of the Union Address as well as that of many others in the late twentieth and early twenty first century, directive rhetoric is used to clearly identify groups from whom the president needs or expects support and compliance.

In 1992, Bush continued his use of directive rhetoric and, quite to the contrary of the overall presidential average of directive rhetoric of 0.23%, his State of the Union Address consisted of over 1.2% directive rhetoric, a level matched only by Washington. In this speech, Bush used directive rhetoric to directly propose policy recommendations to Congress as well as to issue specific commands for policy passage. He used the rhetoric in address of the economy, saying, "*You* must, *you* must pass the other elements of my plan to meet our economic needs. *You* must cut the capital gains tax on the people of this country. And so I'm asking *you* to cut the capital gains tax to a maximum of 15.4%. This then is my short-term plan. *Your* part, members of Congress, requires enactment of these common-sense proposals...And I submit my plan tomorrow. And I am asking *you* to pass it by March 20." And he also used directive rhetoric throughout his other proposals concerning such issues as nuclear arms, "I remind *you* this evening that I have asked for *your* support in funding a program to protect our country from limited nuclear missile attack," human services, "I ask *you* tonight to fund our HOPE housing proposal and to pass my enterprise-zone legislation, which will get businesses into the inner city," pork barrel politics, "I call on Congress to adopt a measure that will help put an end to the annual ritual of filling the budget with pork-barrel appropriations. We all know how these things get into the budget, and maybe *you* need someone to help *you* say no. I know how to say it. And *you* know what I need to make it stick. Give me the same thing 43 governors have—the line-item veto—and let me help *you* control spending," and families and education, "I ask *you* tonight to raise the personal exemption by $500 per child for every family. It's time to allow families to deduct the interest they pay on student loans. And I'm asking *you* to do just that…And, I'm asking *you* to allow people to use money from their IRAs to pay medical and educational expenses, all without penalties." Clinton followed up Bush's example by utilizing more directive rhetoric (0.73%) on the average than even his predecessor.

The illustrations above show us several things regarding the use of directive rhetoric in the State of the Union Address. First of all, Washington and Bush's combination of directive and authority rhetoric is characteristic of most of the presidents throughout presidential history who often utilize a mix of those forms of popular address rhetoric as well as an integration of identification rhetoric to communicate their message. Contrary to the "traditional/ modern" divide, the illustration of the use of directive rhetoric in the State of the Union Address proposes that presidents during the nineteenth and twentieth centuries utilized very similar percentages of directive rhetoric in their speeches. It also suggests that there were no groundbreaking presidencies who originated the use of directive rhetoric. Instead, presidents of all eras utilized varying amounts of the popular address rhetoric in their speeches. In addition, the figure above suggests that, if anything, presidents today resemble their founding counterparts more than almost any other executives of the past. Again, this contradicts the allegation of the "traditional/ modern" divide that presidents, especially during the founding, were constrained in their address by some constitutional mandate that they not use popular address rhetoric or be policy active in their speech.

Figure 2.13

The Average Percentage of Directive Rhetoric in Presidential Inaugural Addresses

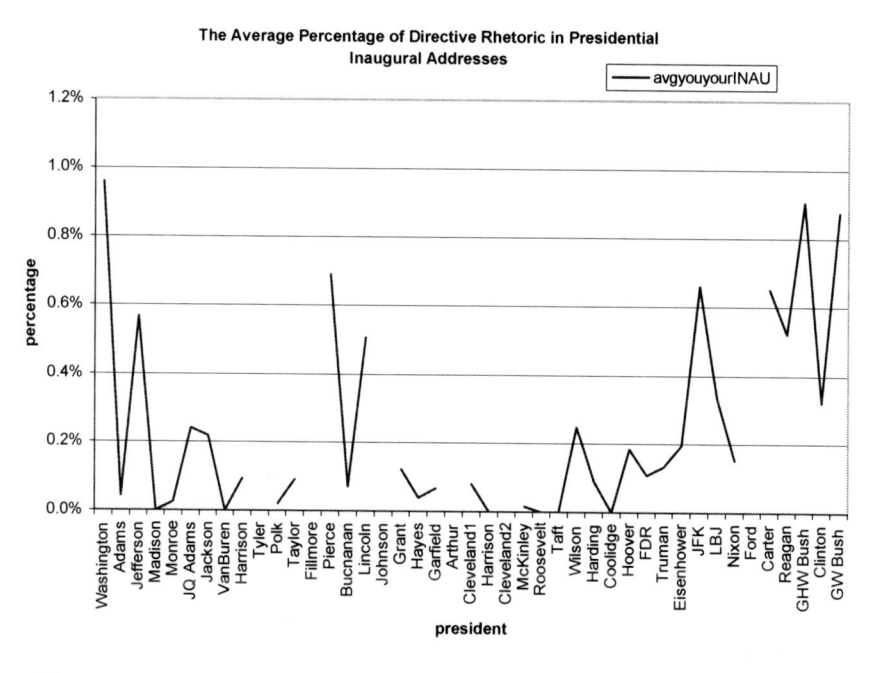

Figure 2.13 illustrates the average percentage of directive rhetoric per president in the Inaugural Address. Perhaps more than any other examination of popular address rhetoric to this point, Figure 2.13 shows an amazing amount of variability in the percentage of directive rhetoric used by presidents throughout history. Similarly to the other figures that examined different forms of popular address rhetoric, Figure 2.13 also does not provide either the picture of two clear eras of presidential rhetoric, nor a single presidential administration that could be seen as groundbreaking or establishing a new pattern of behavior. Instead, the figure shows that presidents such as George Washington, Thomas Jefferson, Franklin Pierce, and Abraham Lincoln used high levels of directive rhetoric, similar to the addresses of JFK, Carter, GHW Bush and GW Bush. In addition, it shows that presidents throughout the nineteenth and twentieth centuries used levels of directive rhetoric in their addresses that varied from 0% to nearly 1% of their Inaugural address.

During the nineteenth century, presidents like Washington (0.95%), Jefferson (0.56%), Pierce (0.69%) and Lincoln (0.50%), used some of the highest levels of directive rhetoric of presidents during any time period. The average percentage of directive rhetoric during the entirety of presidential history is only 0.2% in comparison to these early presidents whose levels double and nearly quadruple the overall average. In fact these "traditional" executives rivaled the percentages of twentieth century presidents like JFK (0.65%), Carter (0.65%), Reagan (0.52%), GHW Bush (0.9%), and GW Bush (0.88%).

In terms of the highest percentage of directive rhetoric used on the average, George Washington reached levels that no president has ever mimicked. In his Inaugural Address of 1789, Washington spoke almost directly to the Congress in suggesting what they need to do in the first session and the duties with which they were entrusted. He began by addressing the abstract powers of the Congress, saying that "The circumstances under which I now meet *you* will acquit me from entering into that subject further than to refer to the great constitutional charter under which *you* are assembled, and which, in defining *your* powers, designates the objects to which *your* attention is to be given." However, he quickly abandoned the abstract for the specific and suggested that Congress begin to take action on several issues immediately. He proposed that Congress, almost from the outset, deliberate upon the fifth article of the Constitution and whether it demanded that alterations of the document be made. He stated that "Besides the ordinary objects submitted to *your* care, it will remain with *your* judgment to decide how far an exercise of the occasional power delegated by the fifth article of the Constitution is rendered expedient at the present juncture by the nature of objections which have been urged against the system...I shall again give way to my entire confidence in *your* discernment and pursuit of the public good; for I assure myself that whilst *you* carefully avoid every alteration which might endanger the benefits of an united and effective government, or which ought to await the future lessons of experience, a reverence for the characteristic rights of freemen and a regard for the public harmony will sufficiently influence *your* deliberations on the question how far the former can be impregnably fortified or the latter be safely and advantageously promoted."

Although a commanding presence might be expected from the first president of the United States, a significant percentage of directive rhetoric from the likes of Franklin Pierce is a bit more of a surprise. Yet, upon close examination, his use of directive rhetoric does not differ significantly from that of the first president of the country. In 1853, Pierce delivered an Inaugural address which was unique not only in its use of directive rhetoric, but to whom the address was directed. Pierce speaks, not to the people or the Congress, but to the country itself, contriving a dialogue with the country herself, and issuing directives for policy and behavior for her to follow. He begins this strange diatribe by suggesting that he will need the nation throughout his tenure. He states in the opening that "*You* have summoned me in my weakness; *you* must sustain me by *your* strength. When looking for the fulfillment of reasonable requirements, *you* will not be unmindful of the great changes which have occurred, even within the last quarter of a century, and the consequent augmentation and complexity of duties imposed in the administration both of *your* home and foreign affairs."

He followed this with more abstract contemplation on the past and future of the country, saying "It is not *your* privilege as a nation to speak of a distant past. The striking incidents of *your* history, replete with instruction and furnishing abundant grounds for hopeful confidence, are comprised in a period comparatively brief. But if *your* past is limited, *your* future is boundless." After several more broad comments directed to the country in general, he specifically addressed policies of his administration. In one instance, he addressed the propriety of maintaining an active and enlarged military, saying that "The Army as organized must be the nucleus around which in every time of need the strength of *your* military power, the sure bulwark of *your* defense--a national militia--may be readily formed into a well-disciplined and efficient organization. And the skill and self-devotion of the Navy assure *you* that *you* may take the performance of the past as a pledge for the future." In another, he commented on the necessity of an accountable and responsible civil service, stating that "*You* have a right, therefore, to expect *your* agents in every department to regard strictly the limits imposed upon them by the Constitution of the United States." Although he delivered the Inaugural address in very interesting fashion, he still produced a speech that contained percentages of directive rhetoric above many twentieth century presidents and similar to many contemporary ones.

In comparison, presidents at the end of the twentieth century and beginning of the twenty-first century used levels of identification rhetoric that approached the high percentages utilized by George Washington himself. In his Inaugural address of 1989, GHW Bush used almost 0.9% of directive rhetoric. Further, his son, George W. Bush also used levels reminiscent of Washington by making 0.88% of his Inaugural addresses directive rhetoric on the average. In his address, GHW Bush used directive rhetoric to speak not only to the Congress, but to the people in abstract terms about the future of the country and the relations between a Democratic Congress and his Republican presidency. He began the Inaugural by looking to a positive vision of the future, saying to the American people that "There are times when the future seems thick as a fog; *you* sit and wait, hoping the mists will lift and reveal the right path. But this is a time when the future seems a door you can walk right through into a room called tomorrow." And later, he extended his vision to all people, exclaiming "And to all I say, No matter what *your* circumstances or where *you* are, *you* are part of this day, *you* are part of the life of our great nation." The only other area that has a clear focus of directive rhetoric occurred in his conversation with congressional leaders. In the middle of the address he spoke to the leaders directly, saying "I put out my hand. I am putting out my hand to you, Mr. Speaker. I am putting out my hand to you, Mr. Majority Leader. For this is the thing: This is the age of the offered hand. And we can't turn back clocks…Mr. Majority Leader, the Congress and the Executive were capable of working together to produce a budget on which this nation could live. Let us negotiate soon and hard. But in the end, let us produce."

GW Bush seemed to pick up with the high levels of directive rhetoric used by his father in his Inaugural addresses as well. In a statement that was eerily similar to the example of directive rhetoric from his father's State of the Union Address examined above, GW Bush again addressed the youth of the nation, saying, "I ask our youngest citizens to believe the evidence of *your* eyes. *You* have seen duty and allegiance in the determined faces of our soldiers. *You* have seen that life is fragile and evil is real and courage triumphs. Make the choice to serve in a cause larger than *your* wants, larger than *yourself*, and in *your* days you will add not just to the wealth of our country but to its character."

Although GW Bush did speak in abstract terms in his first Inaugural in 2001 to the people of the United States, saying things like "What *you* do is as important as anything government does. I ask *you* to seek a common good beyond your comfort; to defend needed reforms against easy attacks; to serve *your* nation, beginning with *your* neighbor. I ask *you* to be citizens," the lion's share of his directive rhetoric is contained within the second Inaugural address of 2005; it is used in the address of other countries and other peoples. He opened by speaking of the willingness of the United States to help the cause of freedom everywhere, saying "Today, America speaks anew to the peoples of the world. All who live in tyranny and hopelessness can know:

The United States will not ignore *your* oppression or excuse *your* oppressors. When *you* stand for *your* liberty, we will stand with *you*. Democratic reformers facing repression, prison, or exile can know: America sees *you* for who *you* are, the future leaders of *your* free country." This is a direct communiqué to those in other countries, as opposed to the country itself or the citizens of this nation. He then followed up with a direct address to the leaders of hostile and friendly nations alike. "The leaders of governments with long habits of control need to know: To serve *your* people, *you* must learn to trust them. Start on this journey of progress and justice, and America will walk at your side. And all the allies of the United States can know: We honor *your* friendship; we rely on *your* counsel; and we depend on *your* help." The Inaugural of GW Bush is similar to his father's Inaugural and those of the nineteenth century in the abstract address of the people at large. However, it is unique in that the people that it addresses with Directive rhetoric are largely the citizens and the leaders of *other* countries around the globe.

The data above illustrate important points regarding the development of the Inaugural address and also the usage of directive rhetoric by presidents within that address. First of all, as with the State of the Union Address, the use of directive rhetoric exhibits none of the patterns of use that would insinuate that there would be different eras of its use as popular address rhetoric. Instead, it shows an ebb and flow throughout presidential history that can be seen by some presidents of the nineteenth century using amounts greater than or equal to percentages of directive rhetoric used by many of the presidents of the twentieth and twenty-first century. In addition, the similarities to the use of directive rhetoric in the State of the Union Address continue, as some modern presidents of the late twentieth and early twenty first centuries returned to percentages of directive rhetoric not seen since the founding Inaugurals of the nation. It is important to note, however, that just because the percentages between the two time periods appear similar, this by no means suggests that the Inaugurals are returning to the form or style of the founding addresses. Instead, as with the other forms of popular address rhetoric, the history of directive rhetoric in the Inaugural address is one of an evolution of presidential personalities which use directive rhetoric when and if they see fit. Recently, it seems as though the directive rhetoric of the founding presidents that addressed the duties of Congress and the people of the new nation, is being adapted to address the emergent countries and struggling peoples around the worlds as they begin their own "founding."

96 *The Evolutionary Rhetorical Presidency*

Figure 2.14

The Average Percentage of Directive Rhetoric in Presidential Proclamations

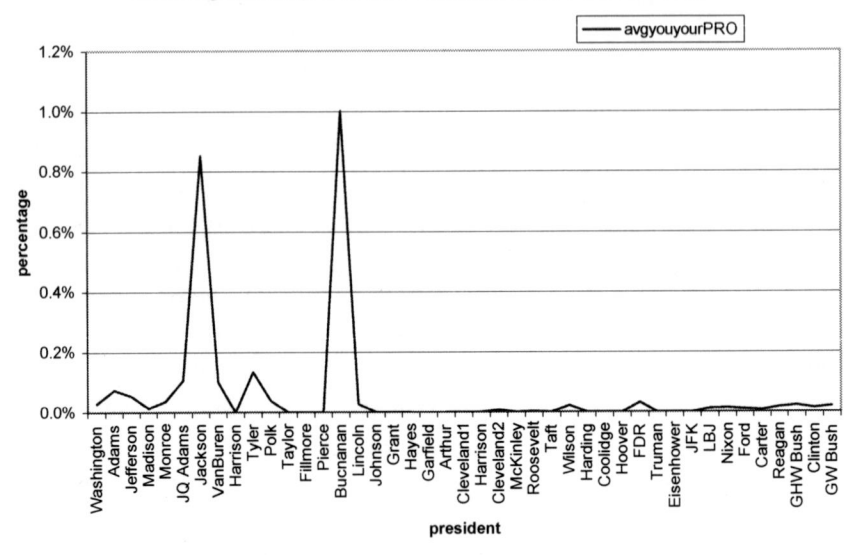

Figure 2.15

The Average Percentage of Directive Rhetoric in Presidential Executive Orders

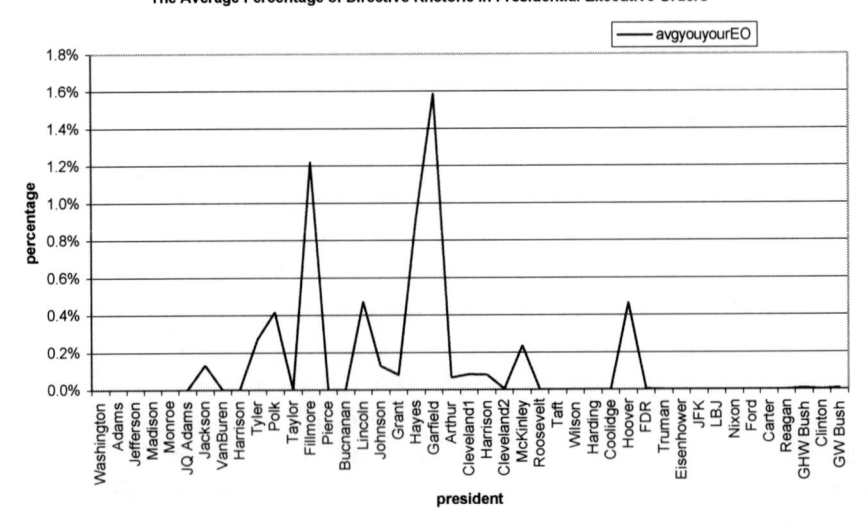

Figure 2.14 and Figure 2.15 show the average percentage use of directive rhetoric in presidential proclamations and in executive orders, respectively. Both figures are similar in that, overall, presidents from the founding to the present day have used extremely low levels of directive rhetoric in their proclamations and executive orders, if they have used any at all. The previous examinations of the State of the Union Addresses and the Inaugural Addresses illustrated that contemporary presidents used directive rhetoric in ways that were similar to nineteenth and even founding presidents. Figures 2.14 and 2.15 also show that today's presidents use levels of directive rhetoric similar to may of the presidents of the past. However, this similarity is also in the extremely low levels of directive rhetoric that they use as opposed to their peers, instead of higher levels of this form of popular address rhetoric.

In Figure 2.14 we can see that directive rhetoric and presidential proclamations have had little, if any, real interaction in the presidential past. The average percentage use of this form of popular address rhetoric in the proclamations is only .06% across all of the presidents. This is the smallest percentage use of any of the forms of popular address rhetoric we have seen thus far. Indeed, even if we separate the presidents into different eras according to the "traditional/ modern" tenets, which suggest that presidents in the "modern" period should use this form of popular address rhetoric in much higher percentages than their predecessors, we find results that are to the contrary of this assumption. The average percentage of directive rhetoric that was used in the proclamations prior to 1900 was 0.1%, and the average percentage used after 1900 was 0.008%. First of all, this difference, again, exhibits a weakness in the division of presidents, as presidents during the eighteenth and nineteenth centuries had a higher average use of directive rhetoric. However, because of the low percentages of the use of directive rhetoric overall, this should not be read as a substantive demarcation that can be shown between the two time frames, nor any others that we might choose to use. Instead, a large contributor to the difference in averages may come from the examination of individual presidents and their use of directive rhetoric.

In addition to illustrating a general lack of use of directive rhetoric in the proclamations, Figure 2.14 also challenges the "traditional/ modern" divide and the classification that comes with that paradigm of all presidents into specific groups that behave exactly alike. It shows that, even though presidents on the whole refrained from utilizing this form of popular address, some individual presidents of the nineteenth century chose to use percentages of directive rhetoric that had never before been seen and would not be used again. Contrary to their predecessors or their successors, Andrew Jackson and James Buchanan used extremely high levels of directive rhetoric in their proclamations.

A look at the proclamations of Andrew Jackson, with an average use of 0.85% of directive rhetoric, give use a better understanding of his deviation from the presidential average. In his proclamation of December 10th, 1832, Jackson used an incredible amount of directive rhetoric in his address of the right of the states to "nullify" federal law at their own behest. After discussing the constitutional framework which was in contradiction to the theory, he appealed directly to the senses and sensibilities of the people, asking, "I do not ask *you*, fellow-citizens, which is the constitutional disposition; that instrument speaks a language not to be misunderstood. But if *you* were assembled in general convention, which would *you* think the safest depository of this discretionary power in the last resort? Would *you* add a clause giving it to each of the States, or would *you* sanction the wise provisions already made by *your* Constitution?" This example illustrates just how much Jackson thought of himself as a true "man of the people," and also shows the tremendous amount of confidence that he had in their reasoning ability. He continued his direct address and questioning of the people saying "If this should be the result of *your* deliberations when providing for the future, are *you*, can *you*, be ready to risk all that we hold dear, to establish, for a temporary and a local purpose, that which *you* must acknowledge to be destructive, and even absurd, as a general provision? Carry out the consequences of this right vested in the different States, and *you* must perceive that the crisis your conduct presents at this day would recur whenever any law of the United States displeased any of the States, and that we should soon cease to be a nation."

He finished the proclamation by asking (or telling) the people themselves to review the policy that has been proposed for its value or detriment. He stated that, "The ordinance, with the same knowledge of the future that characterizes a former objection, tells *you* that the proceeds of the tax will be unconstitutionally applied...These are the allegations contained in the ordinance. Examine them seriously, my fellow-citizens; judge for *yourselves*. I appeal to *you* to determine whether they are so clear, so convincing, as to leave no doubt of their correctness; and even if *you* should come to this conclusion, how far they justify the reckless, destructive course which *you* are directed to pursue." In addition to these examples, in that proclamation, Jackson continued this question and answers session with the people of the nation and specific states, and also continued his extraordinarily high use of directive rhetoric to do so.

In his proclamations, Buchanan utilized even higher percentages than those illustrated by Jackson above. In fact, nearly 1% of his proclamations consist of directive rhetoric. An examination of his proclamations also provides insight into why his use of directive rhetoric is nearly seventeen times that of the presidential overall average. Just as Jackson used directive rhetoric to appeal to the people regarding nullification and its propriety, the high percentage of directive rhetoric used by Buchanan can be traced to his address directed at the citizens of Utah on April 6th, 1858. In his attempt to quell the uprising taking place, Buchanan spoke directly to the people saying, "Fellow-citizens of Utah, this is rebellion against the Government to which *you* owe allegiance; it is levying war against the United States, and involves *you* in the guilt of treason. Persistence in it will bring *you* to condign punishment, to ruin, and to shame; for it is mere madness to suppose that with *your* limited resources *you* can successfully resist the force of this great and powerful nation." He then appealed to the citizens as having been mislead and mistaken, saying "If *you* have calculated upon the forbearance of the United States, if *you* have permitted yourselves to suppose that this Government will fail to put forth its strength and bring *you* to submission, *you* have fallen into a grave mistake. *You* have settled upon territory which lies, geographically, in the heart of the Union. The land *you* live upon was purchased by the United States and paid for out of their Treasury; the proprietary right and title to it is in them, and not in *you*. Utah is bounded on every side by States and Territories whose people are true to the Union. It is absurd to believe that they will or can permit *you* to erect in their very midst a government of *your* own."

After having justified his opposition to the uprising in terms of United States dominion, Buchanan then also relayed to the citizens of Utah that this was not an attack on their faith. He spoke firmly and directly to them, stating "Do not deceive *yourselves* nor try to mislead others by propagating the idea that this is a crusade against *your* religion. The Constitution and laws of this country can take no notice of *your* creed, whether it be true or false. That is a question between *your* God and *yourselves*, in which I disclaim all right to interfere. If *you* obey the laws, keep the peace, and respect the just rights of others, *you* will be perfectly secure, and may live on in *your* present faith or change it for another at *your* pleasure. Every intelligent man among *you* knows very well that this Government has never, directly or indirectly, sought to molest *you* in your worship, to control *you* in *your* ecclesiastical affairs, or even to influence *you* in *your* religious opinions."

He also provided an account of the equal treatment and representation that they had received in the past. He suggested to those in Utah that "This rebellion is not merely a violation of *your* legal duty; it is without just cause, without reason, without excuse. *You* never made a complaint that was not listened to with patience; *you* never exhibited a real grievance that was not redressed as promptly as it could be. The laws and regulations enacted for *your* government by Congress have been equal and just, and their enforcement was manifestly necessary for *your* own welfare and happiness. *You* have never asked their repeal. They are similar in every material respect to the laws which have been passed for the other Territories of the Union, and which everywhere else (with one partial exception) have been cheerfully obeyed. No people ever lived who were freer from unnecessary legal restraints than *you*. Human wisdom never devised a political system which bestowed more blessings or imposed lighter burdens than the Government of the United States in its operation upon the Territories." Finally, he offered an olive branch to the citizens of Utah as he was "anxious to save the effusion of blood and to avoid the indiscriminate punishment of a whole people for crimes of which it is not probable that all are equally guilty, I offer now a free and full pardon to all who will submit themselves to the just authority of the Federal Government. If *you* refuse to accept it, let the consequences fall upon *your* own heads. But I conjure *you* to pause deliberately and reflect well before *you* reject this tender of peace and good will." Buchanan used directive rhetoric here to not only warn the people of Utah against criminal intent, but also to explain the logic of the constitution, and make them aware of the penalties of defiance and the rewards for obedience.

Figure 2.15, which examines the average percentage use of directive rhetoric in the executive orders, appear very similar to that of Figure 2.14. The overall average is 0.16% however, which is almost double that of the proclamation average. This increased average is not the result of presidents from the founding to the present using higher levels of directive rhetoric in the executive orders than their proclamations however. Again contrary to the "traditional/ modern" divide, the increased average is also not due to an overall increase in the use of this form of popular address rhetoric with the presidents of the twentieth century. Indeed, the average percentage use of directive rhetoric during the twentieth century is .037% and that of the nineteenth century is about eight times higher at 0.28%. This finding would actually suggest the opposite assumption to that given by the "traditional/modern" divide; instead of presidents utilizing more of this form of popular address rhetoric during the mid to late 1900's, it appears as though its primary use was in the executive orders that were delivered prior to 1900.

The reason for the increased average in the nineteenth century comes from the variation that can be seen between presidential uses of directive rhetoric, especially during the nineteenth century. Many of the presidents were in line with the overall presidential average, however there were many more presidents who surpassed that average during the nineteenth century (Jackson (0.13%), Tyler (0.27%), Polk (0.42%), Fillmore (1.22%), Lincoln (0.47%), Johnson (0.13%), Hayes (0.92%) and Garfield (1.59%)), than there were presidents who rose significantly above the overall average in the twentieth and twenty-first centuries, like McKinley (0.24%) and Hoover (0.47%). Fillmore and Garfield are notable examples of highest levels of directive rhetoric during the nineteenth century. Indeed, in their executive orders they used levels of directive rhetoric (1.2% and 1.6% respectively) that were far above the average presidential use. Although Garfield's spike can be explained as the result of a small number of executive orders combined with only a few uses of directive rhetoric, Fillmore provides a much better look at how this form of popular address rhetoric was used in the nineteenth century.

In his executive orders, Fillmore used directive rhetoric to instruct individuals as to what should be done regarding specific situations. In his Executive order of May 17th, 1852, Fillmore spoke directly to the secretary of war, informing him that he had given "an authority to Hugh Maxwell, collector at New York, under the eighth section of the act of April 20, 1818, to arrest any unlawful expedition that may be attempted to be fitted out within his district... I will thank *you* to issue the necessary instructions to the proper military officer in that district." In another executive order of June 29th 1852, Fillmore directly addressed his cabinet members on the death of Henry Clay, Stating that "I am sure all hearts are too sad at this moment to attend to business, and I therefore respectfully suggest that *your* Department be closed for the remainder of the day." And in yet another executive order on September 13th, 1852, Fillmore addressed one of his Generals, and ordered him to look into infrastructure improvements. He stated that "I have to acknowledge the receipt of *your* favor of the 13th instant and to say that I shall be pleased if *you* will cause the necessary surveys, projects, and estimates for determining the best means of affording the cities of Washington and Georgetown an unfailing and abundant supply of good and wholesome water to be made as soon as possible."

From the founding to the present day, Presidential Proclamations and Executive orders share a history of use, confusion, and also, as illustrated above, a lack of the use of directive rhetoric in their formation and delivery. The average use of this form of popular address rhetoric in the proclamations or executive orders is far below that of directive rhetoric in the Inaugural, the State of the Union, or the levels of identification rhetoric or authority rhetoric found in any form of presidential address here examined. However, regardless of the low levels of its incorporation, the figures above do illustrate an important statement regarding the separation of the presidents into eras of behavior. More than anything else, the findings above prevent us from doing so. Figures 2.14 and 2.15 illustrate no pattern of significant increase or decrease, nor do they suggest that there was a groundbreaking president who originated the incorporation of directive rhetoric into proclamations or executive orders. Instead, the figures show a history of presidential rhetoric that emphasizes the importance of individual study of each president for a better understanding of how they used not only their proclamations and executive orders, but also how they utilized directive rhetoric in different contexts and for different ends.

Popular Rhetoric and Presidential Address

The findings above relating to popular and congressional address, identification rhetoric, authority rhetoric, and directive rhetoric indicate important changes in the understanding of presidential communication, as well as the "modern/traditional" paradigm. Popular rhetorical address is an undeniable technique that presidents today use to make the public aware of an issue or to pressure the Congress to action through a direct appeal to the constituents of those congressional members. However, this study suggests that different forms of "popular address" were present in the eighteenth and nineteenth century in amounts that mirror or surpass those of the twentieth and twenty-first centuries.

Although the "traditional" and the "modern" presidential distinctions may seek to provide scholars with "new terms with which to assess the character and development of the constitutional order and the president's place within it," (Tulis, 1987, 4), my study suggests that this paradigm may be overly simplistic and have a misappropriated emphasis on only the twentieth century. By categorizing presidents into two distinct periods, characterized by certain behavior, certain policy activity, and certain ways of speaking, the "traditional/modern" demarcation suggests that we are able to easily separate presidents. Dahl proposes that presidents of the twentieth century are important to differentiate from past presidents, saying that "particularly in recent decades, the task of shaping presidential address to influence and manipulate public opinion, has become a central element in the art and science of presidential conduct...Thus the presidency has developed into an office that is the very embodiment of the kind of executive the Framers, so far as we can discern their intentions, strove to avoid" (Dahl, 1990, 369).

In his writings, Tulis "tried to show that nearly all of the presidents in the nineteenth century spoke and wrote differently than nearly all the presidents in our [twentieth] century" (Tulis, 1996, 4). Thus, he suggests that there was once a "non-rhetorical" presidency where all of the "modern" elements (policy proposal and popular address) were absent, and that the rhetorical and the non-rhetorical can be easily discriminated (Medhurst, 1996, xiii).

However, my data show that this inclination toward the employment of popular address rhetoric is not only *present* in the State of the Union Addresses, Presidential Inaugurals, Presidential Proclamations, and Executive Orders in the eighteenth and nineteenth century, it is sometimes found in *larger* frequency in founding and "traditional" presidential addresses than in the twentieth and twenty-first century rhetoric of "modern" successors. This suggests that the alleged passive eighteenth and nineteenth century behavior proposed by the "traditional/modern" paradigm might be less generalizable and in contrast to the assertions of Tulis, Greenstein, and others. Early presidents were not only aware of popular address rhetoric, but they employed it within their speech. In fact, the data demonstrate that presidents such as Adams, Polk, Fillmore Buchanan, and Cleveland used similar or higher percentages of popular address rhetoric than did presidents such as Wilson, Coolidge, and Hoover.

These findings also seem to hint at more substantial commentary on political communication and the presidency as a whole. Instead of seeing presidential rhetoric as an innovation of a single executive (which was not supported here), it might behoove scholars to place more focus on the singular president and look with more care at the presidents of the eighteenth and nineteenth centuries who are often overlooked. Similar to Laracey's conclusions regarding the presidential veto, I find that with popular address rhetoric, "its use has waxed and waned depending on strategic circumstances and the proclivities of individual presidents" (2002, 171). Indeed, the data here present a varying and fluctuating evolutionary rhetorical presidency whose inclusions or dismissals appear to depend on the individual decisions of the individual officeholders. Although advocating the "traditional /modern" paradigm, Greenstein does seem to subliminally hint at the same conclusion in the very last sentence of his 2006 article. He states that "the American Presidency has evolved into a powerful instrument of governance not only as the result of changes in society and the political system, but also of the entrepreneurship of individual chief executives" (2006, 588).

The rhetorical findings here suggest that presidents from the founding have used the constitutional provisions of the State of the Union Address and the Inaugural Address as well as the informal powers of the Executive Order and the Presidential Proclamation to promote their own policy initiatives and use popular address rhetoric, and also that they have done so in different ways and utilizing different rhetoric. Zarefsky correctly concludes that "It is worth re-examining earlier presidencies—not only to appreciate them more and see from whence we came—but to realize striking similarities and recurrent patterns of rhetorical innovation" (2002, 39). Indeed "we get closest to the language of the politics not by looking for paradigms nor by stringing our best writers together in traditions, but by noticing what the talkers and scribblers are doing with the big words at their disposal" (Rodgers, 1987, 11).

The recognition of the individual contribution of each president to the concept and powers of the "Chief Executive" is of utmost importance in the research of the presidency. "The presidency is less an outgrowth of the constitutional design and more a reflection of ambitious men, demanding times, exploited opportunities, and changing international circumstances…The presidency has been shaped by the varied individuals, operating within a dynamic system under changing circumstances." (Genovese, 2001, 14; 16) Indeed, in his State of the Union Address, a president must deal not only with precedent set by prior executives and the evolution of society since his last address, he must view these changes though the lens of his own ambition and capabilities, as well as his own goals. "A rhetorical context is a unique array of forces—rhetorical, historical, sociological, psychological, strategic, economic, and personal—that exists at any given moment in time and that impacts the speakers selection and presentation of topics" (Medhurst, 1996, xviii).

This chapter illustrates that attempts to parse presidential communication history are questionable endeavors at best. I find that use of popular address rhetoric within the presidential address suggests that there is no easy trend that can encapsulate all of presidential history, dismissing some presidents while embracing others. By examining the challenges faced by presidents like Polk, Fillmore, Cleveland, Garfield and others, who might be viewed as less important under a "traditional/modern" (or similar) delineation, we are provided with a richer picture of how the president today behaves as well as similarities between this behavior and that of presidents of the past. Advocating a "traditional/modern" demarcation weakens the intrinsic value of studying presidents who do not fit a certain criteria, and allows scholars to dismiss many presidents who may make incredibly valuable and nuanced contributions to understanding the presidency and executive communication. This kind of approach is hazardous to the study of the executive and presidential rhetoric, and need be approached with caution, if at all.

CHAPTER III

Excavating the Bully Pulpit: The Foundation and Evolution of Policy Proposal

> *Leaders are visionaries with a poorly developed sense of fear and no concept of the odds against them...they make things happen.*
> —Thomas Jefferson

> *If he [the President] speaks to Congress, it must be in the language of truth.*
> —Andrew Jackson

NEWLY ELECTED presidents often claim that they have a mandate from the people of the United States as a result of their victory (Kelly, 1983). They then use this mandate to propose the policies and push the agendas of their administration. However, as was referred to in previous chapters, the interpretation of presidential history that presents a "traditional" and "modern" way of doing things suggests that only recently has the executive actively pursued his own policy agenda and discarded the trappings of constitutional constraint for the freedom to pursue his own goals. However, as this chapter explains, this characterization of political activity may tend to overlook important nuances in presidential policy proposal and behavior and may assume a presidential pacifism of the 18th and 19th that is not completely supported.

As an example, when Andrew Jackson succeeded John Quincy Adams to the office of the presidency of the United States in 1828, he entered the position on the heels of some of the most partisan and assumedly corrupt politics in a presidential election that the nation had seen. Only four years earlier,

Jackson had lost the presidential election, not by losing the popular vote or the electoral college in which no majority was achieved, but by a vote in House of Representatives that was decided by a political deal between the president-elect Adams and Henry Clay (Adams' soon to be Secretary of State). The time of reverent governing by the founding fathers was through; partisanship had entered the American scene. Jackson had won the popular and the electoral plurality and had still not won the election in 1824.

Four years later, Jackson entered the office of the presidency as a "man of the people," claiming a popular uprising from the common man against the aristocracy that had encompassed the presidency for nearly 50 years. From the inauguration speech in which "some twenty thousand people from all parts of the country converged on Washington to witness the triumph of their candidate," to the raucous reception at the White House in which Jackson was "nearly pressed to death and almost suffocated and torn to pieces by the people in their eagerness to shake hands with Old Hickory" (Remini 1971, 435), the election of Jackson was a vocalization from the average citizen that had seemingly been unrealized up to that point in presidential history. The people had spoken (he had won by estimates of nearly two to one), and they wanted Jackson as a president who would lead them away from the corrupt caucus and aristocracy that had stigmatized the presidency. "The majority is to govern," he said in his 1829 State of the Union Address. Indeed, "Jackson insisted that it was the president who was the direct representative of the people and as such spoke for the people" (Genovese, 2001, 60).

Jackson, claiming the mandate from the public, went on to propose amounts of policy in his State of the Union Addresses previously unrealized. The average number of total policy proposals from 1789-1828 was about 33 policies proposed per State of the Union Address. Yet Jackson, in his eight years in office from 1829-1836 proposed an average of almost 120 policies per State of the Union Address. It was an average number of policies unmatched by the likes of presidents such as JFK (97), Franklin Roosevelt (53), Wilson (71), LBJ (102) and even Reagan (99) in the 20th century, and a un-"traditional" and very "modern" showing from Jackson only 50 years into the country's lifespan.

This chapter examines the policy propositions made by the presidents in four different forms of presidential address. According to the conception of the "traditional" president, the presidents of the 18th and 19th centuries do not propose policy, nor do they actively advocate popular policy. In his examination of the two periods, Tulis asserted that "the architects of the constitutional order and most 19th century presidents believed that a strong national government led by a strong executive was compatible with, indeed *required*, the proscription of most of the rhetorical practices that have now come to signify leadership" (Tulis, 1987, 27).

In addition, Tulis, Greenstein, and others find that this "modern" policy-proposing president begins as late in presidential history as the early 20th century. Edwards and Wayne (1997) propose that Theodore Roosevelt set the stage for the "modern" presidency and that by "assuming an assertive posture in both foreign and domestic affairs, Roosevelt expanded the president's policy making roles" (6). They quote Roosevelt himself, espousing the position that his "view was that every executive officer, and above all, every executive officer in high position, was a steward of the people bound actively and affirmatively to do all he could for the people, and not to content himself with the negative merit of keeping his talents undamaged in a napkin" (1997, 7). This proactive stance by Theodore Roosevelt continued to succeeding presidents, and Edwards and Wayne find that "with the exception of three Republican presidents of the 1920's, occupants of the oval office of the 20th century have assumed active political and policy making roles" (1997, 7).

However, even as active as Theodore Roosevelt was, Edwards and Wayne propose that the "modern" presidency truly began with the other Roosevelt—Franklin Delano. They assert that Franklin Roosevelt's "modern" presidency "is characterized by presidential activism in a variety of policy making roles. Many of the practices that Roosevelt initiated or continued have been institutionalized by his successors and/or required by Congress" (1997, 7). This is the same position earlier touched on by Greenstein, who also posits that the true "modern" presidency begins with the leadership and governance of Franklin Roosevelt. During Franklin Roosevelt's terms, "the chief executive became the principle source of policy initiative, proposing much of the legislation considered by Congress. Presidents began to make an increasing amount of policy independent of the legislature" (2000, 3). Michael Genovese also echoes this conclusion, concluding that "FDR established what many refer to as the 'modern presidency,' a strong, activist model of leadership most of his successors felt compelled to try and emulate" (2001, 139).

Accordingly, the assertion is that the "modern" presidency, the trappings of the contemporary presidency, and especially the initiative of the president to propose policy in his addresses did not begin until the early 1900's. How

110   *The Evolutionary Rhetorical Presidency*

then can we attempt to take into account the policy proposals made by Andrew Jackson almost 100 years prior to this rhetorical revolution? Before looking at the policies that were being proposed in presidential address, the first indication that the "traditional" presidents might not be as constrained by the constitution and presidential precedent comes in the simple examination of the number of words of one of the first forms of presidential rhetoric that will be examined: The State of the Union Address.

The Length of the State of the Union Address

Although this study initially looked at the examination of the number of words used in the State of the Union Address over time simply to have the complete data on each form of presidential address, once the data was collected, the changes that had taken place since the founding exhibited an interesting result.

Figure 3.1

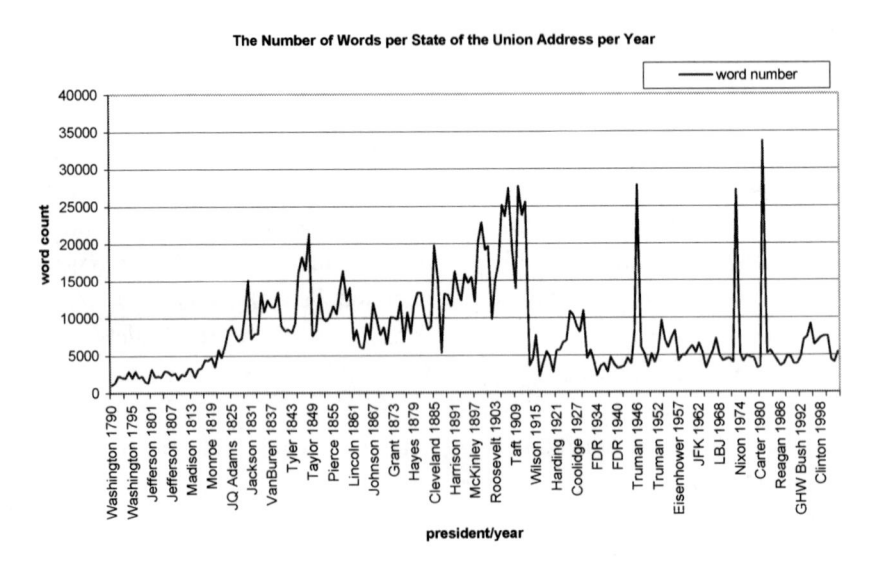

The Number of Words per State of the Union Address per Year

Figure 3.2

The Average Word Number per State of the Union Address per President

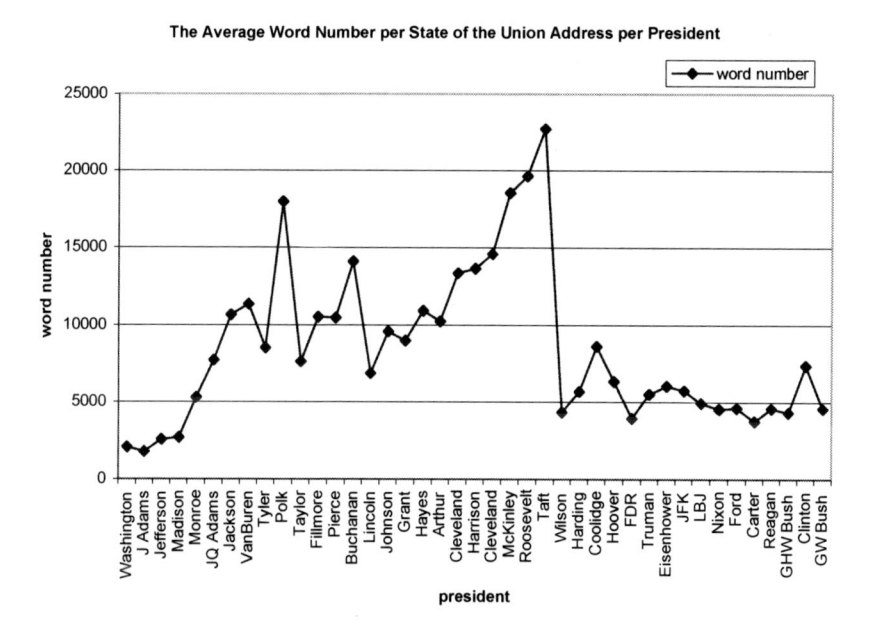

[Chart: word number vs. president, from Washington to GW Bush, ranging from ~2000 words for early presidents, peaking at ~22,500 for Taft, then dropping to around 4000-8000 for modern presidents]

Figure 3.1 illustrates the number of words per State of the Union Address from 1790-2003. Figure 3.2 is an examination of the average number of words used in the State of the Union Address per president.[1] The above figures show several important points. First of all, we see that the founding presidents presented State of the Union Addresses of short length; the average length of the State of the Union Address from Washington through Monroe was just over 3,000 words. From 1790 until 1820, the length did not even reach 5,000 words. However, this brevity soon appears to end and, beginning with John Quincy Adams in 1825, the number of words in the State of the Union Address jumps to almost 9,000 words. Andrew Jackson follows Adams with an address almost double that length with around 15,000 words.

---

[1] Because of the similarity in the patterns that occur in graphs detailing each year as well as each president, unless there is a significant discrepancy between the pattern shown per year as opposed to per president, those which are compiled by president are more relevant to the discussion and will be used from this point.

This sudden rise in address length which was begun by Adams and Jackson is the next consistent finding of the figures and, as seen above, the number of words increases steadily following the Adams presidency until 1914. During the period between 1825 and 1912, the length of State of the Union Addresses grew from the founding (1790-1824) average of 3,000 words to an average of over 12,700 words per State of the Union Address. This increase in number of words is important to observe because it insinuates that there may have been a challenge to a "traditional" presidency constitutionally bound to pithiness. Although the founding participants who became president did indeed keep their messages "short and sweet," the presidents immediately following them felt more and more comfortable giving lengthier addresses.

There may be several reasons for the sudden increase witnessed with the presidencies of Adams and Jackson. First of all, spurred on by the circumstances surrounding the election of 1824, the presidential election became a popular vote contest and the nominations were the result of national convention and not congressional caucus. As a possible result of this new awareness that the public held the keys to the White House, the State of the Union Addresses not only lengthened, they accordingly contained more issues, positions, and activity then in previous addresses.

In addition, in Figures 3.1 and 3.2 we see that with Woodrow Wilson, the number of words of the State of the Union Address per year and per president undergoes a significant and permanent decline. The word count dropped from 25,518 words in the address of 1912 to 3,553 words in the address of 1913. Furthermore, the average length of the State of the Union Address for the Taft presidency was almost 23,000 words to just over 4,000 words per address in Wilson's tenure. However, the drop in address length is not solely attributable to the presidency of Wilson, because it was also in 1913 that the State of the Union Address changed from a written to an orally delivered format.

It may well be that Wilson was responsible for making the decision to change the form of delivery of the State of the Union Address from written form sent to Congress to orally delivered format. Indeed this is consistent with the style that many scholars attribute to him of seeking "to inject new energy in government by viewing the president as the 'only governmental officer with a national mandate,' whose function was to understand the 'true majority sentiment' and explain it to the people" (Crockett, 2002, 112). However, this does not necessarily indicate that Wilson had originated a "modern" style of leadership to be imitated by successive officeholders. In fact, shortening of address length may simply indicate that convention and format of personal delivery did not allot the same kind of address seen in previous presidencies. An address consisting of 30,000 words would neither be practical nor probable for presentation in a public address. Instead, a State of the Union Address would necessarily be shorter, and presented within a manageable time span.

The permanent decline in the length of the State of the Union Address following its return to oral delivery can be seen also in the fact that there has been no hint of a return to the address lengths of the 19th and early 20th centuries. We can see that there have been some presidents in the modern-day era whose verbosity in single situations (Truman 1946, Nixon 1973, and Carter 1980) has returned the address to the length of "traditional" addresses in single State of the Union Addresses (27,841, 27,150, and 33,675 respectively). However, without these rare spikes (which are not included in Figure 2 because they are addresses that the president delivered in written format to Congress at various points during that year), the presidents of the 20th century appear not to mimic the lengths of 19th century presidents, but instead resemble those of the original founding period. In fact, the average, as discussed above, between 1825 and 1914 was over 12,000 words per address, whereas the average length of the State of the Union Address including and following Wilson (1913-2003) was almost half of that at just over 6,000 words per address.

Because of the extended Address lengths that existed prior to Wilson, and the significant change with the return of the State of the Union Address to oral delivery, questions arise as to what the presidents during the 19th century period were doing in addresses that tripled and sometimes quadrupled the lengths of 20th century presidents. The "traditional/modern" paradigm seems to suggest that the presidents of the 19th century were policy inactive and constrained by the formality of precedent as well as constitutionally mandated duty. However, as seen above, these presidents were making State of the Union Addresses that almost quadrupled the lengths of those of the 20th century presidencies. As a result of this initial finding regarding the State of the Union Addresses, it gives warrant to examine the number of policies that are actually proposed in those State of the Union Addresses and the other forms of presidential address in order to conclude whether or not the increasing address lengths of the 19th century are indeed indicative of a policy active president that may be unrecognized by many scholars today.

The Presidency and Policy Proposition in the State of the Union Address

In order to fully evaluate the changes that have taken place in policy proposal and advocacy over the history of the rhetorical presidency, it is first important to look at the total number of policies that were proposed by the presidents in their State of the Union Addresses and the implications of any patterns. Although it will be necessary shortly to control the number of policies proposed for the length of the addresses, as presidents delivering the Address orally were constrained by lengths that written deliveries were not, it is important that the general view of policy totals be examined for their possible contribution to our understanding of presidential activity.

Figure 3.3

The Average Number of Policies Proposed per State of the Union Address per President

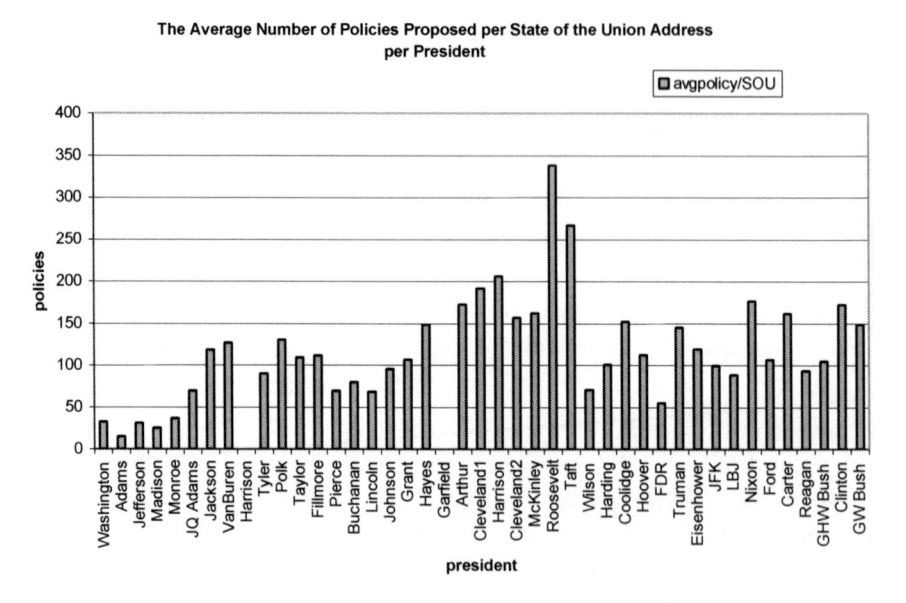

Figure 3.3 is a comparison of the average number of policies proposed in the State of the Union Address per president. When the data are compiled to individual presidents, we see that there is a correlation between the number of words used in the State of the Union Address and the number of policies that are proposed in the address. When looking at the figure above, the founding period appears to be an era of presidential history in which total

policy proposal was dramatically lower than any other. In fact, the average from 1790 to 1824, was only about 30 policies proposed per State of the Union Address. This may initially suggest that the founders did indeed refrain from policy proposal as suggested by the tenets of the "traditional/ modern" divide. However, the fact that there were actually policy propositions by presidents during the founding period cannot be denied, and presents a challenge to a completely policy inactive president that might be assumed under the standard characterization of a "traditional" pattern of behavior. As examined earlier in this study, in his State of the Union Address, Washington proposed policy relating to the military, education, and the economy. In one sweeping statement in his State of the Union Address in 1797, Adams also addressed both defense and the economy stating that, "I should hold myself guilty of a neglect of duty if I forbore to recommend that we should make every exertion to protect our commerce and to place our country in a suitable posture of defense as the only sure means of preserving both…it is necessary that provision be made for fulfilling these obligations."

Other presidents of the founding period did indeed also exhibit "modern" characteristics by advocating various policies in their State of the Union Address, and approached the policies from both a general and a specific perspective. Jefferson gives example of this abstract intonation in his address of the issues of tariffs in his State of the Union Address of 1802 by stating that, "it rests with the Legislature to decide whether they will meet inequalities abroad with countervailing inequalities at home, or provide for the evil in any other way." As illustrated here, although he broached the topic of the tariffs and duties, no specifics for remedy were offered; he only suggested generally that Congress do something about the subject and deferred to the legislative power. Madison also took this broad approach to some policies as well, addressing the economy and stating in his State of the Union Address of 1811 that, "the decrease of revenue arising from the situation of our commerce, and the extraordinary expenses which have and may become necessary, must be taken into view in making commensurate provisions for the ensuing year; and I recommend to your consideration the propriety of insuring a sufficiency of annual revenue at least to defray the ordinary expenses of Government, and to pay the interest on the public debt, including that on new loans which may be authorized." Again, we are presented with generalities instead of specific policy details.

However, as opposed to consistently speaking in the abstract, presidents of the founding also addressed the specifics of policy when dealing with several topics and almost always when discussing the military. In the same 1802 State of the Union Address by Thomas Jefferson examined above, he states, "a small force in the Mediterranean will still be necessary to restrain the Tripoline cruisers, and the uncertain tenure of peace with some other of the Barbary Powers may eventually require that force to be augmented. The necessity of procuring some smaller vessels for that service will raise the estimate, but the difference in their maintenance will soon make it a measure of economy." Madison also proposed specific changes to the commissioning of officers in the military suggesting that, "toward an accomplishment of this important work I recommend for the consideration of Congress the expediency of instituting a system which shall in the first instance call into the field at the public expense and for a given time certain portions of the commissioned and non-commissioned officers." (Madison 1810).

Madison continued with military specifics in 1811 recommending, "accordingly, that adequate provisions be made for filling the ranks and prolonging the enlistments of the regular troops; for an auxiliary force to be engaged for a more limited term; for the acceptance of volunteer corps, whose patriotic ardor may court a participation in urgent services; for detachments as they may be wanted of other portions of the militia, and for such a preparation of the great body as will proportion its usefulness to its intrinsic capacities." Although some other realms of policy were relegated to general propositions, the military was an area in which the founding presidents, and almost every president succeeding them, felt free to propose specifics and give details of action.

In contrast to the brief average number of policy proposals of the some of the founders, beginning with the extremely partisan contested election of 1824 and the entrance into presidential office of John Quincy Adams, the average number of policies proposed in each State of the Union Address begin to rise significantly. Indeed, Adams' entrance in a highly politically charged election signified more than the end of the "Virginia Dynasty" (called such because every one of the presidents before John Quincy Adams except his father, John Adams, originated from Virginia). It also signaled the beginning of significant policy increase in the State of the Union Addresses of the presidents.

As seen in Figure 3.3, Adams himself proposed almost 69.5 policies per State of the Union Address and began his term by proposing 95 policies in his annual address in 1825. Adams began his very first address in contrast to the generality based State of the Union Addresses of his predecessors, giving detailed changes that he saw as necessary concerning tariffs and trade. "The removal of discriminating duties of tonnage and of impost is limited to articles of the growth, produce, or manufacture of the country to which the vessel belongs or to such articles as are most usually first shipped from her ports. It will deserve the serious consideration of Congress whether even this remnant of restriction may not be safely abandoned, and whether the general tender of equal competition made in the act of 1824-01-08, may not be extended to include all articles of merchandise not prohibited, of what country so ever they may be the produce or manufacture." This is an example of a statement that not only proposes three different policies, but also gives specifics on acts of Congress that he feels are lacking and precise changes in policy that may be necessary.

He continued to advocate explicit policies in addressing veterans pay—"I submit to Congress the expediency of providing for individual cases of this description by special enactment, or of revising the act of 1820-05-01, with a view to mitigate the rigor of its exclusions in favor of persons to whom charity now bestowed can scarcely discharge the debt of justice." He also proposed detailed policies relating to such subjects as education and science, "connected with the establishment of an university, or separate from it, might be undertaken the erection of an astronomical observatory, with provision for the support of an astronomer, to be in constant attendance of observation upon the phenomena of the heavens, and for the periodical publication of his observances."

Adams also made specific policy recommendations relating to the military as seen in his proposal "to counteract the prevalence of desertion among the troops it has been suggested to withhold from the men a small portion of their monthly pay until the period of their discharge; and some expedient appears to be necessary to preserve and maintain among the officers so much of the art of horsemanship as could scarcely fail to be found wanting on the possible sudden eruption of a war, which should take us unprovided with a single corps of cavalry." In this example, we can see how an early president like Adams was able to propose specific presidential policy that dealt not only with the military, which prior presidents also tended to do, but also to the subjects of the economy, science, education, health, the frontier, Indians, and trade. He gave each of these issues in-depth examinations with proposals including dollar amounts and reference to congressional acts of the past, instead of simply addressing them generally as subjects into which Congress should inquire.

Jackson not only followed Adams into the White House, he also imitated Adams' tendency to utilize the State of the Union Address for specific policy proposal. In fact, he began his presidency by proposing 217 policies in his inaugural State of the Union Address, and, as illustrated in Figure 3.3, proposed an average of 119 policies per address over his tenure. In his State of the Union Address of 1829, Jackson claimed his election was a victory for the common man and wasted no time in framing his policy propositions as programs for and supported by the populous. He began the Address claiming that "in discharging the responsible trust confided to the Executive in this respect it is my settled purpose to ask nothing that is not clearly right and to submit to nothing that is wrong; and I flatter myself that, supported by the other branches of the Government and by the intelligence and patriotism of the people, we shall be able, under the protection of Providence, to cause all our just rights to be respected."

He again claimed the trust of the people when he addressed policy relating to Great Britain, stating "with Great Britain, alike distinguished in peace and war, we may look forward to years of peaceful, honorable, and elevated competition. Every thing in the condition and history of the two nations is calculated to inspire sentiments of mutual respect and to carry conviction to the minds of both that it is their policy to preserve the most cordial relations. *Such are my own views, and it is not to be doubted that such are also the prevailing sentiments of our constituents.*" (emphasis added). In advocating policy in this way, Jackson not only contributed to the evolution of the State of the Union and presidential rhetoric by arguing that his policies were obviously supported by the people, but he also used their goodwill and support to propose policy numbers never before seen in the State of the Union Address.

The proposal of specifics in policy advocacy can be illustrated further in Jackson's discussion of the necessity for revision of the method of election of the vice-president and president. "I would therefore recommend such an amendment of the Constitution as may remove all intermediate agency in the election of the President and Vice-President. The mode may be so regulated as to preserve to each State its present relative weight in the election, and a failure in the first attempt may be provided for by confining the second to a choice between the two highest candidates." He appears neither bound by precedent nor constitutional restraint from making specific policy suggestions even relating to alteration of the Constitution itself.

Roosevelt and Taft were two of the most prolific presidents in terms of both the number of words in their State of the Union Addresses (Figures 3.1 and 3.2) as well as the sheer number of policies that they were able to propose in each (Figure 3.3). As seen above, they were the pinnacle of both length and policy proposition throughout the history of the presidency and the State of the Union. The average length of a State of the Union Address during the tenure of Roosevelt and Taft was 20,675 words. Figure 3.3 illustrates that the average number of policies proposed by the two men was 338 and 266 policies per State of the Union Address, respectively.

In their State of the Union Addresses, Theodore Roosevelt and Taft ran the gambit of general and specific policy proposals, touching on many different and diverse subjects and issues; they even provided subheadings so that the readers might not forget which topic was being discussed. To repeat the example given in the introduction, Theodore Roosevelt's State of the Union Address in 1902 shows how he would often encapsulate three or four policy proposals within one sentence of the address. For example, he states that "1)It is suggested, however, that all future legislation on the subject should be with the view of encouraging the use of such instrumentalities as will automatically supply every legitimate demand of productive industries 2) and of commerce, 3) not only in the amount, 4) but in the character of circulation; 5)and of making all kinds of money interchangeable, 6) and, at the will of the holder, convertible into the established gold standard" (There were six policies proposed in this single sentence alone).

In addition, Roosevelt would explain in extraordinary detail the policy propositions that he was making or the issues that he wanted to see acted upon by the Congress. In one discussion of the Panama Canal, in his seventh State of the Union Address on December 3, 1907, he gave the following detailed description of the locks in the canal:

> "The chief engineer and all his professional associates are firmly convinced that the 85 feet level lock canal which they are constructing is the best that could be desired. Some of them had doubts on this point when they went to the Isthmus. As the plans have developed under their direction their doubts have been dispelled. While they may decide upon changes in detail as construction advances they are in hearty accord in approving the general plan. They believe that it provides a canal not only adequate to all demands that will be made upon it but superior in every way to a sea level canal. I concur in this belief."

Was this level of detailed policy advocacy necessary to inform the Congress on the state of the union? It is debatable. However, it was considered a necessity by Roosevelt in order to achieve exactly those policies that he wanted and to see them completed in exactly the way that he desired. This finding seemingly contradicts the view of Theodore Roosevelt as one of the "traditional" presidents that might have shied away from policy proposal and political initiative. It is contrary to the assertion that "Theodore Roosevelt's 'middle way' was, in fact, a campaign for moderation—moderate use of popular rhetoric, moderate appeals for moderate reform" (Tulis, 1987, 96). Indeed, the figure above suggests that Roosevelt was actually quite far from moderate in the number of total policies he proposed as well as the details that he used to propose them.

Taft continued the ostentatious style of State of the Union Addresses of his predecessor and continued with lengths and policy propositions that are unmatched in State of the Union Addresses to this day. In 1910, Taft's State of the Union Address was 27,651 words long, containing 397 policy proposals. In addition, Taft continued the format, begun in the eighth State of the Union Address of Theodore Roosevelt, of providing headings and subheadings for the subject matters of which he spoke and for the policies that he wanted to propose.

In Taft's first Address, he had over 35 headings detailing his policy proposals. *Europe, The Near East, Latin America, The Far East, the Department of State, Other Departments, Government Expenditures and Revenues, Frauds in the Collection of Customs, Maximum and Minimum Clause in Tariff Act, Use of the New Tariff Board, War Department, The Navy, Department of Justice, Expedition in Legal Procedure, Injunctions Without Notice, Anti-Trust and Interstate Commerce Clause, Jail of the District of Columbia, Post Office Department, Second Class Mail Matter, Postal Savings Banks, Ship Subsidy, Interior Department, New Mexico and Arizona, Alaska, Conservation of Natural Resources, Department of Agriculture, Department of Commerce and Labor, The Light House Board, Consolidation of Bureaus, The White Slave Trade, the Bureau of Health, Civil Service Commission, Political Contributions, Freedman's Savings and Trust Company, Semi-Centennial of Negro Freedom,* and *Conclusion* were all subject headings used by Taft during his first State of the Union Address in 1909. Each heading was followed by a detailed examination of the subject as well as many detailed policy propositions for the Congress to examine.

Although the figures above suggest that this activist stance towards policy proposal continued with relative consistency until 1913 with Woodrow Wilson, the decline seen in average policy proposals per State of the Union Address corresponds again with the average length of the address itself. Wilson's addresses, out of a necessity that probably would not have allowed the listener to maintain attention for a 20,000 word Roosevelt-like address, dropped to an average of 4,342 words. Wilson's addresses were almost five times shorter that what the written State of the Union Address had grown to prior to 1913. In fact, Wilson proposed only 74 policies in his first State of the Union Address and, as seen in Figure 3.3, averaged only about 71 policy propositions per State of the Union Address, with some addresses, like that of 1917, proposing as few as 30 policies. This was almost five times less than the average number of policies proposed per year during the presidencies of Theodore Roosevelt and Taft.

Figure 3.3 also illustrates that these shorter, and orally delivered addresses, continue to the present day, as seen in the fact that George W. Bush proposed around only 80 policies in his 2003 State of the Union Address and averaged only 100 policies per Address; this is a far cry from the 200 and 300 policy propositions in State of the Union Addresses given in the written format period by such presidents as Roosevelt or Taft. As a result, it appears that presidents in the early to late 20th century, into the 21st century, have proposed almost 35 fewer total policies, on average, in their State of the Union Address than the presidents of the mid-to-late 19th and early 20th centuries.

These findings present evidence that the presidents of the 19th century may not have been the policy-shy and "propositionally challenged" executives suggested by their categorization as "traditional." It appears as though there are no clear patterns of policy proposition proclivity presented to suggest that the presidents of the 19th century proposed on the average more policies in their State of the Union Addresses than their counterparts in the 20th and 21st century. In fact, if we examine the *total* number of policies proposed throughout presidential history, as well as broken down into a "modern" and "traditional" period, we are given a clearer picture of the similarities that all presidents have had as well as the slow evolution that their forms of speech may take.

Figure 3.4

The Average Total Number of Policies Proposed per "Traditional" and "Modern" Period With Wilson as Demarcation Point

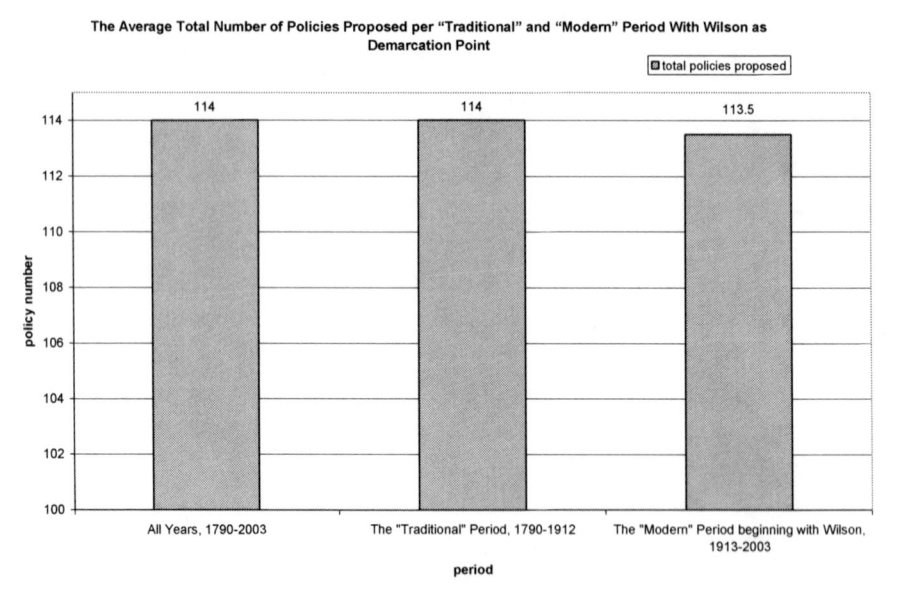

Period	Total Policies Proposed
All Years, 1790-2003	114
The "Traditional" Period, 1790-1912	114
The "Modern" Period beginning with Wilson, 1913-2003	113.5

Figure 3.4 is an illustration of the average number of total policies proposed per State of the Union Address from 1790-2003, a "traditional" period from 1790-1912, and a "modern" period from 1913-2003. If we consider the totality of State of the Union Addresses, we see that the results do not support a difference in total policy proposal activity between a pre- and post-Wilson period, nor a significant difference between an oral and written presentation of the State of the Union Address. In fact, the total number of policies proposed in the "traditional" period from the founding to Wilson mirrors the average number of total policies overall, and still presents a higher average than the period including and succeeding Wilson. As a result, a consideration of State of the Union Addresses in the aggregate finds little support for Wilson's presidency as an administration that had a dramatically different production on policy proposal. In addition, the same lack of a conclusive transformative presidency could be said for scholars advocating the division of presidential history in the "traditional" and the "modern" periods who use presidents such as Theodore Roosevelt and Franklin Delano Roosevelt as the benchmarks and beginnings of the "modern" period. None of these presidencies represented significant pre- and post-presidency differences.

However, even though the total average number of policy proposals in the State of the Union Address present a challenge to the "traditional/ modern" paradigm, it is important to look even more closely at the act of proposing policy within the State of the Union Addresses and what that act tells us about presidential policy activism as well as environmental factors that might affect it. In order to address these issues, it is important to view policy proposal in the State of the Union Address in a controlled comparison. To present a more comparable picture of the presidents and their policy proposals, it is especially important that we control for the type of delivery that was utilized in the State of the Union Address. The data presented above provide an examination of the total number of policies proposed in the State of the Union Address without any effort to take into account the length differences as a result of the format change of the State of the Union Address. With this in mind, the Figures showed that those presidents from Jefferson until Wilson who delivered the State of the Union Address in written format continuously increased the address length. As noted earlier, when Wilson changed the delivery of the State of the Union Address from written form to the orally delivered format, this made a 20,000-word address impractical and implausible for personal delivery. As a result, in the early 20th century, the address length dropped to around 5,000 words per address and this trend has continued to the present day.

In order to account for the format shift and more clearly see exactly what is taking place regarding policy proposal in the State of the Union Address, the next step is to control for that change. By dividing the number of policies by the number of words of each State of the Union Address we are able to get a consistent measure of policy proposal with which to compare across addresses and presidents.

124   The Evolutionary Rhetorical Presidency

Figure 3.5

The Average Policy Numbers Proposed per 1000 Words per President in the State of the Union Address

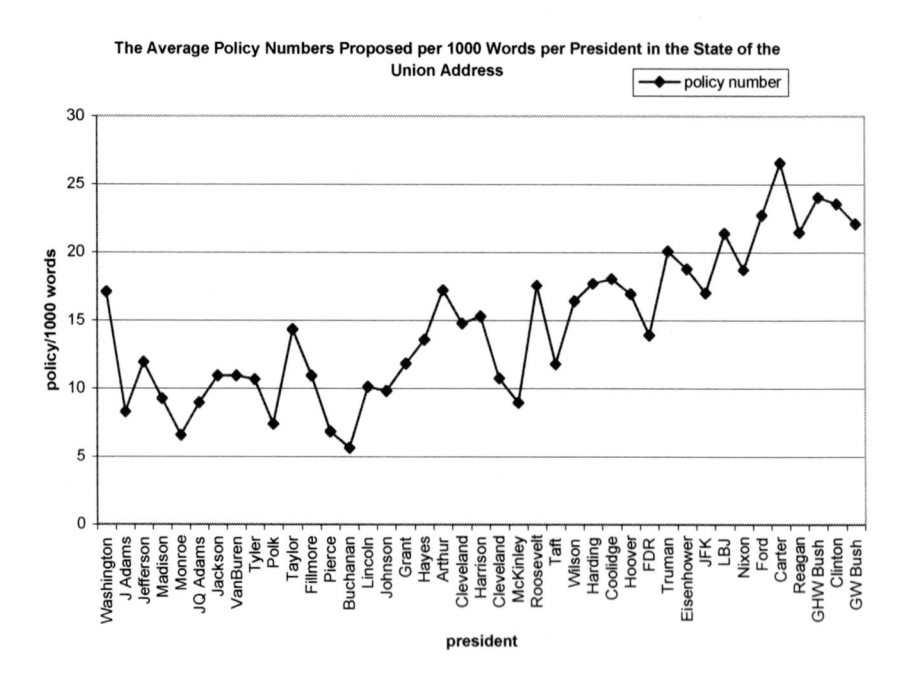

Figure 3.5 illustrates the average number of policies proposed per 1,000 words of the State of the Union Address per president. The graph exhibits a pattern much different from the trends illustrated in Figure 3.3 above. Instead of providing significant demarcations of policy proposal that appear to be based on the form of delivery that was selected by the president, Figure 3.5 shows a much clearer illustration of a consistent evolution of policy proposal activity in the State of the Union Address. Although there are several variable increases and decreases in the number of policies proposed per 1,000 words of the address, there is nothing substantive enough to indicate separate times of policy proposal, nor is there anything that would indicate or enable a grouping of presidents according to a specific characterization of policy proposal activity.

What we can see from the figure above, is what appears to be a general increase in the number of policies proposed in the State of the Union Address per president from the founding to the present day. From John Adams onward, there is a slow and consistent rise in the number of policies that are proposed per 1000 words of the State of the Union Address. Indeed, the average number of policies grows from around 10 policies proposed per 1000 words of the state of the union address to around 20 policies proposed in the State of the Union Addresses of the 21st century. Although we saw earlier that contemporary presidents propose fewer total policies overall than many of their predecessors in the nineteenth century, the data above suggest that presidents today are proposing more and more policies within fewer and fewer words.

This evolution in the State of the Union Address is truly an indication of several things, each of which challenge the belief that the rhetorical presidency may be easily parsed into two separate eras of presidential behavior as well as the assertions that there might have been an individual president who introduced a new way of rhetorically doing things in the early twentieth century. First of all, the figures that examine the average total number of policies that are proposed in the State of the Union Address without controlling for length, provide an important insight into the presidents of the eighteenth and nineteenth centuries. The "traditional/ modern" dichotomy would suggest that the presidents of the 18th and 19th centuries were inactive in terms of policy, and it proposes that the presidents who delivered the State of the Union Address in written format were prevented from having any real opportunity to be policy active or push their own agenda. However, the increase in the number of total policies that can be seen from the founding to the time when Wilson changed the State of the Union Address to oral delivery, suggests that the presidents of the eighteenth and nineteenth centuries were indeed extremely policy active. In fact, presidents as early as Washington, Adams, and Jefferson all proposed and pushed very specific policies in their State of the Union Addresses. In addition, the consistently increasing total policy propositions that culminate in the incredibly policy-full addresses of Roosevelt and Taft show that, even though presidents may have been bound to a written delivery of the State of the Union Address, they utilized this medium to its fullest extent. They delivered Addresses that were longer than ever before, and Addresses that contained more policy propositions than at any time in presidential history.

A second finding is that, although Wilson did change the format of delivery of the State of the Union Address from written to oral delivery, the presidents that followed behaved in a manner almost exactly similar to the behavior of the eighteenth and nineteenth century presidents regarding the written address. When the State of the Union Address was delivered in written form, it had no page limit; thus presidents continued to use the message as a rhetorical and policy proposal weapon by simply increasing the length of the State of the Union Address, thereby increasing the number of subjects that could be covered and the number of policies that could be proposed. After Wilson, presidents again sought to maximize the use of the State of the Union within the confines that oral delivery placed on its length. In doing so, contemporary presidents have evolved the ability to use less words to say more. Therefore, although their overall total policy numbers are less than that of the presidents of the nineteenth century, contemporary presidents have almost double the average policies proposed per 1000 words of the address. The presidents of today have found a way to do more with less, just as the presidents of the nineteenth century found ways to do more with more. In addition, no single individual emerges as a "father" of policy proposal and activity. Although Jefferson can be credited for changing the State of the Union Delivery to written format and Wilson can be credited as changing it back to oral delivery, this is where their credit for change must end. Instead, the slow increase in policy proposal in the State of the Union shows that every president enters the office with an agenda and policies that they would like to see accomplished. They then use whatever tools are at their disposal to accomplish this goal.

The Presidency and Policy Proposition in the Inaugural Address

The examination of the State of the Union Addresses suggests that the history of policy proposition in presidential rhetoric may exhibit more variability than a separation and classification into separate eras of rhetorical behavior will allow. To add depth and detail to the full examination of the policy proposing president, it is important to look at the policy propositions in the Inaugural address as well for the similar or disparate characteristics and conclusions that might be found therein. Although the State of the Union Address is usually associated with the proposal of policy, the Inaugural address is not. In his work, Tulis states that the Inaugural "emphasized popular instruction in constitutional principle and the articulation of the general tenor and direction of presidential policy, while tending to avoid discussion of...particular policy proposals" (1987, 47). Because this claim again suggests important differences between presidential behaviors in different eras, it is important that the policy proposal in the Inaugural address be as closely examined as the State of the Union Address to evaluate its evolution and use.

Figure 3.6

The Average Number of Total Policies Proposed in the Inaugural Address per President

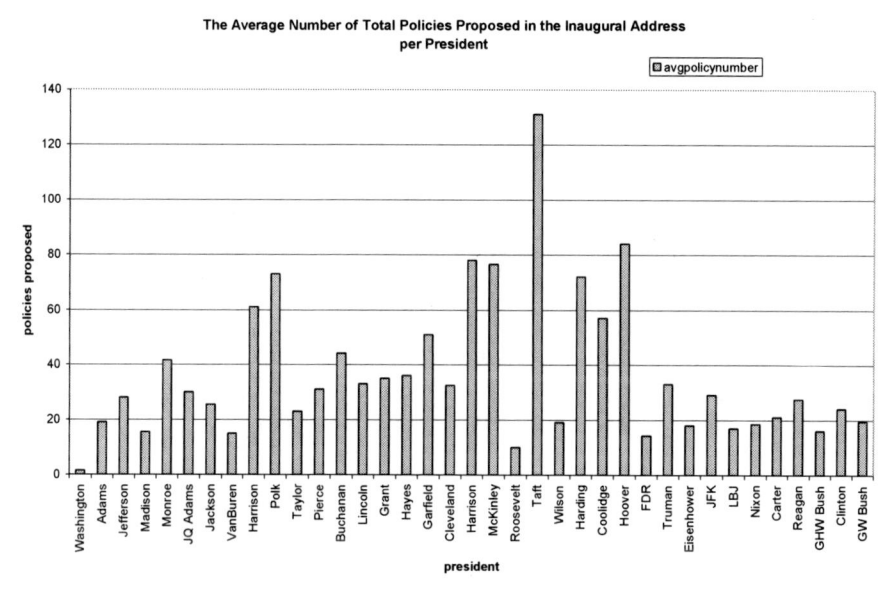

Figure 3.6 is a comparison of the average number of policies proposed in the Inaugural Address per president. The first finding of the chart above is that presidents tend to propose less policy in their Inaugural address than they do in their state of the union address. In fact, the average number of policies that are proposed by presidents in their Inaugural Address are anywhere from one-half to one-third as many as were proposed in their State of the Union Address. However, this lower level of policy proposal in this kind of presidential speech in no way detracts from the fact that the chart above shows that every president from George Washington to George W. Bush, except for those who took the office unexpectedly and therefore did not give an Inaugural Address, used this form of presidential address to propose the themes for their administration and notify the nation of what they believe needed to be done. Regardless of the ceremonial nature associated with the address, the Figure above shows that presidents do indeed utilize their Inaugural address to pursue policy and administrative objectives.

In his Inaugural addresses, James Monroe not only proposed an average number of policies higher than any "modern" president since FDR (41.5), he also engaged in very un-"traditional" behavior in his proposal of policies that addressed many different subject matters as well as the manner in which he provided specifics on those propositions. Although Monroe did begin his Inaugural in a more general and abstract sense, stating that "Let us by all wise and constitutional measures promote intelligence among the people as the best means of preserving our liberties. Our distance from Europe and the just, moderate, and pacific policy of our Government may form some security against these dangers, but they ought to be anticipated, and guarded against," he soon grew increasingly specific with policy requests and the details of that policy.

Similar to the finding in the examination of the State of the Union Address that the founders were often very specific in terms of military policy, Monroe also addressed many different policies that were related to the defense of the country and the reinforcement of the existing military. In the opening of his first Inaugural, he suggested that "our coast and inland frontiers should be fortified, our Army and Navy, regulated upon just principles as to the force of each, be kept in perfect order, and our militia be placed on the best practicable footing." He continued to specify military policy by proposing how the size of the military should be delineated, saying "Our land and naval forces should be moderate, but adequate to the necessary purposes...In time of war, with the enlargement of which the great naval resources of the country render it susceptible, and which should be duly fostered in time of peace, it would contribute essentially, both as an auxiliary of defense and as a powerful engine of annoyance, to diminish the calamities of war and to bring the war to a speedy and honorable termination. But it ought always to be held prominently in view that the safety of these States and of everything dear to a free people must depend in an eminent degree on the militia. It is of the highest importance, therefore, that they be so organized and trained as to be prepared for any emergency."

In addition to the discussion on the general appropriate nature of the military in colonial life, Monroe also seized the role of commander in chief in his Inaugural by dictating the specifics of where the military presence need be on an international scale. After detailing where international naval bases and Navy outposts should be located, he stated that "we should present to other powers an armed front from St. Croix to the Sabine, which would protect in the event of war our whole coast and interior from invasion." This is very much a legislatively active president who has a firm grasp of the role he would like to see played by the military, and what policy would be best enacted for the country.

Monroe also proposed policy dealing with many other facets of domestic life and his administrations' goals for the country as well. He started another section of the Inaugural by explaining that "Other interests of high importance will claim attention, among which the improvement of our country by roads and canals, proceeding always with a constitutional sanction, holds a distinguished place." He made comment on trade, saying "Our manufacturers will likewise require the systematic and fostering care of the Government. Possessing as we do all the raw materials, the fruit of our own soil and industry, we ought not to depend in the degree we have done on supplies from other countries. It is important, too, that the capital which nourishes our manufacturers should be domestic. Equally important is it to provide at home a market for our raw materials, as by extending the competition it will enhance the price and protect the cultivator against the casualties incident to foreign markets." He also spoke to the situation with the Indian-Americans, stating that "With the Indian tribes it is our duty to cultivate friendly relations and to act with kindness and liberality in all our transactions. Equally proper is it to persevere in our efforts to extend to them the advantages of civilization."

Monroe used the commander in chief function illustrated above to dictate military policy, and he also used his Inaugural address to propose that other realms of policy and national interest might be best suited if he were given the power over them. In discussing the extensive lands of the new nation, Monroe asserted his own authority and the propriety of that authority. He stated, "The vast amount of vacant lands, the value of which daily augments, forms an additional resource of great extent and duration…To meet the requisite responsibility every facility should be afforded to the Executive to enable it to bring the public agents intrusted with the public money strictly and promptly to account." He followed this statement on what needed to be done with a statement of how he could do the job best. "I shall do all I can to secure economy and fidelity in this important branch of the Administration, and I doubt not that the Legislature will perform its duty with equal zeal. A thorough examination should be regularly made, and I will promote it."

In addition to these suggestions that he, as president was best suited to deal with certain issues, Monroe also felt free to give his opinion to the Congress and the people regarding what should be done. On the issue of international relations Monroe said that "Respecting the attitude which it may be proper for the United States to maintain hereafter between the parties, I have no hesitation in stating it as my opinion that the neutrality heretofore observed should still be adhered to." This declaration of his own position and the suggestion that it should be followed also continued on later in the address when Monroe informed the people that "With every power we are in perfect amity, and it is our interest to remain so if it be practicable on just conditions. I see no reasonable cause to apprehend variance with any power, unless it proceed from a violation of our maritime rights. In these contests, should they occur, and to whatever extent they may be carried, we shall be neutral."

Monroe's Inaugural Address is interesting and enlightening for a number of reasons. First of all, the Inaugural shows little restraint on policy proposal or advocacy that suggest he should, or could, be placed within a "traditional" time period with other presidents who were allegedly intimately tied by the "constitutional restraints" placed on their activity. Instead, Monroe used his Inaugural address to propose both abstract and specific policies for domestic and international affairs. Secondly, Monroe's address shows a president who seemed eager not only to expand the powers of his office, but to give his unique position and opinion on policy and program to the Congress and the American People. Either of these activities suggest that Monroe was more of an activist president than one seemingly tied to a tradition of inactivity and meekness. As with the State of the Union Address, it appears as though the Inaugural address, even as early as the founding, was seized upon by presidents as a way to exercise their powers, expand their influence, and accomplish their goals.

After Monroe, the Inaugural address saw an incredible variation in the amount of policies that were proposed in it by successive presidents. Some presidents such as Van Buren, Teddy Roosevelt, and George HW Bush proposed very little policy at all in their Inaugural addresses. Instead, much of what was said during the Inaugural address was of an abstract and general nature about the proper course of action for the country. Van Buren spoke as one of the country in his Inaugural, simply stating general positions that the country need to take. He stated that in international relations, "We sedulously cultivate the friendship of all nations as the conditions most compatible with our welfare and the principles of our Government. We decline alliances as adverse to our peace. We desire commercial relations on equal terms, being ever willing to give a fair equivalent for advantages received. We endeavor to conduct our intercourse with openness and sincerity, promptly avowing our objects and seeking to establish that mutual frankness which is as beneficial in the dealings of nations as of men." All of these proposals addressed the policies that the nation should follow, but were more guiding principals of his administration than specific mandates for action.

GHW Bush also followed that same form of Inaugural address in 1989. In his Inaugural, he proposed a "thousand points of light" program for the country to follow. He, as with Van Buren, did not however offer significant specifics in the address. Instead, he too spoke as one of the country and in general terms, suggesting that "all the community organizations are spread like stars throughout the Nation, doing good. We will work hand in hand, encouraging, sometimes leading, sometimes being led, rewarding. We will work on this in the White House, in the Cabinet agencies. We need a new engagement, too, between the Executive and the Congress." Bush did dabble in specific subjects such as the economy, however he did not propose specific tenets of action, stating that "we must bring the Federal budget into balance...Mr. Majority Leader, the Congress and the Executive were capable of working together to produce a budget on which this nation could live. Let us negotiate soon and hard. But in the end, let us produce." This too was the approach that he took to international relations as well saying "To the world, too, we offer new engagement and a renewed vow: We will stay strong to protect the peace. While keeping our alliances and friendships around the world strong, ever strong, we will continue the new closeness with the Soviet Union, consistent both with our security and with progress." While none of these policy lines was specific, they were still the President's enumeration of the direction that he would like to see taken and a way to go about doing so.

While Van Buren and Bush represent presidents who did not propose much policy in their Inaugural address, or did so largely in abstract, the majority of the presidents of the nineteenth and twentieth centuries utilized the speech for specific policy advocacy and dictation. In addition, ten presidents since Monroe have proposed over 40 policies per Inaugural address and nearly eighteen have proposed over thirty policies on the average in their Inaugural. Notable Inaugural addresses that proposed policy numbers far above the overall average were presidents such as Polk (73), Harrison (78), McKinley (76.5), Taft (131), Harding (72), and Hoover (84). In these addresses, we see the combination of abstract and specifics that were utilized by Monroe and examined above.

However, these presidents also focused much more on the details of the policies that they were proposing and how the policies themselves should be enacted. In 1929, Hoover delivered an Inaugural address that is characteristic of the others who proposed high levels of policy in their speech. Although the Inaugural does contain general comments on some policy initiatives, the majority deals with specific ways to enact or accomplish the policy goals of the administration and the president. In the Inaugural, Hoover first spoke to the issue of fairness and equality of the judicial branch and the problems that the country faced in terms of prohibition. In order to battle the lax enforcement of the law, Hoover proposed "to appoint a national commission for a searching investigation of the whole structure of our Federal system of jurisprudence, to include the method of enforcement of the 18th amendment and the causes of abuse under it. Its purpose will be to make such recommendations for reorganization of the administration of Federal laws and court procedure as may be found desirable." In addition, Hoover stated that "In the meantime it is essential that a large part of the enforcement activities be transferred from the Treasury Department to the Department of Justice as a beginning of more effective organization." In this instance, Hoover not only used the Inaugural to warn those citizens not adhering to the national policy of prohibition against its violation, he also proposed a transfer of power between agencies for more efficiency.

In addition to the subject of prohibition, Hoover utilized the Inaugural address to direct the attention of the Congress and the people to specific issues of domestic concerns aligned with his own goals and policies. Speaking of campaign proposals, he stated that "Action upon some of the proposals upon which the Republican Party was returned to power, particularly further agricultural relief and limited changes in the tariff, cannot in justice to our farmers, our labor, and our manufacturers be postponed. I shall therefore request a special session of Congress for the consideration of these two questions. I shall deal with each of them upon the assembly of the Congress." In addition, Hoover's Inaugural runs the gambit by addressing many different policies that need be enacted or acted upon in a single sentence. If we number these policies we see that Hoover not only proposed activity on many different areas of domestic policy, but also that he did so with the parsimony that is similar to the way that the presidents of the twenty-first century have moved towards the proposal of more policy with less words in their State of the Union Address. He stated that "1) It appears to me that the more important further mandates from the recent election were the maintenance of the integrity of the Constitution; 2) the vigorous enforcement of the laws; 3) the continuance of economy in public expenditure; 4) the continued regulation of business to prevent domination in the community; 5) the denial of ownership or operation of business by the Government in competition with its citizens; 6) the avoidance of policies which would involve us in the controversies of foreign nations; 7) the more effective reorganization of the departments of the Federal Government; 8) the expansion of public works; 9) and the promotion of welfare activities affecting education and the home." In this single sentence, Hoover not only proposed nearly ten policies on which he believed the nation must act, but he was able to advocate both general (avoidance of controversies with foreign nations) and specific (the reorganization of the federal bureaucracy and prevention of monopolies) plans of action in one statement. This concentrated form of policy proposal is also a hallmark of the other presidents who were more policy active than any of their peers in the Inaugural address overall.

Another observation that can be made from Figure 3.6 is the lack of a dynamic shift or significant increase that occurs as the result of a singular presidency or individual office holder. Even if we look to the presidencies that are avowed to be the beginning of a "new," "modern," way of doing things for their contributions and innovations regarding policy proposal and activity in the Inaugural address, we are not presented with any findings that could confirm this proposition. Indeed, the average number of policies that are proposed in the Inaugural addresses of Wilson (19) and FDR (14.25), two of the champions of the "origins of the modern," are far below the overall presidential average of 36.8 policies per Inaugural address. In fact, not only are they lower than the overall average, but Wilson and FDR also propose fewer policies in their Inaugural address than any of the presidents during the twentieth and twenty-first century. While it is important to note that the findings above need to be controlled for length in order to give more accurate averages, the examination of the total number of policies that were proposed in the presidential Inaugural addresses does suggest that Wilson and FDR may not have been walking on such groundbreaking rhetorical paths that had not been trodden before.

134   *The Evolutionary Rhetorical Presidency*

Figure 3.7

The Average Number of Policies Proposed per 1000 Words of the Inaugural Address Per President

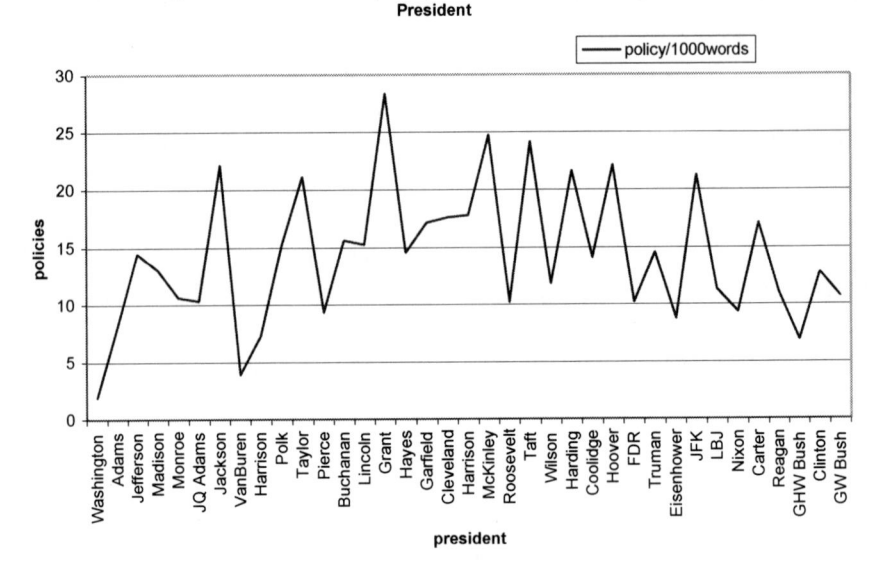

Figure 3.7 illustrates the average number of policies proposed per 1,000 words of the Inaugural Address per president. Contrary to the difference that appeared with the earlier comparison of the policies proposed in the State of the Union Address, the figure above controlling the policies for speech length shows no significant trend in policy proposal or policy activity over eras of time or between presidents. Instead, Figure 3.7 illustrates that when number of words is controlled for, the proposal of policy exhibits variability between presidents, and shows that, on the whole, from the founding to the present day, presidents have not significantly shifted the number of policies per 1000 words that they propose in their Inaugural addresses.

If Figure 3.7 is compared to Figure 3.6, we can see that the presidents who proposed high amounts of overall policy numbers in their presidential Inaugurals are, on the whole, presidents who also propose higher numbers of policy once the number of words has been controlled for. Presidents like Taft, Harding, and Hoover, who, as was shown above, proposed some of the highest overall levels of policy, were also individuals who did so with a high number of policies proposed per 1000 words. This in effect, is a picture of two different kinds of policy active presidents. The first types of presidents are those, such as Harding and Hoover, who delivered short speeches with a large number of policy propositions. Harding and Hoover delivered Inaugural addresses that were 3325 and 3795 words respectively. In these Inaugurals, they proposed 72 and 84 total policies, giving them an average of 21.7 and 22.1 policies proposed per 1000 words. Grant was one of the only presidents to be more succinct in his incorporation of policy into his Inaugural addresses. In his two Inaugurals of 2265 words total, Grant proposed 70 policies. This averaged out to nearly 28.4 policies proposed per 1000 words of the Inaugural address. No other president before or after was able to as tersely propose policies in the Inaugural address. The spikes that occur in Figure 3.7 are also the result of verbose presidents like Taft, who delivered an incredibly long Inaugural address that was also imbued with large amounts of policy proposal. Taft's Inaugural address of nearly 5500 words is one of the longest in history, second only to Harrison's infamous Inaugural of 1841 that contained nearly 8500 words and ended up costing Harrison his life. In Taft's long Inaugural, he also proposed more policies in a single address, with 131, than any other president to date, and more total policies than every other president except McKinley who proposed 154 policies in two combined Inaugurals.

Again, if we look for this figure to illustrate either two different eras of policy proposal in the Inaugural Address, or to show us an individual presidency that set a standard of rhetorical behavior that was not present before that administration and that every succeeding president followed, we cannot reach either of those conclusions. Figure 3.7 shows us that the average number of policies proposed in the Inaugural address per 1000 words of the Inaugural address is 14.2 policies. If we separate the presidential past into a "traditional" period that encompasses the eighteenth and nineteenth centuries and a "modern" period that begins at around 1900, we see that the average for the early era is 13.9 policies per thousand words, and the average for the later time period is 14.6 policies proposed per thousand words of the Inaugural address. This slight difference, most probably due to the small number of policies proposed by Washington in the earlier time and the large number proposed by Taft in the later, is neither significant, nor suggests that there has been major change throughout presidential history in the use of the Inaugural or the role that it has played in the proposition of presidential policy. In addition, the lack of the emergence of a single president who can be credited with creating the form of Inaugural used today, because it literally began with the inception of the presidency and evolved from that point, does not in any way support the proposition that early presidents were policy averse, nor that a permanent transformation in the way this rhetoric was used occurred with any single administration.

The Presidency and Policy Proposition in Presidential Proclamations

When we examine presidential proclamations for policy proposal, the first issue that must be reconciled is the change that they have seen from the founding to the present. As discussed in Chapter 2, originally, proclamations were used in much the same manner as executive orders. This, in effect, made both forms of presidential address viable rhetorical weapons by which the presidents could unilaterally make policy and communicate the goals and ambitions of their administrations. This similarity between the two presidential directives also is one of the main reasons for the confusion between them in the past. However, as presidents and proclamations evolved, the presidential proclamation began to take a ceremonial and holiday-related tone. In fact, the finding that over 90% of the proclamations that are issued today are holiday related might lead us to assume that they have lost their policy proposal potency.

Although individual holiday proclamations may outnumber those non-holiday proclamations that are made, if there are significantly more policies proposed and enacted in the few non-holiday related proclamations, the suggestion would be that the true function of holiday in proclamations is simply commemorative and functions in addition to the normal policy and unilateral lawmaking ability that proclamations have had since the founding. However, if these holiday proclamations are as dense with policy proposition as their counterparts, this hearkens to insinuations that the proclamation itself has evolved to become a new weapon of pander as well as policy proposition as opposed to a useless and largely decorative rhetorical tool.

Figure 3.8 is an illustration of the percentage of policies that were proposed in non-holiday presidential proclamations from the founding to the present day. Just as with the State of the Union Addresses and the Inaugurals, each presidential proclamation received a line-by-line reading in order to determine how many policy proposals it contained. Once again, this phrase-level examination proved useful in fully fleshing out the number of policies that were proposed in the proclamations.

Figure 3.8

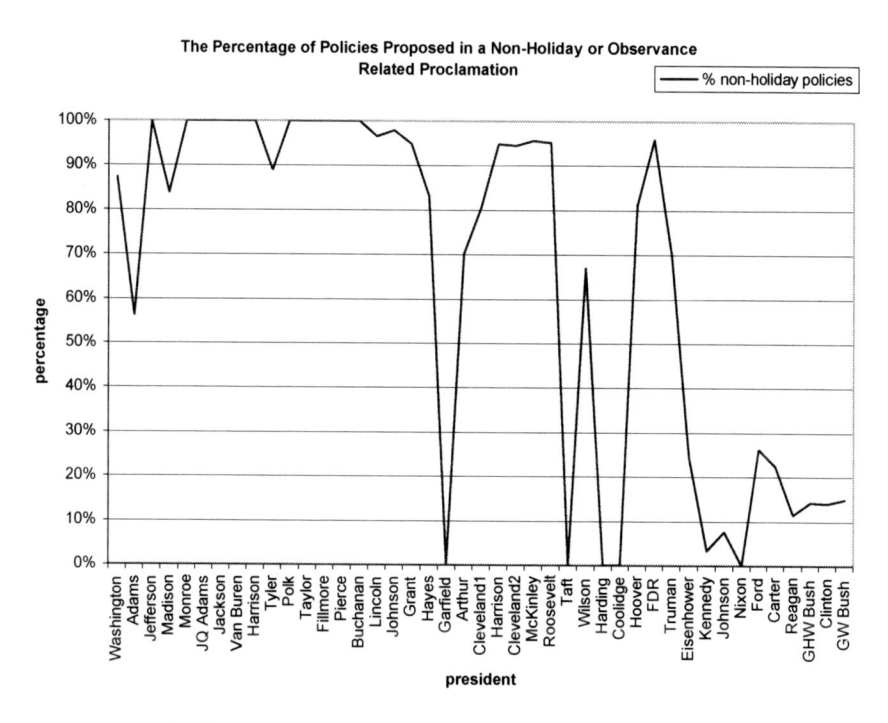

The Percentage of Policies Proposed in a Non-Holiday or Observance Related Proclamation

— % non-holiday policies

For example, in a presidential proclamation on August 19th, 1893 dealing with the administration of land, Grover Cleveland set forth guidelines relating to how towns could obtain land for their usage. If policy propositions were coded by sentence, this policy proposal would count as one. However, if the sentence is examined more closely, one can see that there are nearly nine policies that emerge from a single sentence. Each policy is, in itself, a separate and binding mandate regarding the overall subject. The following is the sentence itself with my listing of policy numbers for that single sentence:

1. "The land must be paid for at the Government price per acre,
2. and proof must be furnished relating, first, to municipal occupation of the land;
3. second, number of inhabitants;
4. third, extent and value of town improvements;
5. fourth, date when land was first used for town-site purposes;
6. fifth, official character and authority of officer making entry;
7. sixth, if an incorporated town, proof of incorporation,
8. which should be a certified copy of the act of incorporation, and,
9. seventh, that a majority of the occupants or owners of the lots within the town desire that such action be taken."

As can be seen from the illustration above, although the sentence itself is addressing the topic of land procurement, there are nearly nine policy proposals, enactments, and requirements, each with the force of law, that must be undertaken in order for the city to obtain its land.

Figure 3.8 illustrates that, as opposed to the presidents of the founding and the 18th and 19th centuries, who proposed over 80% of their policies in presidential proclamations in non-holiday rhetoric, today's presidents do not seem to use their proclamations to do the same. In fact, since Kennedy, over 75% of the policies that are proposed in presidential proclamations are announced in holiday or observance related statements. Although the data in the chart above suggest that the vast majority of today's proclamation policies are proposed in the context of holiday and observance proclamations, the question of true importance is whether or not this evolution infers that the proclamation is indeed a weapon in disrepair, used only for the ceremonial, or whether it has simply become something new with which to propose policy.

Based upon the findings above, a conclusion that we might wish to draw would be that the presidents of today have chosen to use other means than the presidential proclamation in order to propose important policy and unilaterally make law. This would suggest that the presidential proclamation has become a rhetorical waste of time, and that presidents use proclamations to pander to subject specific crowds in meetings in the rose garden or other locales. However, in order to say with surety that the proclamations of today, in their holiday-related format, are less valuable, and that the holiday proclamations are of less worth than the specifically worded proclamations of the past, it is necessary to grant them the same close examination that was given to the State of the Union Addresses and the Inaugurals.

Figure 3.9 is the average number of policies that were proposed per presidential proclamation from George Washington to George W. Bush. This is an examination of the number of overall policies that were proposed in the proclamations from the founding to the present.

Figure 3.9

The Average Number of Policies Proposed per Presidential Proclamation per President

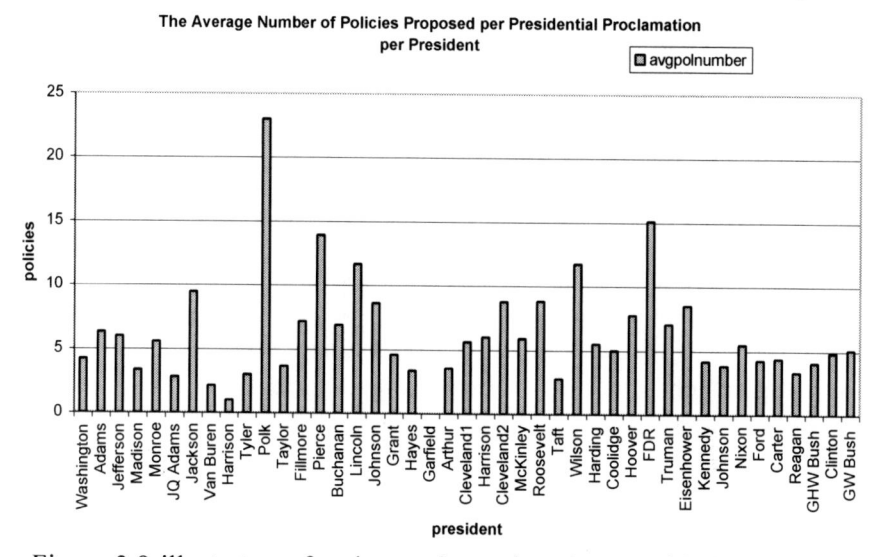

Figure 3.9 illustrates a few interesting points that provide important understanding of the use of proclamations and policy proposal throughout presidential history. First of all, one of the primary findings is that, although proclamations have become increasingly holiday related, presidents today propose generally as many policies per presidential proclamation as many of their eighteenth and twentieth century counterparts. The overall average number of policies proposed per presidential proclamations is 6.2 policies. If indeed the data would have supported one of the main tenets of the "traditional/ modern" divide, there should be a significant difference in this average, due to the "new" empowerment of policy activity in the "modern" period, between the eighteenth and nineteenth and twentieth and twenty-first centuries. However, if we look at the average number of policies proposed per proclamation before 1900, it is about 6.27 policies. Contrary to being lower than the overall average, the presidents prior to 1900 actually proposed slightly more policies per proclamation. In addition, contrary to being above the overall average or even that of the eighteenth and nineteenth centuries, presidents in the "modern" period after 1900 actually proposed slightly less policy (6.1 policies per proclamation) than their predecessors. The major finding in this regard is not the fact that presidents during the eighteenth and nineteenth centuries appeared more policy-active than their successors. Instead, because the difference between no presidential eras is significant, there

is no opportunity to conclusively nor should even be demarcated separately. Instead, Figure 3.9 shows that, although times have changed and the way in which the proclamation is couched has changed, presidents on the whole, continue to use the proclamation today to propose levels of policy that resemble not only presidents of the early twentieth century, but presidents of the eighteenth century and founding as well.

Another finding that has also appeared in many of the other figures in this chapter is that, although presidents have generally used policy proposal in the proclamation consistently, there is extensive variability according to the president issuing the proclamations. While there are some presidents like Van Buren, Harrison, Tyler, and Taft who used their proclamations for very little policy activity, there are others who, similarly to the State of the Union and Inaugural, choose to propose much higher levels of policy in their proclamations. At first glance, the illustration that Wilson (11.8) and FDR (15.1) proposed more policy in their proclamations than any other presidents after 1900 looks to give hope to the claim that they might have originated a new way of speaking. However, when we look at all of the presidents, we see that their styles were not followed by subsequent presidents, as should be the case when a president transforms the way things are done. Also presidents in the nineteenth century like Polk (23.0) and Pierce (13.9) not only propose as much policy in their proclamations as Wilson and FDR, they sometimes propose much more.

When the proclamations of these four presidents are examined much more closely, we can see a similarity between many of the proclamations in which they proposed a significant number of policies; mainly, international conflict was the subject around which many of the policy proposals were concerned. Polk and Pierce both issue proclamations that address issues with Mexico, whether in war or facing rebellion. In his proclamation of May 14, 1846, Polk announced to the country that "by the act of the Republic of Mexico a state of war exists between that Government and the United States." He then went on to "proclaim the same to all whom it may concern; and I do specially enjoin on all persons holding offices, civil or military, under the authority of the United States that they be vigilant and zealous in discharging the duties respectively incident thereto; and I do, moreover, exhort all the good people of the United States, as they love their country, as they feel the wrongs which have forced on them the last resort of injured nations, and as they consult the best means, under the blessing of Divine Providence, of abridging its calamities, that they exert themselves in preserving order, in promoting concord, in maintaining the authority and the efficacy of the laws, and in supporting and invigorating all the measures which may be adopted by the constituted authorities for obtaining a speedy, a just, and an honorable peace." This incredibly long sentence produces many policy directives, from making sure the people of the United States feel patriotic, to making sure that there is obedience to all of the country's laws in the trying time.

In his proclamation of January 18th, 1854, Pierce also issued a proclamation regarding Mexico. In this proclamation though, he was addressing, not the entire people of the United States, but those who, he had been informed, were planning "an unlawful expedition [that] has been fitted out in the State of California with a view to invade Mexico, a nation maintaining friendly relations with the United States." In much the same way and with the same format as Polk, Pierce warned the people of the country to obey the laws and "warning all persons who shall connect themselves with any such enterprise or expedition that the penalties of the law denounced against such criminal conduct will be rigidly enforced; and I exhort all good citizens, as they regard our national character, as they respect our laws or the law of nations, as they value the blessings of peace and the welfare of their country, to discountenance and by all lawful means prevent such criminal enterprises; and I call upon all officers of this Government, civil and military, to use any efforts which may be in their power to arrest for trial and punishment every such offender." Once again, a single sentence is utilized by Pierce to dictate and propose policy and issue a mandate of behavior that he expected to be followed.

Although they do not address Mexico, Wilson and FDR also utilized significant policy proposals in their proclamations to address issues of international conflict and war. In Proclamation number 1364, issued on April 6, 1917, Wilson addressed the war against Germany. As with Polk and Pierce, Wilson used very few sentences to propose many policies relating to the proper relations between Germany and the United States. The following illustration provides not only the proclamation itself, but also the number of policies that were proposed in it:

1. Now, therefore, I, Woodrow Wilson, President of the United States of America, do hereby proclaim to all whom it may concern that a state of war exists between the United States and the Imperial German Government;
2. and I do specially direct all officers, civil

3. or military, of the United States that they exercise vigilance and zeal in the discharge of the duties incident to such a state of war;
4. and I do, moreover, earnestly appeal to all American citizens that they, in loyal devotion to their country, dedicated from its foundation to the principles of liberty and justice, uphold the laws of the land,
5. and give undivided and willing support to those measures which may be adopted by the constitutional authorities in prosecuting the war to a successful issue and in obtaining a secure and just peace;
6. And, acting under and by virtue of the authority vested in me by the Constitution of the United States and the said sections of the Revised Statutes, I do hereby further proclaim and direct that the conduct to be observed on the part of the United States toward all natives, citizens, denizens, or subjects of Germany, being males of the age of fourteen years and upwards, who shall be within the United States and not actually naturalized, who for the purpose of this proclamation and under such sections of the Revised Statutes are termed alien enemies, shall be as follows:
7. And pursuant to the authority vested in me, I hereby declare and establish the following regulations, which I find necessary in the premises and for the public safety:
8. First. An alien enemy shall not have in his possession, at any time or place, any firearm,
9. weapon
10. or implement of war,
11. or component part thereof,
12. ammunition,
13. maxim
14. or other silencer,
15. bomb
16. or explosive
17. or material used in the manufacture of explosives;
18. Second. An alien enemy shall not have in his possession at any time or place, or use or operate any aircraft
19. or wireless apparatus,
20. or any form of signaling device,
21. or any form of cipher code,
22. or any paper,
23. document
24. or book written
25. or printed in cipher
26. or in which there may be invisible writing;
27. Third. All property found in the possession of an alien enemy in violation of the foregoing regulations shall be subject to seizure by the United States;
28. Fourth. An alien enemy shall not approach or be found within one-half of a mile of any Federal
29. or State fort,
30. camp,
31. arsenal,
32. aircraft station,
33. Government
34. or naval vessel,

35. navy yard,
36. factory,
37. or workshop for the manufacture of munitions of war or of any products for the use of the army or navy;
38. Fifth. An alien enemy shall not write,
39. print,
40. or publish any attack or threats against the Government
41. or Congress of the United States, or either branch thereof,
42. or against the measures or policy of the United States,
43. or against the person or property of any person in the military, naval or civil service of the United States,
44. or of the States
45. or Territories,
46. or of the District of Columbia,
47. or of the municipal governments therein;
48. Sixth. An alien enemy shall not commit or abet any hostile acts against the United States,
49. or give information,
50. aid,
51. or comfort to its enemies;
52. Seventh. An alien enemy shall not reside in or continue to reside in, to remain in, or enter any locality which the President may from time to time designate by Executive Order as a prohibited area in which residence by an alien enemy shall be found by him to constitute a danger to the public peace and safety of the United States,
53. except by permit from the President and except under such limitations or restrictions as the President may prescribe;
54. Eighth. An alien enemy whom the President shall have reasonable cause to believe to be aiding or about to aid the enemy,
55. or to be at large to the danger of the public peace or safety of the United States,
56. or to have violated or to be about to violate any of these regulations, shall remove to any location designated by the President by Executive Order,
57. and shall not remove therefrom without a permit,
58. or shall depart from the United States if so required by the President;
59. Ninth. No alien enemy shall depart from the United States until he shall have received such permit as the President shall prescribe,
60. or except under order of a court, judge, or justice, under Sections 4069 and 4070 of the Revised Statutes;
61. Tenth. No alien enemy shall land in or enter the United States,
62. except under such restrictions and at such places as the President may prescribe;
63. Eleventh. If necessary to prevent violation of the regulations, all alien enemies will be obliged to register;
64. Twelfth. An alien enemy whom there may be reasonable cause to believe to be aiding or about to aid the enemy,
65. or who may be at large to the danger of the public peace or safety,
66. or who violates or attempts to violate,
67. or of whom there is reasonable ground to believe that he is about to violate, any regulation duly promulgated by the President, or any criminal law of the United States, or of the States or Territories thereof, will be subject to summary arrest by

the United States Marshal, or his deputy, or such other officer as the President shall designate,
68. and to confinement in such penitentiary,
69. prison,
70. jail,
71. military camp,
72. or other place of detention as may be directed by the President.
73. This proclamation and the regulations herein contained shall extend and apply to all land and water, continental or insular, in any way within the jurisdiction of the United States.

In his proclamations, FDR also followed suit by addressing not only the policies of the United States related to the wars with which country was a party, but also by addressing the policies of America as they related to the wars that exist between other countries. In Proclamation 2141 on October 5th, 1935, FDR stated that:

1. Now, therefore, I, Franklin D. Roosevelt, President of the United States of America, acting under and by virtue of the authority conferred on me by the said Joint Resolution of Congress, do hereby proclaim that a state of war unhappily exists between Ethiopia and the Kingdom of Italy;
2. and I do hereby admonish all citizens of the United States or any of its possessions and all persons residing or being within the territory or jurisdiction of the United States or its possessions to abstain from every violation of the provisions of the Joint Resolution above set forth, hereby made effective and applicable to the export of arms, ammunition, or implements of war from any place in the United States or its possessions to Ethiopia
3. or to the Kingdom of Italy,
4. or to any Italian possession,
5. or to any neutral port for transshipment to,
6. or for the use of, Ethiopia
7. or the Kingdom of Italy.
8. And I do hereby declare and proclaim that the articles listed below shall be considered arms, ammunition, and implements of war for the purposes of Section 1 of the said Joint Resolution of Congress: CATEGORY I (1) Rifles
9. and carbines using ammunition in excess of cal. 26.5, and their barrels;
10. (2) Machine guns,
11. automatic rifles,
12. and machine pistols of all calibers,
13. and their barrels;
14. (3) Guns,
15. howitzers,
16. and mortars of all calibers,
17. their mountings
18. and barrels;

Excavating the Bully Pulpit 145

19. (4) Ammunition for the arms enumerated under (1) and (2) above, i.e., high-power steel-jacketed ammunition in excess of cal. 26.5;
20. filled and unfilled projectiles and propellants with a web thickness of .015 inch or greater for the projectiles of the arms enumerated under (3), above;
21. (5) Grenades,
22. bombs,
23. torpedoes,
24. and mines, filled
25. or unfilled,
26. and apparatus for their use or discharge;
27. (6) Tanks,
28. military armored vehicles,
29. and armored trains.
30. Vessels of war of all kinds, including aircraft carriers
31. and submarines.
32. Aircraft, assembled
33. or dismantled, both heavier
34. and lighter than air,
35. which are designed, adapted, and intended for aerial combat by the use of machine guns
36. or of artillery or for the carrying and dropping of bombs,
37. or which are equipped with, or which by reason of design or construction are prepared for, any of the appliances referred to in paragraph (2), below;
38. (2) Aerial gun mounts
39. and frames,
40. bomb racks,
41. torpedo carriers,
42. and bomb
43. or torpedo release mechanisms.
44. Revolvers
45. and automatic pistols of a weight in excess of 1 pound 6 ounces (630 grams), using ammunition in excess of cal. 16.5, and ammunition therefor.
46. Aircraft assembled
47. or dismantled, both heavier
48. and lighter than air, other than those included in Category III;
49. (2) Propellers
50. or air screws,
51. fuselages,
52. hulls,
53. tail units,
54. and under-carriage units;
55. (3) Aircraft engines.
56. Livens projectors
57. and flame throwers;
58. Mustard gas,
59. lewisite,
60. ethyldichlorarsine,
61. and methyldichlorarsine.

62. And I do hereby enjoin upon all officers of the United States, charged with the execution of the laws thereof, the utmost diligence in preventing violations of the said Joint Resolution, and this my proclamation issued thereunder,
63. and in bringing to trial and punishment any offenders against the same.
64. And I do hereby delegate to the Secretary of State the power of prescribing regulations for the enforcement of Section I Of the said joint resolution of August 31, 1935, as made effective by this my proclamation issued thereunder.

In addition to Figure 3.9 showing the high levels of policy proposed in the proclamations of the above discussed presidents, even though proclamations of contemporary presidents are holiday centered, this does not mean that they do not propose policy as well. In fact, although there have been significant changes in the subject matter on which presidential proclamations are based, presidents today are generally as policy active in their proclamations as presidents of the past. Despite their holiday focus, presidents of the contemporary presidency still use the platform of the proclamation as a weapon by which to propose policy and attempt to institute change.

As one example, we can look at Proclamation 8068, where George W. Bush discussed National Energy Awareness Month. However, far from being a simple statement, similar to the Thanksgiving proclamations of old that asked for a day to reflect, this proclamation proposed policy and reinforced the administration's position on energy production and conservation. Similarly to Cleveland's proclamation discussed above, Bush's statement on energy had several policies in a single sentence and addressed many different issues at once by stating the following:

1. My Administration is working to improve energy efficiency
2. and conservation,
3. increase our domestic supply of energy,
4. and diversify our energy supply through advanced technologies.
5. My Administration's Advanced Energy Initiative seeks to diversify energy resources by substantially increasing funding for clean-energy research.
6. To change how we power our homes and offices, we will invest more in zero-emission coal-fired plants,
7. revolutionary solar
8. and wind technologies,
9. and clean, safe nuclear energy.
10. We will focus on improving hybrid
11. and hydrogen technologies for our automobiles
12. and increasing the use of biofuels.
13. Now, Therefore, I, George W. Bush, President of the United States of America, by virtue of the authority vested in me by the Constitution and laws of the United States, do hereby proclaim October 2006 as National Energy Awareness Month.

14. I encourage Americans to take steps to conserve energy
15. and develop responsible habits that will reduce energy consumption in their everyday lives.

Although Bush is directing these comments at a specifically interested audience, he is still using the proclamation to propose his own policy and state what will be done by his administration. Although not done in the same ways as Washington, this is still presidential unilateral policymaking and policy proposal. It is simply using the new medium of the holiday and observance address with which to do the same things.

Despite the findings above that suggest a strangely consistent behavior of past presidents regarding proclamations, it is important to take the same step as was undertaken with the examination of the State of the Union Addresses and Inaugurals; mainly, it is important to once again control for proclamation length to look for more comparable patterns or results.

Figure 3.10 is the average number of policies that were proposed per 1000 words of the presidential proclamations from George Washington to George W. Bush. This is, in effect, a standardization of the number of policies that were proposed in the proclamations from the founding to the present. Although Figure 3.10 has been controlled for by length, the results that it presents and the important conclusions that it reaches are incredibly similar to those of Figure 3.9 above. First of all, Figure 3.10 presents no evidence of a significant increase or decrease in the levels of policy that are proposed per 1000 words of presidential proclamation. The only shift that is present is that presidents from the founding to the present, again, generally propose the same amounts of policy in their proclamations. There is also no indication of different eras or support for a "modern" or a "traditional" period where policy activity is significantly different. The overall average in this chart is 13.6 policies proposed per 1000 words of presidential proclamation.

Figure 3.10

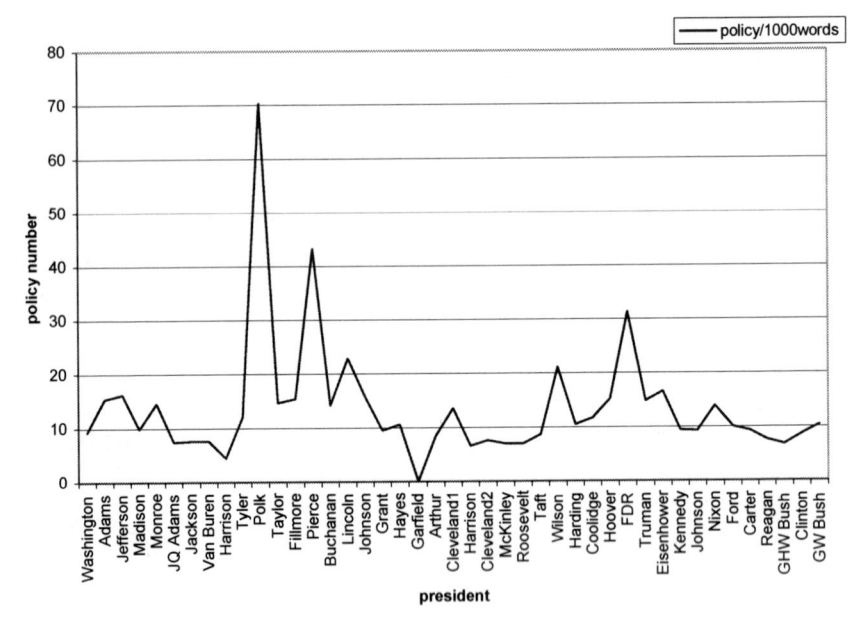

The Average Number of Policies Proposed per 1000 Words of Presidential Proclamations per President

There is no significant difference when we examine the averages that would be associated with a "traditional" period where presidents were not policy active or a "modern" period where they were. Once again, the data suggest not only that there are no observable classifications that can be made, but also that, in this case, presidents during the nineteenth century are as policy active, if not more so, than their twentieth century counterparts.

Yet again, the Figure also lacks evidence of an individual presidency or a way of speaking or proposing policy that seems to act as a transformative benchmark that not only changes the way that things were done, but sets a new precedent for the way things will be done after that point. This is not to say that there were not presidents that proposed policy numbers far above the average. As we can see, the same presidents who proposed the highest levels of policy when overall proposals were examined in Figure 3.9 are still those who proposed the most policy once that address length was controlled for. Polk, Pierce, Wilson and FDR maintain their increased policy activity in this

Figure largely due to the fact, as with the Inaugural, that they proposed lots of policy while maintaining a shorter address length.

There is no conclusive evidence that can be reached that there was any individual president whose behavior was new and followed by all other presidents, as would need to be discovered under a "traditional/ modern" paradigm. Instead, we see again what we have seen in the examination of almost every other fact of presidential speech and policy proposal. Mainly, there is too much variability between presidents to be able to categorize them into any eras of behavior. In addition, it is this very variability that is so important to enriching our understanding of the presidency and its evolution. By looking at both the presidents who seem to demonstrate similar behavior to their peers as well as those who, for one reason or another, appear significantly above or below that norm, we can see how changing context, personalities, and proclivities all impact presidential rhetoric and its evolution to contemporary use.

The Presidency and Policy Proposition in Executive Orders

The last of the four types of presidential address to be examined for policy proposal and advocacy is the executive order. As mentioned above, until the beginning of the twentieth century these were sometimes used and confused in form and function with presidential proclamations. However, over the course of presidential history, the proclamations evolved to take on an extremely ceremonial character and to deal almost exclusively with holidays when used by twenty-first century presidents. However, this by no means followed that the proclamations were devoid of policy advocacy and proposal. As the focus of the proclamation began to shift to the memorialization of specific days on the calendar, the executive order slowly became the means by which the presidents of the United States amended existing law, created commissions for specific duty and unilaterally sought to impose policy changes and administration goals. The question examined here becomes whether or not the use of the executive order as a much more sterile form of presidential address (see Chapter 2 on its lack of popular address rhetoric) means that presidents used this tool for more or less policy proposal than the others.

150   *The Evolutionary Rhetorical Presidency*

Figure 3.11

The Average Number of Policies Proposed per Executive Order per President

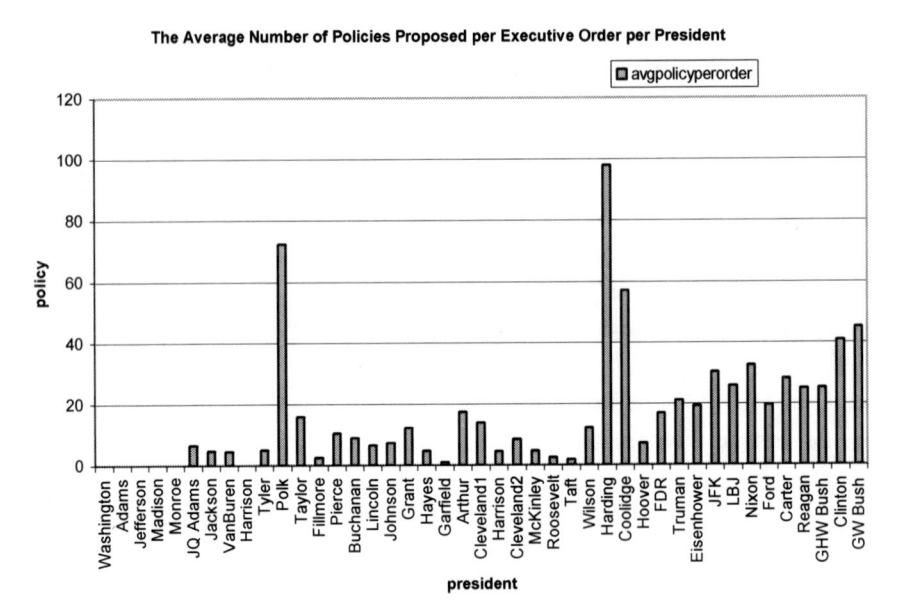

Figure 3.11 is an illustration of the average number of overall policies proposed per executive order per president. Immediately, an interesting observation that can be made is that, overall, the average number of policies per executive order is higher than the number of policies proposed per proclamation; totals are even close to the overall number of policies that presidents proposed in the Inaugural addresses. This Figure also provides data that is consistent with the other three other forms of presidential address that have been examined herein, in that it fails to provide support for a dramatic shift in policy proposal and advocacy that would appear either across two distinguishable time periods or following the "transformative" presidency of a single officeholder.

One of the first conclusions that this Figure illustrates is that there is no significant difference between the average numbers of overall policies proposed during the addresses of presidents during any era of presidential history. Instead, there were presidents during both the nineteenth and twentieth centuries that proposed similar numbers of overall policies in their executive orders. In fact, there are several presidents during the nineteenth century that propose similar number of policies in their addresses to the presidents who were supposedly responsible for the origins of the "modern" rhetorical presidency. There were several "traditional" presidents like Taylor (16.0), Pierce (10.5), Grant (12.2), Arthur (17.5), and Cleveland (14.0) that all averaged similar numbers of policies proposed in their executive orders to "modern" presidents such as Wilson (12.2), FDR (17.0), Hoover (7.1), and Ford (19.6). Indeed, the findings provide little evidence that Wilson, FDR, or any other of their twentieth century contemporaries differentiated themselves significantly from the behavior and rhetorical proclivities and tendencies of presidents from any other period.

In addition to illustrating similarities between the presidents of the "traditional" era and presidents of the "modern" era, another finding that the Figure does present is that, consistent with every other form of presidential address, there is an extremely high variation between the policy proposals of presidents in their executive orders that poses a challenge to any overarching assumptions that can be made regarding long periods of presidential history. In fact, the figure shows that the presidents who proposed the highest average levels of policies in their executive orders, Polk (72.3) and Harding (98.0), were not from a single era in presidential history, but were from both the nineteenth and twentieth centuries.

A closer look at the reasons behind the high levels of policy proposal also reinforces the variation in utilization of the executive order for many different policy purposes. In Polk's executive order of March 30th, 1847, we can see an example of where his high number of overall policy proposals originates. In that executive order, Polk commented on the proper trade relations between Mexico and the United States in the time of conflict. He carefully enumerated all of the specific Mexican goods that would be subject to a new military tax to aid in the funding of the war and discourage trade with the warring country. For example, one section of the order looks at the many different types of goods that would be affected and, due to the fact that they would all be either produced or traded by different interested parties, they must all be counted as separate policies. He states:

1. "That the duty on silk,
2. flax,
3. hemp
4. or grass,
5. cotton,
6. wool,
7. worsted
8. or any manufactures of the same,

9. or of either or mixtures thereof;
10. coffee,
11. teas,
12. sugar,
13. molasses,
14. tobacco
15. and all manufactures thereof,
16. including cigars
17. and cigarritos;
18. glass,
19. china,
20. and stoneware,
21. iron
22. and steel
23. and all manufactures of either not prohibited, be 30 per cent *ad valorem* ;
24. on copper
25. and all manufactures thereof,
26. tallow,
27. tallow candles,
28. soap,
29. fish,
30. beef,
31. pork,
32. hams,
33. bacon,
34. tongues,
35. butter,
36. lard,
37. cheese,
38. rice,
39. Indian corn
40. and meal,
41. potatoes,
42. wheat,
43. rye,
44. oats,
45. and all other grain,
46. rye meal
47. and oat meal,
48. flour,
49. whale
50. and sperm oil,
51. clocks,
52. boots
53. and shoes,
54. pumps,
55. bootees
56. and slippers,

57. bonnets,
58. hats,
59. caps,
60. beer,
61. ale,
62. porter,
63. cider,
64. timber,
65. boards,
66. planks,
67. scantling,
68. shingles,
69. laths,
70. pitch,
71. tar,
72. rosin,
73. turpentine,
74. spirits of turpentine,
75. vinegar,
76. apples,
77. ship bread,
78. hides,
79. leather
80. and manufactures thereof,
81. and paper of all kinds, 20 per cent *ad valorem*;"

Polk used the executive order here to make international policy dictates and suggestions. One thing that should be noted is that, even though the executive order has the unilateral weight of actual law, the goods above are also policy proposals, because presidents often used executive orders to amend other executive orders if they found parts or elements of them to be contrary to their original policy goal.

Harding appears as a president whose levels of average policy proposal in the executive orders are much higher than the overall presidential average as well. However, contrary to the way that Polk utilized his executive order for trade discussion, Harding uses his policymaking and proposal ability for a much more mundane and administrative task. In executive order number 3669, that Harding delivered on April 29, 1922, he addressed the care of military veterans and said that certain hospitals "now under the supervision of the United States Public Health Service and operated for hospital or sanatoria or other uses for sick and disabled former soldiers, sailors and marines, are hereby transferred to the United States Veterans' Bureau and shall on and after the effective date hereof operate under the supervision, management

154   *The Evolutionary Rhetorical Presidency*

and control of the Director of the United States Veterans' Bureau." This, in itself, is a proposal and enactment of policy. However, the high levels of policy proposal are more evident in the actual description that Harding then gives of the hospitals to be transferred from the Health Service to the Veterans' Bureau. He not only listed the hospitals under construction that would be assumed by the Bureau, he enumerated the following hospitals to be transferred to oversight by the Bureau:

1. No. 13 Southern Infirmary Annex, Mobile, Alabama
2. No. 14 Annex to New Orleans Marine Hospital, Algiers, La.
3. No. 24 Palo Alto, California
4. No. 25 Houston, Texas
5. No. 26 Greenville, South Carolina
6. No. 27 Alexandria, Louisiana
7. No. 28 Dansville, New York
8. No. 29 Norfolk, Virginia (Sewall's Point)
9. No. 30 Chicago, Illinois (4649 Drexel Boulevard)
10. No. 30 Chicago, Illinois (Annex-7535 Stoney Island Avenue)
11. No. 31 Corpus Christi, Texas
12. No. 32 Washington, D. C. (2650 Wisconsin Avenue)
13. No. 33 Jacksonville, Florida
14. No. 34 East Norfolk, Massachusetts
15. No. 35 St. Louis, Missouri (5900 Arsenal)
16. No. 36 Boston, Massachusetts (Parker Hill)
17. No. 37 Waukesha, Wisconsin
18. No. 38 New York, New York (345 West 50th Street)
19. No. 39 Hoboken, Pennsylvania
20. No. 40 Cape May, New Jersey
21. No. 41 New Haven, Connecticut
22. No. 42 Perryville, Maryland
23. No. 44 West Roxbury, Massachusetts
24. No. 45 Biltmore, North Carolina
25. No. 46 Deming, New Mexico
26. No. 47 Markleton, Pennsylvania
27. No. 48 Atlanta, Georgia
28. No. 49 Philadelphia, Pennsylvania (Gray's Ferry Road & 24th St.)
29. No. 50 Whipple Barracks, Arizona
30. No. 51 Tucson, Arizona
31. No. 52 Boise, Idaho
32. No. 53 Dwight, Illinois
33. No. 54 Arrowhead, Springs, California
34. No. 55 Fort Bayard, New Mexico
35. No. 56 Fort McHenry, Baltimore, Maryland
36. No. 57 Knoxville, Iowa
37. No. 58 New Orleans, Louisiana (439 Flood St)
38. No. 59 Tacoma, Washington

39. No. 60 Oteen, North Carolina
40. No. 61 Fox Hills, Staten Island, New York
41. No. 62 Augusta, Georgia
42. No. 63 Lake City, Florida
43. No. 64 Camp Kearney, California
44. No. 65 St. Paul, Minnesota (Dayton & Virginia Avenue)
45. No. 67 Kansas City, Missouri (11th and Harrison Streets)
46. No. 68 Minneapolis, Minnesota (914 Elliott Avenue)
47. No. 69 Newport, Kentucky
48. No. 71 Sterling Junction, Massachusetts
49. No. 72 Helena, Montana (Fort William Henry Harrison)
50. No. 73 Chicago, Illinois (Annex to U.S.Veterans' Hospital #30)
51. No. 74 Gulfport, Mississippi
52. No. 75 Colfax, Iowa
53. No. 76 Edward Hines, Jr. Hospital (Maywood Illinois)
54. No. 77 Portland, Oregon.
55. No. 78 North Little Rock, Arkansas (Fort Logan H. Roots)
56. No. 79 Dawson Springs, Kentucky
57. No. 80 Fort Lyon, Colorado, and
58. The Purveying Depot at Perryville, Maryland.

This listing of each hospital, as well as all of the other details that he adds to this individual executive order, provides a good illustration of why he appears in the Figure as proposing the highest levels of overall policy in his executive orders in presidential history.

Although, according to Figure 3.11, proponents of the "traditional/ modern" divide might be tempted to suggest that the rise in the overall number of policies proposed in the executive orders per president that can be seen after the presidency of FDR is indeed proof of his transformation of the use of the executive order, the reason for this is much less relative. At first blush, Figure 3.11 shows that, after FDR, the average number of policies proposed per executive order has risen. However, this can be traced to the format and collection of executive orders themselves. It is only with the advent of the classification and numbering system that was instituted in the beginning of the twentieth century to differentiate between the proclamations and the executive orders that the number of policies that were proposed in the executive orders began to slowly increase. In 1935, executive orders and presidential proclamations were required to be entered into the *Federal Register*. This new attempt at the collection and the preservation of the executive orders and addresses that occurs during the presidency of FDR does indeed lead to a rise in the number of policies proposed per executive order, because it is largely with this shift that they fully differentiate themselves from proclamations and

156   The Evolutionary Rhetorical Presidency

are used primarily for the enactment of specific policies or amendments to existing law. Just as the proclamations truly began to embrace their role in the ceremonial realms, so did the executive orders evolve to be a tool utilized almost solely for the laying out of detailed changes to policy, or new suggestion and creation of it.

However, as we have seen at earlier points in the chapter, just because the overall policy proposal average illustrates one conclusion, it is important to control for the length of the address to fully examine the changes that have taken place in the executive order.

Figure 3.12

The Average Number of Policies Proposed per 1000 Words of Executive Orders per President

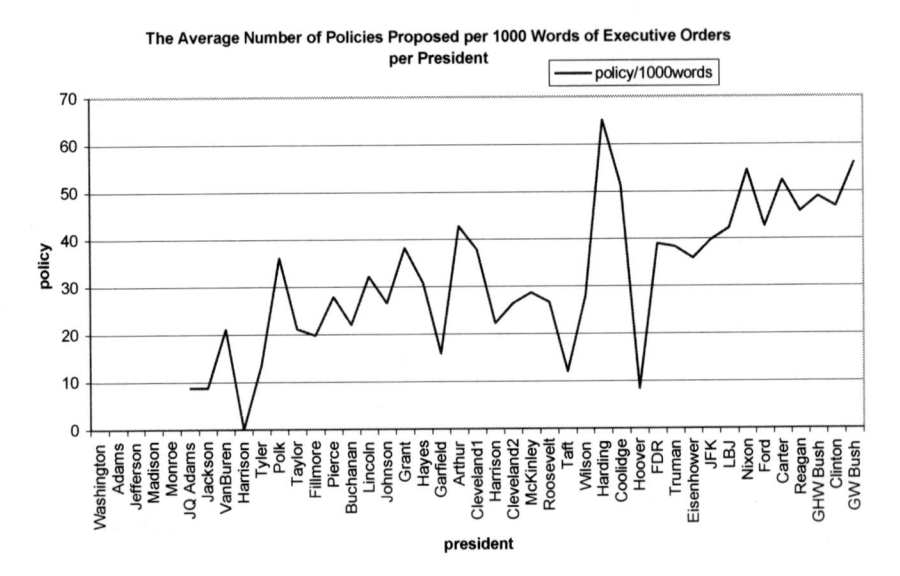

Figure 3.12 is an illustration of the average number of policies proposed per 1000 words of executive orders per president. Once again, the figure above is able to better standardize the results from the prior figure by controlling for number of words in the addresses. This is especially important with the executive orders because of the smaller sample size of executive orders that could be obtained from before their codification in the *Federal Register*. Figure 3.12 notes a couple of important things in our consideration of the executive order and the role of policy proposal in that form of presidential address. First of all, we see the same kind of variation between presidents, yet again, that has been found throughout this book and among each of the

forms of address examined specifically for policy proposal in this chapter. The presidencies of Polk Harding and Coolidge maintain their prominent place among the presidents who proposed the most policy in their executive orders even when address length is controlled for. In addition, in both the nineteenth and twentieth centuries, there are presidents who appear above and below the average of their peers. This variation alone is significant evidence against the separation of presidential history into categories that might not recognize the nuances of speech that each individual president may be responsible for.

In addition to the variation among presidents, this Figure seems to present an image of the evolution of the executive order that is incredibly similar to the evolution of the State of the Union that appeared when we controlled for the length of the address. What figure 3.12 demonstrates is that there is a slow evolutional increase in the amount of policy that is proposed in the executive order. Far from finding two distinguishable eras which exhibit totally similar characteristics within themselves, and far from discovering a singular presidency that invents a way of speaking followed by all successors, the figure suggests that each president from the earliest time of the founding has expanded on the office of the presidency by utilizing the executive order more and more to propose their policy and issue their dictates. The history of the executive order in policymaking, then, is a slow increase in the number of policies that are included within them from the founding to the present. However, even by making this statement, it is important to note that this does not make attempt to generalize this to all of the presidents, only to make a statement about the abstract direction of the evolution of the executive order and policy. If I was to label the development of the executive order as a simple increase over time, that conclusion would be as errant as the "traditional/ modern" divide which it questions. Namely, it misses the specific uses by each president as well as the ways in which each individual personally uses them. Although we can say with confidence that the contemporary executive order has grown over time to include more policy per number of words for each president, there are notable deviations which must be accounted for as well.

Policy and Policymaking in Presidential History

Today's president is generally assumed to initiate and propose policy in his addresses. It seems to be a given that a State of the Union Address will present outlines for programs and policies that the president would like to see Congress take action upon. It seems like a foregone conclusion that the president will deliver an Inaugural address which is ceremonial in tone and avoids direct legislative recommendation. It seems to be a commonly know fact that the presidential proclamations and executive orders will be used to make "secret" unilateral policy away from the prying eyes of the public. However, as we have seen here, these kinds of statements are unfortunate stereotypes regarding each form of presidential address that miss the true evolution of each from the founding to the present.

The "modern" rhetorical presidency presents an image of a presidency which has only recently empowered itself with policy proposal and advocacy. It presents the image of a contemporary president who speaks directly to the people of the issues that the president would like to see enacted, and the paths that Congress and the people must take in order to fulfill this plan, unfettered by constitutional precedent or constraint. This characterization of contemporary presidential policy proposal is not really a misnomer to be disproved; it is really only the assertion that this is a "recent" development that must be questioned. Presidents of today *do* propose policy. Presidents of today *do* advocate positions that they would like to see taken by the Congress. Presidents of today *do* speak of plans for the people of the nation and policies that will improve or alter their lives. In this respect, there is no error with the characterization of today's policy-proposing president.

The inconsistency, it seems, occurs when the allegation is made that this behavior, and the rhetoric that accompanies it, is exclusively the action of presidents of the twentieth and twenty-first centuries, or that it is only the direct result of an innovation by a singular presidency in the early twentieth century. What the data illustrated in this chapter have presented is a significantly different picture of the presidents of the far past than is presented by most scholars of the "traditional/ modern" persuasion. These findings suggest that presidents as early as Adams proposed amounts of policy that rival the policy propositions in State of the Union Addresses today. The data illustrate that the Inaugural address is not used solely for abstract preponderances of the future of the country. The addresses show that the presidential proclamation and the executive order have not only been used by presidents since the founding for policy proposal, but that they have each evolved into their own separate form of presidential weaponry for unilateral legislation and policy advocacy.

The chapter also tells the stories of many presidents in the 18th and 19th centuries that can be characterized by few signs of constraint regarding policy proposal or advocacy in either the State of the Union Address, the Inaugural Address, the Presidential Proclamation, or the Executive Order. In addition, there is not a single president that can be cited as the exception to the definitional behavioral rule. Instead, as the figures above indicate, most of the presidents of today bear a strange resemblance to the presidents of yesteryear when we compare their policy proposition and advocacy in presidential address. It is also equally important that we look at those presidents and those addresses that do not fit into any pattern of speech or behavior for the insights they offer on presidential activity and ambition.

This does not suggest, by any means, that the presidents of today are not different in many ways from those presidents of two centuries ago. There have been technological advances as well issue developments heretofore unseen in the past history of the presidency. In addition, we see that presidents are becoming more frugal with their words by proposing more policy in shorter amounts of rhetoric than the prolific address-writers of the past. However, if we consider that presidents faced changing environments as well as changing issues in their tenure, the findings above propose that presidents overall have similarly proposed expanding numbers of policies on the increasing numbers of subjects with which they were faced since the founding of the nation. Presidents of the past can be considered different less for policy proposition and involvement with issue advocacy than for a simple difference in context and history of the times. Yes, presidents did propose policy on some dramatically different things in 2000 than they did in 1900 and even more so than in 1800. However, there are also many policies like the economy, the military, trade, and immigration, on which presidents since the very inception of the nation have been politically, rhetorically, and legislatively active.

In the end, no findings emerged regarding policy proposal in any of the forms of presidential address that could definitively be read as supporting a "traditional/ modern" divide in any form. Presidents today do not necessarily propose significantly higher total amounts of policy in all of their addresses than did the presidents of the nineteenth century. Eighteenth and Nineteenth century presidents were not seemingly bound by a constitutional constraint that prohibited them from taking political action or being closely involved with issue proposition. In addition, there is not an individual presidency that can be given credit for any kind of transformation of the way presidents propose policy in any of the four forms of address examined herein.

The examination and illustration of my data presented above suggest that beginning as early as presidents such as Washington, Adams and Jackson, the presidency began to break free of the non-political, constitutionally-proper position of the president, whose only duties were codified directly in the constitution, and who stayed away from the limelight and out of the realm of proposition of public policy. It appears as though Tulis, when commenting that Jackson's "reputation as a popular leader derives not from his activities as a popular speaker, but his attempt to address the people through the annual message" (1987, 73-4) was more than accurate in recognizing the fact that Jackson was one of many "traditional" presidents who used a popular message for popular address. Indeed, as opposed to a twentieth-century innovation, it is exactly the presidents like Jackson, Adams, Polk, and Arthur, as well as each individual who followed them, who each weighed the rhetorical and presidential tools at their disposal for policy advocacy and activity, and decided how their individual administration would utilize these to achieve their own goals and ambitions for themselves and the country.

CHAPTER IV

The Bigger Picture: Visions for the Nation and the World

> *Far better it is to dare mighty things, to win glorious triumphs, even though checkered by failure, than to take rank with those poor spirits who neither enjoy much nor suffer much, because they live in the gray twilight that knows not victory nor defeat.*
> —Theodore Roosevelt

IN PRESIDENTIAL speech and address, we see a unique form of rhetoric that has the opportunity to resonate and be reproduced not only at the domestic level, but also at the international level. Often, the president can use his addresses to speak to the specifics of policy and administrative goals that he would like enacted by the Congress or supported by the people, as well as to the larger future of the country and the world; many addresses speak to the things that can be accomplished by both. The president, in effect, presents the people of the United States, and indeed the world, with his vision of the potential of democracy, the path for the future of the country, the course of humankind, and the international relations issues that could change the world.

In George W. Bush's first and second Inaugural address, we see many examples of his use of this "visionary" speech in both policy proposals for his own country and policy suggestions for others. In his first address, before the events of 9/11/01, George W. Bush used this "visionary speech" to define the role of education, the role of the citizen, and the duty of the government. In speaking to the racial, gender, and cultural differences within the United States, as well as its history, Bush proposed a vision for the way that children, citizens, and even immigrants must deal with a "new" melting pot of a country. He directed his comments towards the education of the young, saying that "America has never been united by blood or birth or soil. We are bound by ideals that move us beyond our backgrounds, lift us above our interests and teach us what it means to be citizens. Every child must be taught these principles." He also spoke to the citizens of the nation saying "Every citizen must uphold them" and lastly addressed those who were new to the country, suggesting that "every immigrant, by embracing these ideals, makes our country more, not less, American." Although these are not "specific" policy propositions of the type that were examined in the previous chapter, these statements are "visionary" policy proposals which offer a much more abstract, but no less powerful, dictate on the direction of the country. In his first address, he also offered these visions of education, social programs, and taxes, saying that "Together, we will reclaim America's schools, before ignorance and apathy claim more young lives. We will reform Social Security and Medicare, sparing our children from struggles we have the power to prevent. And we will reduce taxes, to recover the momentum of our economy and reward the effort and enterprise of working Americans."

In Bush's second Inaugural address, and after the events of 9/11, he used his "visionary" speech policy proposal to address the international community as a whole and their duties, as well as America's role regarding their futures. Each of these statements, again, is not a specific action that can be taken similar to "we must keep Lunken Air Force Base in Cincinnati open for the defense of the country." Instead, these are abstract dictates and policy proposals that suggest the proper advance of the people of the United States and the world as a whole. In speaking to the people, he stated that "We will build our defenses beyond challenge, lest weakness invite challenge" and "we will confront weapons of mass destruction, so that a new century is spared new horrors." He also gave visions of defense in the United States, saying that "We will defend our allies and our interests. We will show purpose without arrogance. We will meet aggression and bad faith with resolve and strength." Bush then took the approach of suggesting a vision of policy of international relations that others in the world should follow, directly stating "to all nations, we will speak for the values that gave our nation birth. What you do is as important as anything government does. I ask you to seek a common good beyond your comfort; to defend needed reforms against easy attacks; to serve your nation, beginning with your neighbor." He spoke not only to the direction for the foreign countries, but also for the people of the other countries, saying "I ask you to be citizens: citizens, not spectators; citizens, not subjects; responsible citizens, building communities of service and a nation of character." He finished the address by announcing the United States' position regarding the security of itself as well as the vision of a democratic future for others. He explained his vision, saying that "it is the policy of the United States to seek and support the growth of democratic movements and institutions in every nation and culture, with the ultimate goal of ending tyranny in our world...America will not impose our own style of government on the unwilling. Our goal instead is to help others find their own voice, attain their own freedom, and make their own way. America will not pretend that jailed dissidents prefer their chains or that women welcome humiliation and servitude or that any human being aspires to live at the mercy of bullies. We will encourage reform in other governments by making clear that success in our relations will require the decent treatment of their own people." And lastly, he closed by explaining the position of his administration and the country that "Today, America speaks anew to the peoples of the world. All who live in tyranny and hopelessness can know: The United States will not ignore your oppression or excuse your oppressors. When you stand for your liberty, we will stand with you."

Visionary Speech, Policy Propositions, and Presidential Address

In the introduction of the book, George W. Bush's State of the Union Address that followed 9/11/01 illustrated that the president used the opportunity of the speech to propose policy and address the people with popular rhetoric. Indeed, as examined further in the previous chapters, the President of the United States uses the State of the Union Address, The Inaugural Address, Presidential Proclamations, and Executive Orders to propose policy and inform the electorate and the Congress of the goals of his administration. The results of a close examination of the number of policies proposed within each of those forms of presidential address suggested that there is no clear distinction between presidential behaviors in different eras. It did not reveal the discovery of a single presidential administration that made such dramatic innovations in presidential rhetoric and speech that they created a "new" and permanent way of doing things. In fact, the previous chapter found that presidents since the beginning of the country have used their speech to act with legislative intent and propose policy for the people. This type of activity is surprising in that it would seem to be in direct conflict with a picture of a "traditional" president who was bound to policy subservience by precedents of the founders (whom, themselves, proposed very high numbers of policy in their addresses) or bound by the strict dictates of constitutional propriety.

This study has provided observations that suggest that "traditional" presidents used popular address rhetoric and that they proposed policy. This is contrary to a paradigm that would propose that they would not. However, there is still one more important facet of the contemporary presidency that needs be addressed to discover whether or not it may indeed be only the function of the "modern" period of the presidency. Unlike the presidents of the eighteenth and nineteenth century, there are suggestions that presidents during a "modern" period not only proposed policy, but they also utilized a rhetorical tool in doing so known as "visionary" speech "which would articulate a picture of the future and impel a populace toward it" (Tulis, 1987, 135). As with the other elements of the "modern" rhetorical presidency, this would seem to insinuate that this kind of speech was absent from the address of the eighteenth and nineteenth century presidents. This chapter will not only seek to evaluate that claim, it will look at the history of the use of use of visionary speech in the State of the Union Address, the Inaugural Address, Presidential proclamations, and Executive Orders and the different ways in which presidents have used this kind of speaking to propose visionary policy and further their agendas for the nation and its place in the world.

Visionary Speech in the State of the Union Address

Even though the Inaugural Address is usually seen by scholars as the presidential address in which the president is more likely to speak in visionary terms regarding the future of the country as well as the direction of the administration that the president advocates, this assumption may not be fully accurate when compared with the other forms of presidential address examined herein. Indeed, George W. Bush's State of the Union Address in 2002 that is examined earlier in the chapter gives insight into just how visionary, in terms of international affairs in this case, the State of the Union Address can be. The previous chapter illustrated that, historically, the president of the United States uses the State of the Union Address to propose policy in higher levels than in the Inaugural address, presidential proclamations, or executive orders. The previous chapter also looked at the fact that presidents who delivered the State of the Union Address in written form not only increased the length of the address, but also the number of policies that they proposed in it. However, when controlled for length, it could be seen that, on the whole, presidents from the founding have generally increased the number of policies that they have proposed in the State of the Union Address regardless of the format constraints with which they are faced.

The important examination here will be whether or not the significant increase in the overall number of policies that are proposed in the State of the Union Address, during both the written and the orally delivered periods, is also accompanied by an increase in the visionary policies that are proposed as well. It is important to determine if the written period of the State of the Union Address, usually labeled the "traditional" period by some scholars, really witnessed a lack of visionary speech in the context of policy proposal. In the end, the question is whether or not the use of visionary policy in the State of the Union has undergone a significant increase in the twentieth century and also whether or not the written delivery of the State of the Union Address impacted the visionary speech that presidents utilized in their policy proposal.

Figure 4.1

The Average Number of Visionary Policies Proposed per State of the Union Address

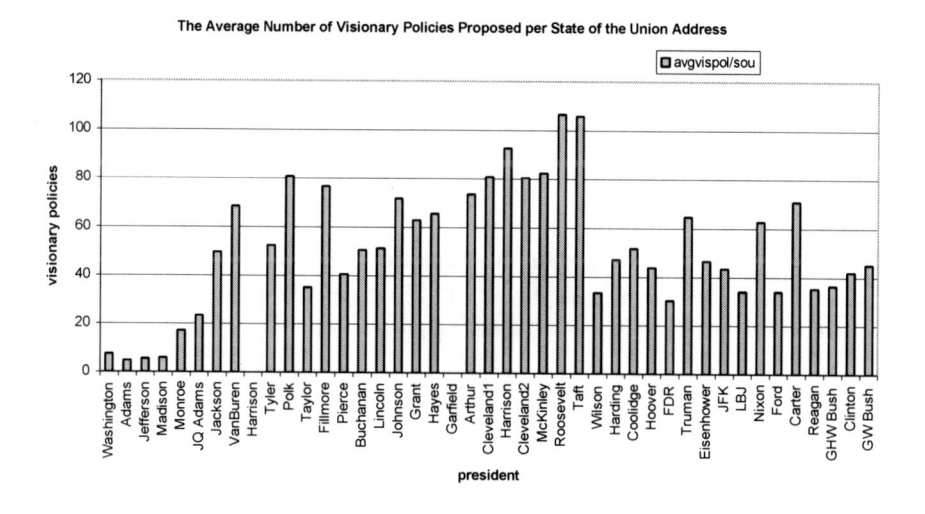

Figure 4.1 is an illustration of the average number of visionary policies that were proposed per State of the Union Address per president. This figure reveals several important comments not only on presidential use of visionary speech in policy proposal, but also in the evolution of the State of the Union

Address itself and the differences between formats. First of all, it must be noted that this figure is extremely similar to the figure which examined the overall average number of policies that were proposed in the State of the Union Address in the previous chapter. However, after having been nearly the highest of all the presidents in terms of number of words of address as well as general policy proposal, Roosevelt and Taft do not differentiate themselves substantively from their peers in terms of visionary speech. In the consideration of overall policy, Roosevelt and Taft proposed nearly 200 more policies in the State of the Union Addresses than any other president. However, Figure 4.1 shows that their elevated levels of policy proposal were not necessarily accompanied by significantly elevated levels of visionary speech as well.

In addition, Figure 4.1 makes a startling commentary on the State of the Union Address during the period when it was delivered in written form. Figure 4.1 shows that, regardless of the written format of the State of the Union Address beginning with Jefferson, presidents who delivered their State of the Union Address in this form utilized the opportunity of the constitutionally mandated speech to propose *their own visions* for the nation and for the world. Indeed, in examining the presidents of the nineteenth century, every one of them uses increasing levels of visionary speech in their policy proposal regardless of the delivery format. In addition, almost all of the presidents after Jackson propose higher numbers of visionary policies than any of the presidents of the twentieth or twenty-first centuries. This not only suggests that the presidents of the nineteenth century utilize visionary speech in their policy proposals, but that they also consistently increased the levels at which they did so.

Harrison's State of the Union Addresses are excellent examples of addresses that were not only delivered at a time when he should allegedly face constitutional restraint, but be confronted by a delivery format of the State of the Union that would prevent him from proposing his own vision for the people and the nation. Yet, Harrison, in his very first State of the Union Address on December 3rd, 1889, proposed many different visions for the country and used this visionary speech to instruct the Congress and the people on future behavior. Harrison first addressed the people's apprehensions regarding the Asian immigrants coming into the country and what role they would play in the future. He stated that "While our supreme interests demand the exclusion of a laboring element which experience has shown to be incompatible with our social life, all steps to compass this imperative need should be accompanied with a recognition of the claim of those strangers now lawfully among us to humane and just treatment." He continued by stating that, in dealing with the new immigrants, "An improper use of naturalization should not be permitted, but it is most important that those who have been duly naturalized should everywhere be accorded recognition of the rights pertaining to the citizenship of the country of their adoption." This was a time period in which almost the entire country, and most certainly the west coast, as a result of feelings of isolationism and William Randolph Hearst's beginning of his propagandized campaign against the "yellow peril" of all of the "Coolie" immigrants that were arriving on the shores and would be released back into the nation after the completion of the railroad, was swelling with opposition to Asian immigrants. Indeed, during WWII, not even FDR stood up for these members of American society when he issued Executive order 9066 which allowed nearly 120,000 Japanese-Americans to be forcibly removed from exclusion zones along the entire west coast. Harrison's statements and policy not only proposed a vision of behavior for those in the country, but a vision of a country where new individuals should be welcomed.

Harrison's vision for the country continued in his consideration of another people in the United States, for whom he also had a vision. After the civil war, presidents tended to moderate their comments on full suffrage and integration in the South largely because of the feeling of a need for national unity following the bloodiest war in United States history. However, Harrison confronted the issue in his State of the Union Address with strong policy proposals and a presentation of his vision for the country that should result. He stated that something must be done "in many parts of our country where the colored population is large the people of that race are by various devices deprived of any effective exercise of their political rights and of many of their civil rights." He followed that although "It has been the hope of every patriot that a sense of justice and of respect for the law would work a gradual cure of these flagrant evils" that adequate effort is not being made on the issue. He voiced his position on the condition of African-Americans in the country and said that "Surely no one supposes that the present can be accepted as a permanent condition."

In order to remedy the problems that were being faced, he first turned to the federal government, saying that "I earnestly invoke the attention of Congress to the consideration of such measures within its well-defined constitutional powers as will secure to all our people a free exercise of the right of suffrage and every other civil right under the Constitution and laws of the United States." In addition, in a rhetorical move not ordinarily used by presidents or the Congress, he placed blame on himself should nothing change with the plight of the former slave. He said that "No evil, however deplorable, can justify the assumption either on the part of the Executive or of Congress of powers not granted, but both will be highly blamable if all the powers granted are not wisely but firmly used to correct these evils."

Harrison concluded this section of the State of the Union Address by both expounding upon the areas of policy that were in the most need and suggested the deserving place of the African-American in the United States. He first proposed policy, stating that "A partial and qualified supervision of these elections is now provided for by law, and in my opinion this law may be so strengthened and extended as to secure on the whole better results than can be attained by a law taking all the processes of such election into Federal control." And, lastly, Harrison spoke directly to the way that they country must properly treat all of its citizens in the present and always in the future. He stated that "The colored man should be protected in all of his relations to the Federal Government, whether as litigant, juror, or witness in our courts, as an elector for members of Congress, or as a peaceful traveler upon our interstate railways." Harrison's use of this visionary speech is an exception to expected behavior in the "traditional" time in which he governed, and is indicative of the visionary speech used by many other presidents during the eighteenth and nineteenth centuries.

Another conclusion from Figure 4.1 is that, although Wilson is responsible for returning the State of the Union Address to orally delivered format, this does not necessarily present a "new" level or use of visionary speech and policy proposal in the State of the Union Address. Instead, the figure shows that, apart from individual deviations in regard to both high and low numbers of visionary policies that were proposed, on the whole, there is a significant similarity between the behavior of the presidents of a "traditional" period and a "modern" period that precludes their separation. The overall average number of visionary policies that were proposed in the State of the Union Address throughout presidential history is around 49 "visionary" policy propositions per State of the Union Address. When we separate the presidents into what could be called a "traditional" era prior to 1900 and a "modern" era after 1900, the data show that they propose 45 and 53 visionary policies respectively. This difference is not only insignificant, but is also so *incredibly* skewed by the high levels of visionary policy proposal from Teddy Roosevelt and Taft, that if they are eliminated from the "modern" average, it drops to 45 visionary policies proposed per State of the Union Address after 1900. This average is exactly the same as that for the presidents before 1900. In effect, figure 4.1 above suggests that presidents from the founding to the present have not only utilized visionary speech in their policy proposals, but also that they have done so with general consistency across time and presidencies. In addition, even if we look to give credit for the use of visionary rhetoric to a singular presidency, none, and especially not the usually championed Wilson or FDR, stand out as responsible for any significant change.

Even though Figure 4.1 provided a look at overall visionary speech as well as presidential visionary policy proposal, it is necessary, once again, to control these findings for the lengths of the addresses to reveal any new insights into the use of visionary speech in the State of the Union Address.

Figure 4.2

The Average Number of Visionary Policies Proposed per 1000 Words of the State of the Union Address

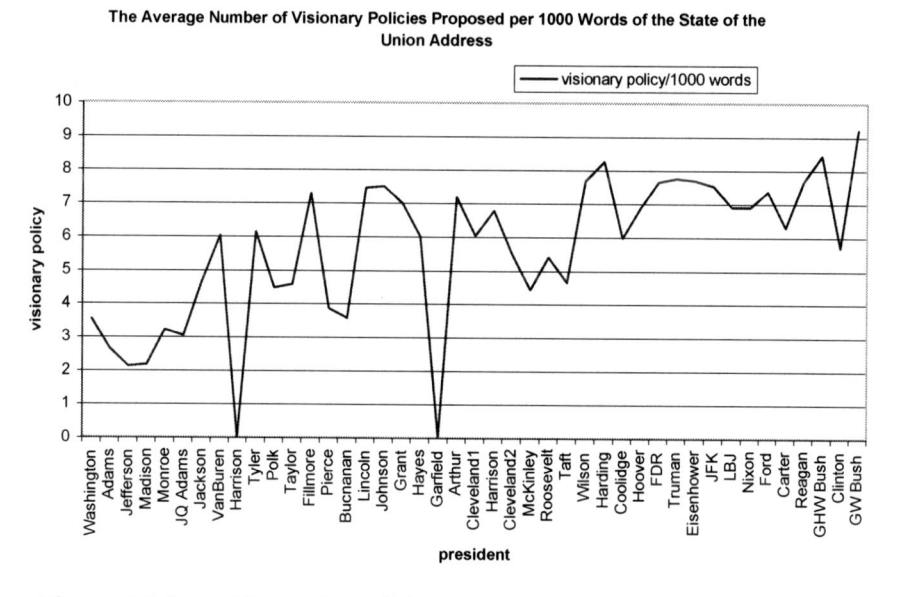

Figure 4.2 is an illustration of the average number of visionary policies proposed by the presidents per 1000 words of their State of the Union Addresses. Once the length of the State of the Union Address is controlled for,

which, in effect, removes the differences between the written and the oral delivery periods, a much clearer image of the evolution of the use of visionary policy in the State of the Union Address appears. Figure 4.1 showed an increase in the number of visionary policies proposed in the State of the Union Address until the change in format from written delivery back to oral delivery. At this point in 4.1, there was a sudden decline in the use of visionary speech in policy proposals. However, Figure 4.2 shows us that, once the length constraints (or possibilities) are standardized, a general trend in the use of visionary policy appears in the State of the Union Address.

Instead of these data providing a picture of presidential use of visionary policy proposals that can be clearly differentiated into two periods, the findings are much more nuanced. Although "modern" presidents do average higher numbers of visionary policy proposals per 1000 words of the State of the Union Address, the figure shows that, not only have presidents since the founding utilized this rhetorical tool, but there is no immediate and significant shift that can be seen in the use of visionary speech. Instead, Figure 4.2 suggests that there has been a general slow evolution of the State of the Union that has come to embody more visionary policy than in the past. Each president builds on the prior administration by including more of a national and international perspective on the proper way to do things in the future and the proper course for the people of the United States. There is no evidenced support for the division of presidential history into time periods on the basis of an alleged impact that would be associated with a "transformative" individual presidency in this regard. It appears as though the use of visionary speech in the State of the Union Address is much less about the contributions of a single executive or time period, and much more about the contributions of each individual executive and their unique impact on the office.

This point is reinforced even more when we see that there have been many presidents during the nineteenth century who used levels of visionary policy proposals with as much frequency, if not more so, than many twentieth century presidents. Even though it appears that contemporary presidents include more visionary policy proposals than the presidents of the past, the increase in the number of visionary policies from presidents as far back as Lincoln to the present is only around 1-1.5 visionary policies proposed in the State of the Union Address. This cannot conclusively support a clear discernment of different presidential habits and behaviors over different time periods. There is neither a visible dichotomy between eras in the use of visionary policy, nor any kind of delineation that clearly separates the behavior of one president from the behavior of others in the use of visionary policy proposal. Although there are some presidents that propose more policy in this fashion, and there are others who propose less policy in this way, the importance of the study lies in determining, like Harrison's examination above, what causes individual shifts in rhetorical use and what each individual executive contributed to the evolution of the State of the Union Address overall.

Visionary Speech in the Presidential Inaugural Address

Although Inaugural addresses are sometimes assumed to be one form of presidential speech in which presidents do not push their policies or administrative agendas, the previous chapter provides illustrations to the contrary and suggests that it, like the State of the Union Address, is, in fact, used by every president for some kind of specific policy proposal. Indeed, one of the reasons for this misjudgment may result from the fact that Inaugural addresses have evolved to become speeches which contain significant numbers policy proposals that are seated in the context of visionary speech and may not seem like explicit policy recommendations on their face. As we have seen above, presidents from the founding to the present day have unabashedly utilized the State of the Union Address for visionary statements. However, it is important to examine whether or not this also holds true for the Inaugural address as well, or whether they may be largely ceremonial and without substance.

Figure 4.3 is an illustration of the average number of visionary policies that were proposed per Inaugural address per president. This figure allows us to make some important conclusions and observations. First of all, we see that although George Washington eschewed the use of visionary policy proposal in his Inaugural addresses, this was by no means a precedent that was followed by subsequent presidents. Indeed, only two presidents later, Thomas Jefferson tripled the average number of visionary policies that had been proposed up to that point with around 7 per Inaugural address. Although there was a decline in this number immediately after his presidency, it was not long until presidents like Van Buren (8), Harrison (12), and Polk (22) pushed the incorporation of visionary policy proposal in the Inaugural address to never before seen heights. In fact, with an average of 22 visionary policies and directives per Inaugural address, Polk utilized more visionary

172   *The Evolutionary Rhetorical Presidency*

speech than any other president in the eighteenth and nineteenth century and more visionary policy speech than every other twentieth century president except Harding (43), Hoover (28), Truman (23), and JFK (29).

Figure 4.3

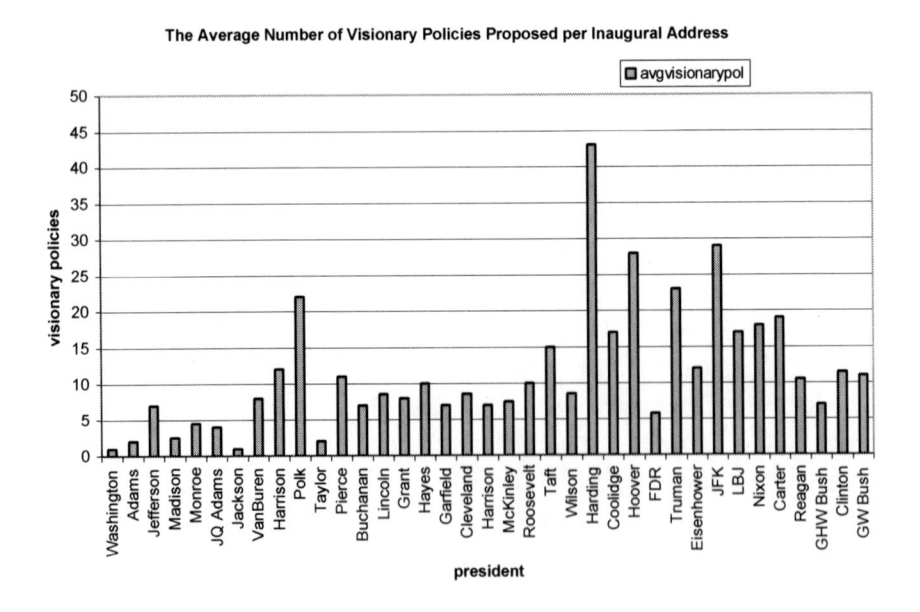

The Average Number of Visionary Policies Proposed per Inaugural Address

An examination of his Inaugural in 1845 clearly illustrates why Polk's presidency ranks among the five highest in presidential history in its use of visionary speech to propose policy. In a form reminiscent of George W. Bush's second Inaugural address examined earlier, Polk uses visionary speech in his Inaugural address to propose and advocate policies that deal with both the domestic and the foreign. Again, these visionary policies are more prescriptions for what is necessary for the good of the country that the president would like to see occur. They are policies because he is suggesting that they are guidelines that need to be followed, and will be, during his administration. They are visionary because they look forward to the future state of affairs, or speak in terms that are more abstract than policy proposals that address specific legislation or budgetary plans. In addressing the taxes that must be administered to the general populace, Polk stated that "The burdens of government should as far as practicable be distributed justly and equally among all classes of our population" and also that "Our patriotic citizens in every part of the Union will readily submit to the payment of such taxes as shall be needed for the support of their Government, whether in peace or in war, if they are so levied as to distribute the burdens as equally as possible among them." These two policy statements suggest Polk's stand on both the behavior of Congress as well as the people. Not only should Congress make sure that the taxes were applied fairly, or Polk would oppose or veto the plan, he also warned the citizens to follow the laws that were passed in the end, and they should refrain from refusal to pay. This is, in effect, Polk's vision for the origination and implementation of national taxes.

In addition to making visionary policy proposals regarding domestic affairs, Polk, as did Bush, spoke to the proper global course of action for international relations. This is not a simplistic policy proposal that suggested that Congress approve a treaty that had been made, or increase the troop levels at a specific locale. Instead, this was Polk's statement on the place of the United States in the world and the place of the world in regard to the United States. In the discussion of the annexation of Texas and its struggle with Mexico, Polk used the opportunity to present his vision on the right of the United States to expand and be free from interference of other countries. He stated that the citizens of Texas "are independent powers competent to contract, and foreign nations have no right to interfere with them or to take exceptions to their reunion." In addition, he explained that "Foreign powers do not seem to appreciate the true character of our Government. Our Union is a confederation of independent States, whose policy is peace with each other and all the world. To enlarge its limits is to extend the dominions of peace over additional territories and increasing millions." Polk also suggested that the United States would be behaving properly if it decided to expand its borders even beyond their present limits, saying that "It is confidently believed that our system may be safely extended to the utmost bounds of our territorial limits, and that as it shall be extended the bonds of our Union, so far from being weakened, will become stronger." He warned other countries who opposed this vision of the nation stating that "All alliances having a tendency to jeopardize the welfare and honor of our country or sacrifice any one of the national interests will be studiously avoided, and yet no opportunity will be lost to cultivate a favorable understanding with foreign governments by which our navigation and commerce may be extended and the ample products of our fertile soil, as well as the manufactures of our skillful artisans, find a ready market and remunerating prices in foreign countries."

Figure 4.3 above raises an important problem with the proposal of a "traditional/ modern" divide. If Polk were not to be dismissed summarily as a "traditional" president, in an era without policy proposal and visionary speech, the clarity with which Polk discussed his stance on international issues and the vision with which he described the future endeavors of the country might very well place those Inaugural statements as a "Polk Doctrine," in the same realms of prominence as the "Monroe Doctrine," the "Truman Doctrine," and the "Bush Doctrine." In fact, if we look the visionary policies that were proposed in the Inaugural address of Truman, they not only resemble Polk's visions in terms of number but also in terms of form and function.

In Truman's Inaugural Address in 1949, we see him address the role of the American people and the international community in ways that are incredibly similar to Polk's. He begun by stating the position of the country, or his vision of that position, saying that "the American people stand firm in the faith which has inspired this Nation from the beginning. We believe that all men have a right to equal justice under law and equal opportunity to share in the common good. We believe that all men have a right to freedom of thought and expression. We believe that all men are created equal because they are created in the image of God. From this faith we will not be moved." Truman then suggested that the problem of communism was not one that should only involve the United States. He addressed other countries saying, "These differences between communism and democracy do not concern the United States alone. People everywhere are coming to realize that what is involved is material well-being, human dignity, and the right to believe in and worship God."

Finally, and similarly to Polk's warning against other countries that might wish to interfere in the development of the United States, Truman proposed a new visionary policy of American involvement around the globe and laid out the points of his plan, saying that "We are ready to undertake new projects to strengthen a free world. First, we will continue to give unfaltering support to the United Nations and related agencies, and we will continue to search for ways to strengthen their authority and increase their effectiveness. Second, we will continue our programs for world economic recovery...In addition, we must carry out our plans for reducing the barriers to world trade and increasing its volume. Economic recovery and peace itself depend on increased world trade. Third, we will strengthen freedom-loving nations against the dangers of aggression...In addition, we will provide military advice and equipment to free nations which will cooperate with us in the maintenance of peace and security. Fourth, we must embark on a bold new program for making the benefits of our scientific advances and industrial progress available for the improvement and growth of underdeveloped areas." In striking similarity to Polk, Truman laid out his plan for the future relations of the country and the role that the United States must play on the international stage; he also utilized visionary speech to do so. This declaration of the role of the citizens of the United States and the country itself within the global community and regarding other countries is also the subject matter of the Inaugural Addresses of Harding and JFK, whose visionary policy numbers are also some of the highest in presidential history.

Another important observation that must be made regarding the data that are presented in Figure 4.3, is that, once again, there does not appear to be enough support for either a distinction between presidential eras of visionary policy proposal, nor the ability to directly associate the origins of this kind of presidential rhetoric with anyone other than George Washington himself and the beginnings of the presidency in general. There are many presidents other than Polk during the nineteenth century such as Harrison (12), Pierce (11), Lincoln (8.5), Hayes (10), and Cleveland (8.5) who propose as many or *more* visionary policies in their Inaugural addresses than presidents of the twentieth and twenty first centuries like T Roosevelt (10) Wilson (8.5), FDR (5.75), Eisenhower (12), Reagan (10.5), GHW Bush (7), Clinton (11.5), and GW Bush (11). The variation between the levels of visionary policy utilized in the Inaugurals suggests that presidents cannot be easily classified by eras or centuries. In addition, some of the presidents who are alleged to be founders of the "modern" rhetorical presidency (such as Wilson and FDR), who allegedly began the use of this type of rhetoric in large quantities, here appear to use less visionary speech than almost any of their presidential peers in the twentieth or any other century.

Although the average number of overall visionary policies does not support the tenets of a "traditional/ modern" paradigm, and even though, on the whole, Inaugural addresses are of fairly similar number of words, it is important to examine how the picture of Inaugural use of visionary speech in policy proposal might change when the analysis controls for number of words.

176   *The Evolutionary Rhetorical Presidency*

Figure 4.4

The Average Number of Visionary Policies Proposed per 1000 Words of the Inaugural Address

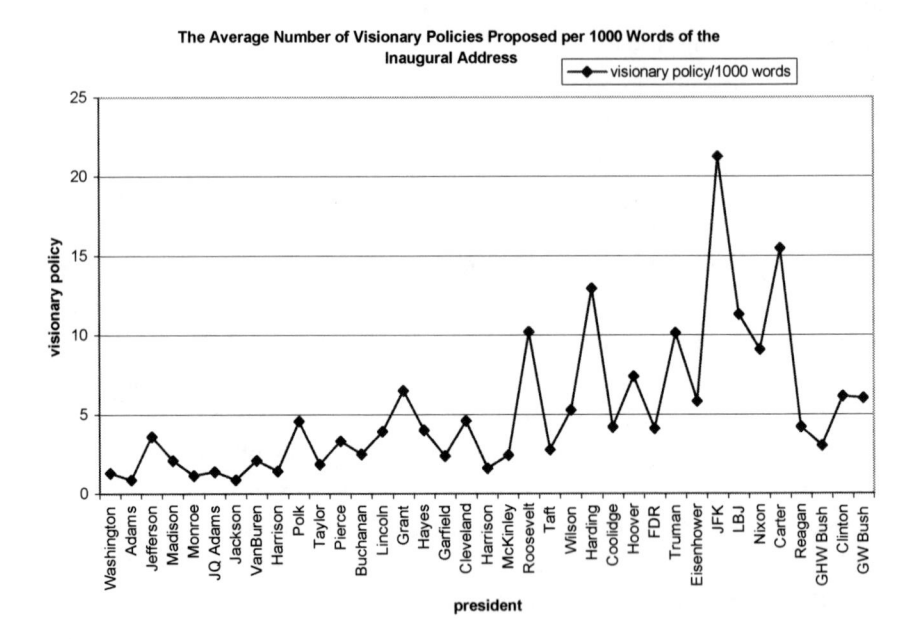

Figure 4.4 is an illustration of the average number of visionary policies proposed per 1000 words of the State of the Union Address. There are several similarities to presidential behavior regarding visionary policy proposal between Figure 4.3 and Figure 4.4. First of all, Harding and JFK, two of the presidents who averaged some of the highest numbers of overall visionary policies per Inaugural address, appear yet again to propose some of the highest levels of visionary policy proposal when length is controlled for. Another finding from Figure 4.3 that appears yet again in Figure 4.4 is that there is an extremely high variation between the use of visionary speech in policy proposals between presidents of both the nineteenth, twentieth and twenty-first centuries. Indeed, there appears to be little support for the conclusion that presidents *all* behaved the same during a certain period of time, nor that an individual like Wilson or FDR set a standard of behavior that was consistently followed by all subsequent presidents. In fact, Wilson (5.3) and FDR (4.1) are yet again far below the average number of visionary policy proposals used by the presidents and are similar in their averages to nineteenth century presidents like Polk (4.6), Hayes (4.0) and Cleveland (4.6).

Figure 4.4 also shows that even though the overall averages of visionary policy proposals seem to increase during the mid to late twentieth century, this does not presuppose that this is a transformative innovation during that period or even that it sets a precedent that contemporary presidents use today. Although presidents like LBJ and Carter are presidents that, similar to Harding and JFK, might be looked at initially as notable for the number of visionary policies that were proposed in their Inaugurals, the reason for the low levels of overall visionary policy in the Figure 4.3, along with the high levels of visionary policy per 1000 words of the Inaugural address in Figure 4.4 illustrate that LBJ and Carter were not necessarily overly active with their visionary policy proposals, but that they were able to propose visionary policies with less words and in shorter Inaugural addresses. In addition, although one might wish to suggest that the twentieth century presidents are increasing the number of visionary policies that they conclude in their Inaugural addresses, this conclusion cannot be supported. As Figure 4.4 illustrates above, presidents like Reagan, GHW Bush, Clinton, and GW Bush do not follow this generalization and actually propose fewer visionary policies than a president like Grant during the nineteenth century. Instead of presidential innovation, the high levels of visionary speech that are used by some presidents in policy proposal must be seen as a function of individual proclivity and preference as opposed to a generational difference between time periods.

Visionary Speech in Presidential Proclamations

Although the examination of the State of the Union Addresses and the study of the Inaugural Addresses illustrated that presidents, since the founding, did indeed use visionary speech to propose policy and speak to the citizens of the United States as well as the international community, these are both addresses with a long history of public delivery. In the previous chapter, we could see that, although the history of the executive order and the Presidential Proclamation is one of confusion and migration into different and specific uses; both of these forms of presidential rhetoric were used, again since the founding, as another means for presidents to propose policy. However, it is important to look at the proclamations and executive orders also as they relate to the use of visionary speech by the presidents themselves for policy advocacy. These two forms of address are rarely nationally disseminated. Further, although few other examinations of addresses here have supported the "traditional/ modern" divide, a comprehensive analysis of the use of visionary speech would not be complete without the examination of the proclamation and the executive order.

Figure 4.5

The Average Number of Visionary Policies Proposed per Presidential Proclamation

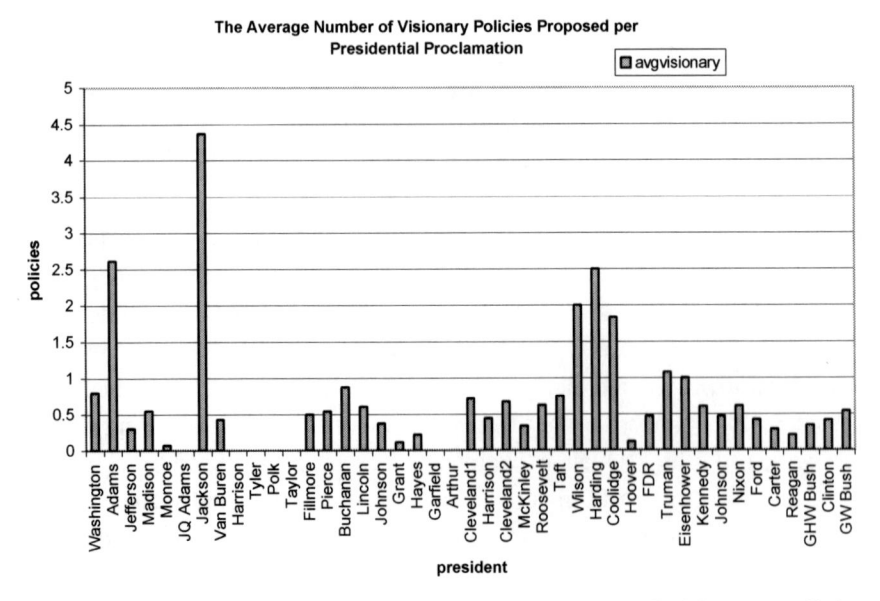

Figure 4.5 is an examination of the average number of visionary policies proposed per presidential proclamation. The first major observation that can be made is that, apart from a handful of presidents like Adams (2.6), Jackson (4.4), Wilson (2.0), Harding (2.5), and Coolidge (1.8), the majority of presidents in both the eighteenth, nineteenth and twentieth centuries propose little, if any visionary policies in their proclamations. In terms of visionary speech, then, the assumption can be made that presidents do not imbue their policy proposals with anywhere near the visionary levels that they associate with policies in their State of the Union Addresses and Inaugurals. Although they do not utilize high levels of visionary speech within their proclamations, the use itself of visionary speech *is* present in the proclamations from the founding to the present time. In fact, presidents of the late twentieth and early twenty first centuries like Johnson (0.5), Nixon (0.6), Ford (0.4), Carter (0.3), Reagan (0.2), both GHW Bush and GW Bush (0.3 and 0.5) and Clinton (0.4), all propose average numbers of visionary policies in their proclamations in

quantities at or below the levels of founding presidents like Washington (0.8) and Madison (0.5), and also nineteenth century presidents like Pierce (0.5), Buchanan (0.9), Cleveland (0.7), and Harrison (0.4).

In addition, although there are variances and presidents who proposed far more visionary policies in their proclamations than others, there is no support for the assertion that this can be labeled behavior of "modern" presidents only. The average number of visionary policies, which, again, is very small compared to the other forms of address, is 0.67 for the entirety of presidential history. If we look for a significant difference between "traditional" and "modern" time periods as the average before 1900 was 0.59 and the average after 1900 was 0.78. This difference is neither numerically strong enough to clearly differentiate any different time periods, nor is it suggestive of any trends that have taken place in the use of visionary speech in the presidential proclamation. What can be said is that presidents from the founding to the present day, regardless of the shifts that have taken place in the use and format of the proclamation, have generally not used visionary speech in their delivery of this form of address.

Figure 4.5 does, however, emphasize the importance of the study of the individual presidents and the variance that can occur as the result of individual presidents. During the founding and the early nineteenth century, Adams and Jackson included levels of visionary policy proposal that were unmatched to this day, and that did not even find presidents behaving similarly until the middle of the twentieth century nearly 100 years later. Almost all of the visionary policies that were proposed in the proclamations of Adams were related to a Thanksgiving proclamation on March 6th, 1799 where he listed a series of things that, with God's blessing, could be different for the country in the year to come. He asked that the people of the United State "call to mind our numerous offenses against the Most High God, confess them before Him with the sincerest penitence, implore His pardoning mercy, through the Great Mediator and Redeemer, for our past transgressions, and that through the grace of His Holy Spirit we may be disposed and enabled to yield a more suitable obedience to His righteous requisitions in time to come." This plea was followed by nearly twenty ways in which the supplication offered to God on Thanksgiving that Adams recommends would benefit the people, the defense of the country, and even the "commerce, manufactures, and fisheries" of the United States.

Adams' use of visionary speech with which to address commerce, domestic relations, and international affairs that were couched in a Thanksgiving Proclamation may have made their presence unclear. However, there is no misunderstanding the statements of policy and vision made by Jackson in his proclamation of December 10th, 1832 which addressed South Carolina's attempt at the nullification of Federal Law. He began by addressing South Carolina directly, and, included with the rhetoric suggesting that he would explain to them all the reasons that nullification is incorrect, was a very real threat and suggestion of what would be done should they disobeyed the laws of the United States. Jackson stated that "Strict duty would require of me nothing more than the exercise of those powers with which I am now or may hereafter be invested for preserving the peace of the Union and for the execution of the laws; but the imposing aspect which opposition has assumed in this case, by clothing itself with State authority, and the deep interest which the people of the United States must all feel in preventing a resort to stronger measures while there is a hope that anything will be yielded to reasoning and remonstrance, perhaps demand, and will certainly justify, a full exposition to South Carolina and the nation of the views I entertain of this important question, as well as a distinct enunciation of the course which my sense of duty will require me to pursue." He continued by describing the general vision of governance and the constitution under which the citizens of the United States had been and would continue to be ruled. He stated that "It is no answer to repeat that an unconstitutional law is no law so long as the question of its legality is to be decided by the State itself, for every law operating injuriously upon any local interest will be perhaps thought, and certainly represented, as unconstitutional, and, as has been shown, there is no appeal."

He then specifically addressed the issue at hand by stating, for the benefit of South Carolina and any state that might have felt the same in the future, that "I consider, then, the power to annul a law of the United States, assumed by one State, incompatible with the existence of the Union, contradicted expressly by the letter of the Constitution, unauthorized by its spirit, inconsistent with every principle on which it was founded, and destructive of the great object far which it was formed... Our Constitution does not contain the absurdity of giving power to make laws and another to resist them... Carry out the consequences of this right vested in the different States, and you must perceive that the crisis your conduct presents at this day would recur whenever any law of the United States displeased any of the States, and that we should soon cease to be a nation." Jackson ended his proclamation with a vision for the country that is very similar to the international visions presented by Polk and Truman in their Inaugural Addresses. He stated that "But each State, having expressly parted with so many powers as to constitute, jointly with the other States, a single nation, can not, from that period, possess any right to secede, because such secession does not break a league, but destroys the unity of a nation...But it has been shown that in this sense the States are not sovereign, and that even if they were, and the national Constitution had been formed by compact, there would be no right in any one State to exonerate itself from its obligations. So obvious are the reasons which forbid this secession that it is necessary only to allude to them...The laws of the United States must be executed. I have no discretionary power on the subject; my duty is emphatically pronounced in the Constitution...Having the fullest confidence in the justness of the legal and constitutional opinion of my duties which has been expressed, I rely with equal confidence on your undivided support in my determination to execute the laws, to preserve the Union by all constitutional means, to arrest, if possible, by moderate and firm measures the necessity of a recourse to force; and if it be the will of Heaven that the recurrence of its primeval curse on man for the shedding of a brother's blood should fall upon our land, that it be not called down by any offensive act on the part of the United States." The policies that Jackson proposed were not only the penalties for disobedience for the people of South Carolina, but also the correct mode of lawful living for the citizens of the country as long as they resided within its borders.

In the twentieth century, presidents like Wilson, Harding, and Coolidge all used higher averages of visionary speech in their proclamation policy proposals than their peers. Upon closer examination, both Harding and Coolidge used almost all of their visionary speech in much the same way as their founding predecessor Adams. They spoke of the plan for the country if it properly thanked God and the direction for the country in the next year if it was again blessed by Him. Wilson did use the Thanksgiving addresses, like that of November 5th, 1919, to state his vision for the country and the world as well, stating that, as the war was closed and things were returning to normal, "the American people devoted their manhood and the vast resources of their country they should, as they give thanks to God, reconsecrate themselves to those principles of right which triumphed through His merciful goodness. These great blessings, vouchsafed to us, for which we devoutly give thanks, should arouse us to a fuller sense of our duty to ourselves and to mankind to see to it that nothing that we may do shall mar the completeness of the victory which we helped to win." He also made an international statement in the Thanksgiving address, stating that "No selfish purpose animated us in becoming participants in the world war, and with a like spirit of unselfishness we should strive to aid by our example and by our cooperation in realizing the enduring welfare of all peoples and in bringing into being a world ruled by friendship and good will." This was Wilson's post-war vision and the policy he advocated for the country and the world.

In addition to taking advantage of the Thanksgiving proclamation to propose policy visions of the future, Wilson, also used visionary speech to comment on proper domestic and international policy. Wilson was able to present his own vision and policy regarding the children and educational system in America, as well as other countries, all within a proclamation issued on May 1st, 1919. On its face, it simply asked for the observation of Boy Scout Week. Within it however, Wilson spoke to the future of the youth of America in times of war, saying "America cannot acquit herself commensurately with her power and influence in the great period now facing her and the world unless the boys of America are given better opportunities than heretofore to prepare themselves for the responsibilities of citizenship." Further, he spoke to the place of the boy across different cultures and the necessary fostering of those of the United States, stating that "Every nation depends for its future upon the proper training and development of its youth. The American boy must have the best training and discipline our great democracy can provide if America is to maintain her ideals, her standards and her influence in the world." He closed by suggesting that "Anything that is done to increase the effectiveness of the Boy Scouts of America will be a genuine contribution to the welfare of the Nation." Although Wilson, Harding, and Polk are all examples of presidents who used visionary speech in much higher percentages than their peers, it is important to control for the length of the addresses to determine if any new findings or patterns emerge as well.

Figure 4.6 presents the average number of visionary policies that were proposed per 1000 words of presidential proclamations. Similarly to Figure 4.5, Figure 4.6 provides several insights into the use of visionary policy proposals in this kind of presidential speech. First of all, it confirms that, contrary to the high levels of visionary speech in the State of the Union Address and the Inaugural Address, presidents do not propose many visionary policies in presidential proclamations.

Figure 4.6

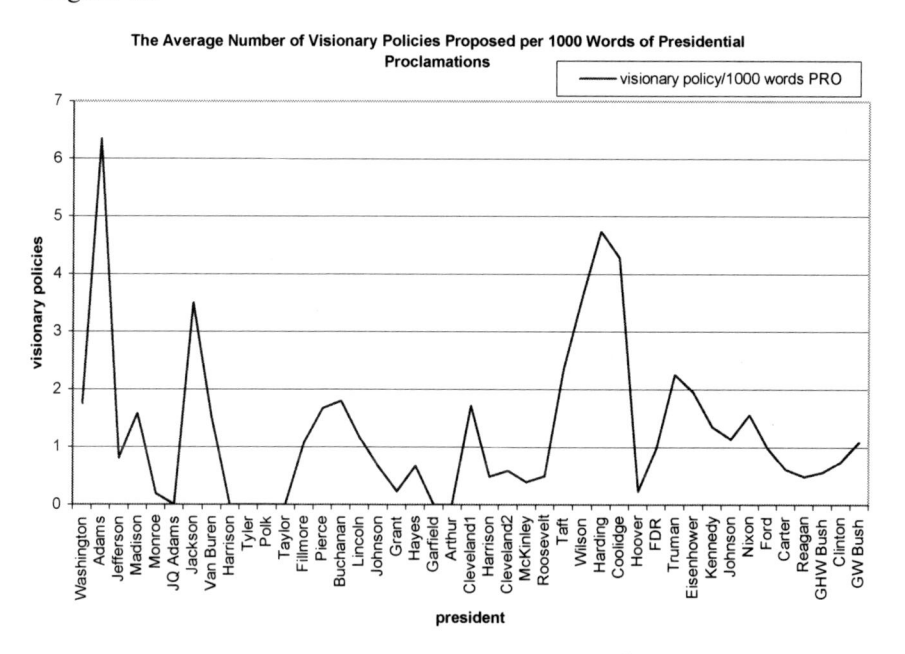

The Average Number of Visionary Policies Proposed per 1000 Words of Presidential Proclamations

In addition, although, as seen in Figure 4.5, presidents like Adams, Jackson, Wilson, Harding and Coolidge, proposed higher numbers of visionary policies per 1000 words of the proclamations, there is no pattern that emerges in the picture of the different levels of the use of visionary policy, nor its changes since the founding, to support the claim that it is, indeed, solely a function of twentieth century presidents. In addition, although Wilson does indeed use one of the highest numbers of visionary policy proposals, the ways in which they are proposed, in the Thanksgiving proclamation for example, set no real precedence or signify any real shift in the rhetoric of the proclamation, as presidents from the founding, and as demonstrated by Adams above, have behaved in similar fashion. Because of the similarities that proclamations shared with executive orders for much of their existence, it is important to again evaluate executive orders as well for any changes, patterns, or insights that they might be able to supply to understanding the development and use of visionary policy proposal in presidential rhetorical history.

184 The Evolutionary Rhetorical Presidency

Visionary Speech in Executive Orders

As other parts of the book have illustrated, executive orders are usually the presidential rhetorical address that is the lightest in terms of its use of popular address rhetoric. However, it is one of the heaviest in terms of the average number of policies that are proposed and enacted within it. Just as the proclamation has evolved to become largely a tool by which presidents cater to specialized groups of voters by creating holidays or observances that are particular to that group's cause, so have the executive orders evolved to become a tool by which the president can circumvent the Congress and the people, as well as the need to speak to either, to make unilateral policy decisions and proposals. To complete the look at visionary speech in presidential address, it is important to determine whether or not the lack of popular address rhetoric results in the finding that presidents do not utilize high amounts of visionary speech and visionary policy proposal in their executive orders.

Figure 4.7

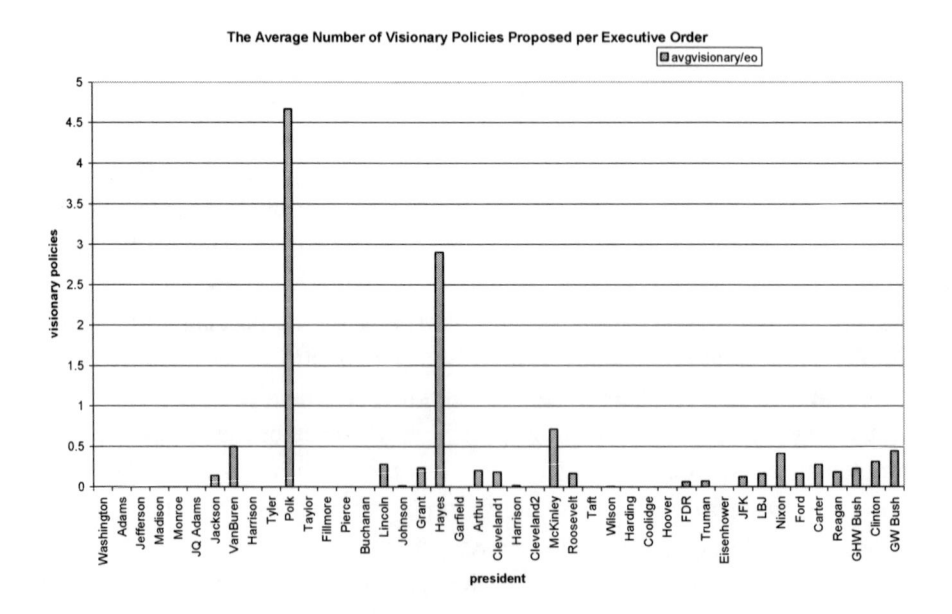

The Average Number of Visionary Policies Proposed per Executive Order

Figure 4.8

The Average Number of Visionary Policies Proposed per 1000 Words of Executive Order

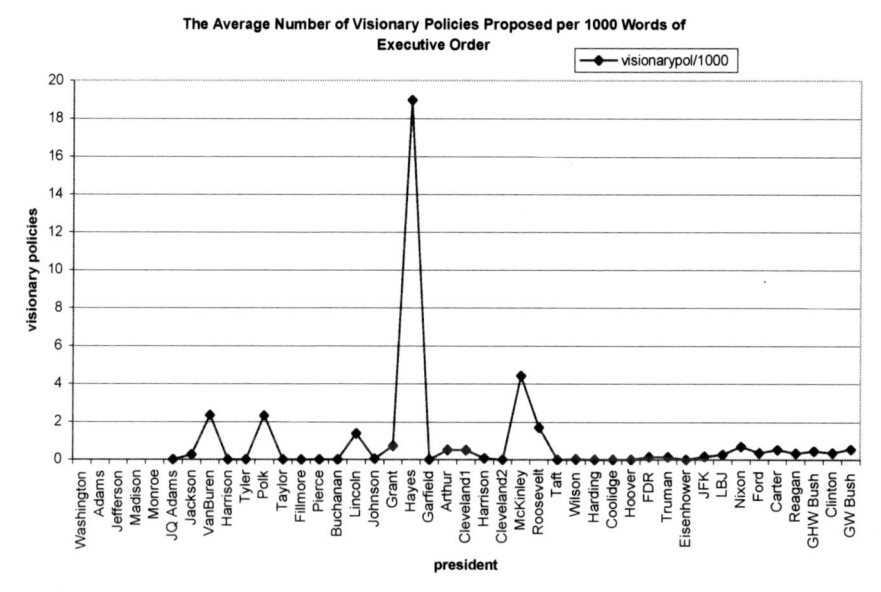

Figure 4.7 depicts the average number of visionary policies that were proposed per executive order for each president. Figure 4.8 illustrates the average number of visionary policies proposed per 1000 words of executive orders. The first conclusion that can be reached as a result of these figures is that, even though executive orders do propose significant numbers of policies as seen in the last chapter, on the whole, they use less visionary speech than found in the averages of the State of the Union Addresses, the Inaugural Addresses, or the Presidential Proclamations. In fact, presidents overall average less than one visionary policy proposal per executive order and less than one half of a visionary policy proposal for every 1000 words of the executive order. Before the figures above are examined for congruence with a generational divide, a general observation on the evolution of the executive orders can be made. The previous chapter found that the average number of *overall* policies proposed per 1000 words of the executive order ranged anywhere from 8 to 60 policies per 1000 words. In Figure 4.8, we can see that, apart from Hayes who averaged 19 visionary policies and policy proposals per 1000 words of executive orders, the next highest president is McKinley who averaged only 4.4 visionary policy proposals per 1000 words. Even this number, the second highest level of visionary speech by a president in the executive orders, is far below the average level of general policy proposal for the presidents. The overall averages involving visionary speech above show

that, while we saw that presidents propose significant numbers of policies in their executive order, they do so largely and almost completely without the use of visionary speech.

One major exception to this average are the executive orders and visionary speech use of Rutherford B. Hayes. There are a couple of reasons why Hayes maintains the highest levels of visionary speech overall even when controlled for by length. First of all, in addition to having lengthy executive orders, the orders proposed significant numbers of policies and almost all of these policies were in visionary terms that explained what Hayes viewed as the proper course of action at the present and also for the future. The visionary proposals and statements used by Hayes largely surrounded one major topic referring to the issue of civil service reform, with which Hayes and many other presidents, on the mid to late nineteenth century, dealt. In several executive orders, he addressed the propriety of the way that the civil service should select employees and also what kind of political involvement was appropriate during campaign cycles for civil servants.

In Executive Orders given on May 26th 1877, and June 22nd, 1877, Hayes made a statement whose intent was a long lasting impact regarding the political involvement of federal employees in political campaigns during the election season. Hayes saw this kind of activity as contrary to the service that ought to be provided. In fact, in both executive orders he repeated the same vision of political propriety saying that "No officer should be required or permitted to take part in the management of political organizations, caucuses, conventions, or election campaigns." This is a statement not just on the present question that needed be settled, but also on Hayes' visions of the propriety of political involvement for all future bureaucrats. He also made it clear in both that the first amendment of the constitution must be honored and identically stated that "Their right to vote and to express their views on public questions, either orally or through the press, is not denied, provided it does not interfere with the discharge of their official duties." He finished the executive orders by issuing a warning statement to those who were in positions of power and said that "No assessment for political purposes on officers or subordinates should be allowed. This rule is applicable to every department of the civil service. It should be understood by every officer of the General Government that he is expected to conform his conduct to its requirements." In these statements, Hayes not only dictated policy to be followed during his own administration, but presented a general course of behavior that he believed proper for politicians of any time period to follow.

Hayes provides a notable example of a president whose behavior and rhetorical proclivities are not similar to nearly any of his peers in office. In addition, he provides further evidence as to why the major categorization that is done by the "traditional/ modern" division may be a misnomer. Attempting sweeping generalizations regarding the behavior of presidents throughout extensive time periods tends to do justice neither to the nuances of the president's themselves, nor to their contributions to our larger understanding of the evolution of the presidencies and the extraordinary differing contexts that each man faced. The study of the presidency already faces the problem of dealing with a very small sample for any aspect of its study and must be cautious not to curtail that population to an even greater degree. In addition, the figures above show no real support for the claim that an individual president may have impacted the use of visionary rhetoric and policy proposal in the executive orders to such a great degree that it transformed the way that address was formed and delivered. In both Figure 4.7 and Figure 4.8, the only generalization that can possibly be made is that, on the whole, presidents do not use very much visionary speech, in either the eighteenth, nineteenth, twentieth or twenty-first centuries, in their executive orders. In addition, apart from deviations provided by the like of Hayes and McKinley, there is nothing to suggest individual impact or transitionary use brought on by any individual president or administration.

Visionary Policy and Presidential Rhetorical History

As the country has grown, so has the world. As the world has grown, so has ability of the United States to access the world. As both the world and the country have grown, so have the number of issues facing presidents, the technology available to them, and the problems that they face. Indeed, it is part of each new president's job to lay a course for the path of the nation in the context of the world. It is something that the people, the Congress, and the rest of the world come to expect. In this effort to seat the place of the United States in the global realm, presidents today use visionary speech to propose their policies and express what mandates they would like to see enacted in the future. Today, presidents voice concern for the nation's citizens regarding issue of education, health care, and the economy. Internationally, presidents today speak of terrorism, democracy, and the global environment that will best foster positive change. George W. Bush is an example of this form of visionary speech and visionary policy proposal. Throughout this book, examples from his Inaugural addresses and from his State of the Union Addresses have shown the vision that he had for peace after 9/11 and for democracy in the world's most volatile locations.

The findings that are presented in this chapter suggest that the separation or classification of presidents into different categories on the basis of similar time periods may miss important nuances of each president and their contributions to the office as a whole. Far from emerging as a rhetorical weapon of presidents only in the twentieth century, the data here propose that visionary speech and visionary policy proposal are, and have been used consistently, in presidential address from the founding to the present day. Although there are presidents who, in the study of each particular form of presidential address, tend to appear above or below the general standard of behavior, the picture regarding visionary policy is one of consistency.

This study does not attempt to begin to claim that all forms of presidential address have seen the same kinds of use of visionary speech and policy proposal in their history. Indeed, there are clear differences not only between the use of policy proposal in the State of the Union Address and Inaugural Address, and the Presidential Proclamations and Executive Orders, but also in each president's incorporation of visionary policy in each of them. Overall, however, addresses have not only consistently used visionary speech from the founding to the present to propose policy, they have also seen a gradual evolution in their format. Instead of witnessing a shift in the use of visionary speech between time periods or following individual presidencies, the figures above suggest that presidents of the United States, regardless of time or context, tend to stand on the shoulders of their predecessors and use increasing levels of visionary speech for policy address and proposal. This incremental shift is not necessarily the result of single presidential initiative, it is the result of an expanding issue base, a shrinking globe, and presidents who wish to do more and fare better than any of their predecessors. The State of the Union Address and the Inaugural Address afford them the platform to make these global statements and propose their visionary initiatives.

The Proclamations and the Executive Orders provide important insights as well, but are different from the State of the Union Address and the Inaugural Address. Instead of consistently utilizing and increasing the use of visionary speech throughout presidential history, as was seen in the State of the Union Addresses and Inaugurals, presidents from the founding to the present have been consistent, on the whole, in the fact that they eschew the use of visionary speech in proclamations and executive orders. Although there are notable examples of exceptions to this rule that have been examined above, proclamations and executive orders contain extremely low levels of visionary speech and visionary policy proposals. However, there is no differentiation in pattern for time periods or even after significant presidencies. Instead, these two forms of address which began their existence in ambiguous confusion between each other, also share the fact that they are not welcome platforms by which presidents can announce visions for the country or directions for the world.

This chapter and the data presented herein propose that rhetoric has evolved and continues to evolve along with the individuals who hold the office of president. Visionary speech is not a new innovation; Washington himself used it on many occasions to speak to his Revolutionary War soldiers about the propriety of their cause. Although the discipline should pride itself on discovering the particular uses of different kinds of speech and looking at the ways in which the presidents speak to the nation and the world, a presidential divide on the basis of time might handicap understanding of the nuances of presidential personality and rhetorical evolution. At worst, it tends to segment the presidents into inappropriate groups that might not, and should not, pretend to be representative of the whole. Any dichotomy of the rhetorical past of the presidency necessarily assumes group followership instead of assuming individual contribution to the office. Each president proposes a unique vision for the office and the country when they come into power. It is this difference that makes the study of the presidency the fascinating subject that it is. A dichotomy endangers these inimitable additions and subsumes uniformity where there is not, nor should be any.

CHAPTER V

Back to the Future: A New Understanding of Presidential Development

> *The [modern] rhetorical presidency is not just a fact of institutional change, like the growth of the White House staff, or the changing career patterns of Congressmen. It is a profound development in American politics.*
>
> —Jeffrey Tulis, *The Rhetorical Presidency*

ALTHOUGH THE "traditional" and the "modern" presidential distinctions may seek to provide scholars with "new terms with which to assess the character and development of the constitutional order and the president's place within it," (Tulis, 1987, 4), this study suggests that this paradigm may tend to miss important nuances and developments in presidential rhetoric. In one of his works, Greenstein proposes that "major changes that, beginning in 1933, produced the modern presidency—increased unilateral policy-making capacity, centrality in national agenda setting...remain central elements of the presidency and of presidential leadership in the final decades of the century" (Greenstein, 1988, 347). Greenstein is correct in his assertion that these elements are indeed important attributes to the contemporary presidency. However, the findings in this book propose that the assumption that these tenets of a "modern" presidency were not present before a certain demarcation may be misleading to the study of presidential policy proposal and rhetoric.

The importance of this examination of presidential address from Washington to G.W. Bush lies in the observation that these findings neither illustrate a "single" presidency from which we can trace the origins of popular address rhetoric, nor an individual president responsible for beginning policy advocacy. Instead, these chapters show that presidents as far back as the founding period proposed policy and used popular address rhetoric with a frequency rivaling some modern-day presidents. In addition to finding that each different form of popular address is used to incorporate varying levels of policy proposal, the study also finds that this use of popular address varies tremendously throughout presidential history and that presidents from the very outset of the country have used this rhetorical tool in the construction of their varying forms of address. These findings tend to suggest a view of presidential history as an evolution rather than a "transformation" during a single presidency.

In the years since the first presidential election, the United States has seen an exponential increase in its citizenry as well as the territory over which it governs. It has risen from the status of rebellious British colony to the paramount world power in 21st century international affairs. Wars have been fought against other nations on foreign soil as well as within America's own borders and between its own people. In addition, the constitution has been amended nearly 30 times to ensure that the imperfect system of government created by the founders is as responsive as possible to the changing times and needs of the people.

These changes in society and government were not overnight developments, however. Indeed, the growth from colony to superpower was a gradual adjustment to context, wherein the government effectively "grew into its skin" by altering social policy, expanding borders, and accepting more and more responsibility on the national and international stages. Correspondingly, the presidency has also evolved from Washington's reluctant leadership that sought to make a stable place for the emerging country on the world stage, to George W. Bush's multitasking presidency where attention is divided between international interactions, domestic concerns, positions on social issues, preparedness for unexpected threats, the and ever-present scrutiny of the rival party in today's "permanent campaign." This evolution did not occur with a single presidential event or individual, but was the result of the changing contexts (war, terrorism, economic collapse), changing powers (budgetary powers, war powers, legislative involvement), and different personalities of each of the individuals who held the executive office. Therefore, presidential history may best be seen as the history of different men with different perspectives facing different times and inheriting and enacting different powers. Just as the United States is a realization of evolution in the face of new and unforeseen challenges, so also the contemporary presidency is an amalgamation of all of the powers, innovations, and personalities of all the men who have held the office.

The Paradigm of the Traditional and the Modern Reconsidered

By categorizing presidents into two distinct periods, characterized by certain behavior, certain policy activity, and certain ways of speaking, a historical demarcation seems to suggest that we are better able to separate presidents on the basis of behavior and activity. According to Fred Greenstein, the best way to trace the origins of the modern-day president's rhetoric and political involvement is to begin with examination of early 20th century presidents when "the presidency began to change in at least four major ways. These added up to so thorough a transformation that a modifier such as 'modern' is needed to characterize the...manifestations of the institution that has evolved from the far more circumscribed traditional presidency" (Greenstein, 1988, 3). Dahl likewise proposes that presidents of the 20th century are important to differentiate from past presidents, saying that "particularly in recent decades, the task of shaping presidential address to influence and manipulate public opinion, has become a central element in the art and science of presidential conduct...Thus the presidency has developed into an office that is the very embodiment of the kind of executive the Framers, so far as we can discern their intentions, strove to avoid" (Dahl, 1990, 369).

As seen from the quote at the outset of the chapter, Tulis also suggests a difference in presidential rhetoric between the presidents of today and those of the 19th century. However, he views the change as much more of an intervention than a simple evolution. "Students of the presidency have nearly all regarded the rhetorical presidency as a logical and benign growth of the institution rather than a fundamental transformation of it. That basic postulate is wrong. The rhetorical presidency signals and constitutes a fundamental transformation of American politics that began at the outset of the twentieth century" (Tulis, 1987, 175). Greenstein echoes this sentiment, saying, "With Franklin Roosevelt's administration...the presidency began to undergo not a shift but rather a metamorphosis" (Greenstein, 1978, 45).

In his writings, Tulis "tried to show that nearly all of the presidents in the 19th century spoke and wrote differently than nearly all the presidents in our

[20th] century" (Tulis, 1996, 4). Thus, this suggests that there once may have been a "non-rhetorical" presidency where "modern" elements, such as policy proposal, popular address, and visionary speech, were absent, and that the rhetorical and the non-rhetorical can be easily discriminated (Medhurst, 1996, xiii). Indeed, Tulis proposes that "the more policy-oriented a speech, the less likely it was to be given in the 19th century...I have suggested that most of the presidents in the 19th century were constrained by the settled practices and doctrine behind them" (Tulis, 1987, 67; 79). He continues, stating that there "was nothing in these speeches ["traditional" addresses] to suggest that the president had a program for the nation, that he was interested in bills before Congress, or even that he wanted popular support for foreign policy" (Tulis, 1987, 72). According to Tulis, it is with Wilson, and not before, that the president *began* to actively initiate policy as well as speak to the people. "The Wilsonian view has replaced the founders' as the basic underpinning of presidential self-understanding and public legitimacy" (Tulis, 1987, 174).

However, the findings in this book show that this inclination toward the employment of policy proposal and popular address in presidential rhetoric is not only *present* in the presidential addresses of the 18th and 19th centuries, but that that these elements are sometimes used and found in *larger* frequencies in founding presidential Addresses and those in the 1800's than their 21st century successors. The data from chapters three and four illustrate increasing word totals as well as the numerable policy proposals by presidents from the 1700s to the early 1900s. Notable examples were the presidencies of Theodore Roosevelt and Taft who proposed two to three times as many total policies on the average than their late 1900s and early twenty first century counterparts. This finding suggests that the passive 19th century behavior proposed by the "traditional/modern" paradigm might be less generalizable than it may seem. In addition, when the differences in total policy proposals that could be attributed to the significant differences in speech lengths were controlled for, "traditional" presidents such as Washington, Taylor, Polk, Arthur, and McKinley proposed as much policy per 1000 words of their State of the Union Address as 20th century presidents like Wilson, Hoover, FDR, and JFK.

Two other significant findings also emerged from the data. First, the examination of the addresses illustrates that there is a general increase in the average number of policies proposed per 1000 words of the State of the Union Address from the founding to the present; this occurred regardless of whether or not these addresses were given in the written or the orally delivered periods of the State of the Union Address. Secondly, the steady increase in the number of policies per 1000 words of the State of the Union Address illustrate that there may be no clear origination point with which policy proposal in the Address begins. Even after surveying each of the policy initiatives and forms of popular address rhetoric used from Lincoln to LBJ, the data illustrated that presidents have incrementally either increased or decreased the number of policies that they proposed; there was no evidence to support an individual president whose policy proposal indicated a significant permanent demarcation or trend that differentiated itself from the overall averages or patterns.

This book also examined the frequency of different popular address rhetoric words within four different forms of presidential address. Aside from discovering important differences in the evolution of such forms of address as the executive orders and the presidential proclamations, the data revealed that that founding presidents were not only aware of popular address rhetoric, but, at times, they employed it within their addresses in significant quantities and in order to propose policy. In fact, the chapters demonstrate that even some presidents such as John Adams and Thomas Jefferson, who should be the most likely of the executives to be bound by some kind of "constitutional constraint," used similar or higher percentages of popular address rhetoric than did many "modern" presidents such as Wilson, Coolidge, and Hoover. In addition, in those forms of address which saw relatively small uses of popular address rhetoric, the data showed that this was neither due to a decision made by an individual president nor could it be generalized to the behavior of only a certain era of presidential behavior. Instead, presidents from the founding to the present behaved similarly, whether in their attempts to increase the proposal of policy and use of popular address rhetoric or in their less than frequent utilization of the same.

Thusly, these findings suggest that presidents from the founding have used the constitutional provision of the State of the Union Address and the Inaugural Address, as well as Presidential Proclamations and Executive Orders to promote their own policy initiatives, make use of popular address rhetoric, make statements on the beliefs of the American people, as well as give general visionary advice as to the course that the country should follow. As a notable example, Washington used his last State of the Union Address in 1796 to make comment on the future relations of the people of the county, their education, and their relations with each other, stating that, "True it is that our country, much to its honor, contains many seminaries of learning highly reputable and useful; but the funds upon which they rest are too narrow to command the ablest professors in the different departments of liberal knowledge for the institution contemplated, though they would be excellent auxiliaries...The more homogenous our citizens can be made in these particulars the greater will be our prospect of permanent union; and a primary object of such a national institution should be the education of our youth in the science of government." Washington, our very first president, used the platform of his final constitutionally mandated address not only to propose policies to benefit mankind, but also to deliver social commentary on the future of the people of the country and their contributions to the stability of that same nation.

Similar examples of presidential use of their rhetoric to address the people as a whole and propose varying policies can be found throughout the founding and the nineteenth century as well. In his Inaugural State of the Union Address in 1801, Jefferson too made assertions that were larger and more abstract than simple policy propositions, but which still proposed a map with which the country be guided. Jefferson referenced the newly acquired census results stating that, "We contemplate this rapid growth and the prospect it holds up to us, not with a view to the injuries it may enable us to do others in some future day, but to the settlement of the extensive country still remaining vacant within our limits to the multiplication of men susceptible of happiness, educated in the love of order, habituated to self-government, and valuing its blessings above all price." In 1882, Chester A. Arthur expounded as well on the future of the people of America and the place of education in the nation's advancement. "No survey of our material condition can fail to suggest inquiries as to the moral and intellectual progress of the people. It is a momentous question for the decision of Congress whether immediate and substantial aid should not be extended by the General Government for supplementing the efforts of private beneficence and of State and Territorial legislation in behalf of education."

This study has shown, through the line-by-line examination of the different forms of presidential address that the examples above are but two of the incredibly varied subjects upon which presidents since the founding have waxed abstractly, made prophetic statements, and enumerated their policy propositions. Although the presidents themselves, their styles, and their foci, have varied even as there have been changes in the different forms of address, their delivery, their lengths, and the technological medium with which they have been delivered, presidents on the whole have used whatever rhetorical tools are available at the time to build on the policy activity of prior presidents and to set their own mark for leadership and legacy.

A Deeper Look at Presidential Study: Past, Present, and Future

In order to better fully understand the development of the power of the contemporary presidency, the innovations and interpretations made by eighteenth and nineteenth century presidents, however slight, must be examined for the impact on the office itself—an institution that was largely framed and begun without its own clear identity. Indeed, from the very origins of the executive position, there has existed an ambiguity in the formal and informal duties of the president that has forced each individual president to re-interpret his position and its meaning from the Constitution. Greenstein suggests that one of the legacies of the founders is "a vagueness, and therefore openness to specification by the president and his politically significant others, of the description of the presidency in the Constitution," and that "the lack of detailed specification of presidential powers and the Delphic references to 'the executive power' and to the power to make treaties, appoint ambassadors and 'other offices,' and be commander in chief have provided license for extensive independent presidential action since the early days of the republic" (Greenstein, 1988, 346). Indeed, there is little clarity provided by the Constitution in the position, expectations, or the duties of the president besides executing the law passed by the legislature. "On a continuum from ambiguity to structured constraint, the presidency is as close to the former as repetitive assembly line work is to the latter. And the more ambiguous the definition of the role, the more it will of necessity be shaped by the personal makeup of the individual who fills it" (Greenstein, 1988, 5).

This vagueness of responsibility and function was not unintentional, however, as the Framers purposely intended the executive to grow and evolve. They felt that the office must change and adapt to new issues, confrontations, or desires of the people. Jefferson explained, "Institutions must advance also, and keep pace with the times. We might as well require a man to wear still the coat which fitted him when a boy" (Quoted in Berman, 1987, 339). The president, as figurative head and literal leader of the country, was expected to watch over the people as well as initiate domestic and foreign policies for their well being; the founders attempted to reconcile this fact by forming an institution with the power to grow. "The presidency is a dynamic, elastic office. Its shape and powers change over time...[the framers] invented an office just ambiguous enough, just flexible enough to adapt, yet not so loose and undefined that it could easily overwhelm the delicate balance of the separation of powers...the constitutional design of the office was left vague enough to give presidents an opportunity to shape and mold the office to conform, in part to the needs of the time, the level of political opportunity, and the skills of each incumbent" (Genovese, 2001, 190).

Even some scholars who advocate a "traditional" and "modern" segregation seem to hint at the important recognition of the differences found between presidents of the past. "Periodically, the presidency has changed, either temporarily or for good. One kind of change has been simple variation from president to president in will and skill to make effective use of the persisting components of the presidential role and to avoid their perils" (Greenstein, 1988, 3). Greenstein further remarks, "A review of the experiences of the modern presidencies makes it clear that presidents and their associates have varied in their capacities to respond to and shape the political environments in which they operate" (Greenstein, 1988, 352). In addition, he finds that "the impact of the president is almost invariably a function of the personal leadership qualities he brings to and displays in office, as well as of the political context of his presidency" (Greenstein, 1988, 1). It is this "variation from president to president" that Greenstein views as important only *after* the rise of FDR. However, this study proposes that it is this "variation" of personality and context that enables the evolution of rhetoric and policy proposal from the *founding* to the modern-day president.

The recognition of the individual contribution of each president to the concept and powers of the "Chief Executive" is of utmost importance in the research of the presidency. "The presidency is less an outgrowth of the constitutional design and more a reflection of ambitious men, demanding times, exploited opportunities, and changing international circumstances...The presidency has been shaped by the varied individuals, operating within a dynamic system under changing circumstances." (Genovese, 2001, 14; 16) Indeed, in his rhetoric, a president must deal not only with precedent set by prior executives and the evolution of society since the last officeholder, he must view these changes though the lens of his own ambition and capabilities, as well as his own goals. "A rhetorical context is a unique array of forces—rhetorical, historical, sociological, psychological, strategic, economic, and personal—that exists at any given moment in time and that impacts the speakers selection and presentation of topics" (Medhurst, 1996, xviii).

In the end, any form of presidential address given by an office-holding president is a personally determined dialogue with the institution's past, present and future, built on the powers, precedents, and rhetoric of the individuals who have held the office in the past. Each executive looks at the political landscape before them and has the ability to choose what rhetorical position they will attempt to play in the overall picture. It is no surprise that those who seek the nation's highest office often attempt to expand or build on the existent powers and precedents of the office. We can "look at the presidency as an institution in which rhetoric plays a major role, asking what can be discovered if we assume that the character of presidential rhetoric has been created, sustained, and altered through time by the nature of the presidency as an institution"(Campbell and Jamieson, 1990, 3). Indeed, "The presidency over time has become larger and more complex than any one of its players, having acquired a portion of identity from each who has won the part. No one person ever fully fills the role; the office includes all its occupants in its encompassing nature" (Fields, 1996, 12). A president's "reflection about the past yields consideration of the principles that should govern the present decision-making about the future," and "in these addresses, one observes presidents justifying initiatives on the basis of a changing view of what the constitution permits" (Campbell and Jamieson, 1990, 63; 57).

This study illustrates that, although it may be an easy way to conceptualize the presidency and presidential history, a modification and re-examination of the "traditional/modern" paradigm may be necessary. The data herein find that the number of policies proposed in the different forms of presidential address as well as the use of popular address rhetoric within those addresses, is, indeed, more an "evolution" of presidential activity than a transformation. In addition, the data exhibit gradual movements and trends as opposed to immediate and permanent increases or decreases in policy proposal or popular address rhetoric. By adopting the perspective that the presidency has undergone an early twentieth century "transformation," consideration of the development of the modern-day president is limited to only those subsequent presidents who exhibit like behavior and tendencies.

Although it is clear that the examination of such presidents as FDR, Wilson, and Theodore Roosevelt provide incredibly important insights into presidential behavior in differing contexts as well as contributions made to the contemporary presidency, it is just as important to examine presidents like Tyler, Taylor, Hayes, and Harrison to see how they themselves approached presidential policymaking and the precedents set by those before them. It is equally important to discover the differing contexts and individual contributions that relatively unknown presidents have made to the presidency as we now know it. Only through a close and complete examination of all of the officeholders of the presidency can the individual rhetorical proclivities, as well as the impact of these personalities on the office overall, be fully understood. By examining the challenges faced by a president as well as the personal motivations and the reasoning of presidents who might be viewed as less important under a generational delineation, we are provided with a richer picture of how the president today behaves as well as the similarities between this behavior and that of presidents of the past. We must be hesitant to follow the constructs of a dichotomy that dismisses close examination of presidents like Hayes, Grant, and Arthur because they are viewed as adding little to understanding of the modern rhetorical presidency. By applying a general partitioning of presidential behavior, divisions such as the "traditional/modern" paradigm tend to overlook rhetorical and behavioral nuances, as well as personal motivations of individual presidents in favor of an easier classification.

Directions for Further Study and Understanding

The presidential rhetorical tradition may not be as simple as a division between certain dates in our history and proposed tenets of behavior to characterize those periods. Instead, the rhetorical presidency must be viewed as each president's response not only to the format of delivery with which he is faced, but his personal rejoinder to context as well as the precedents of policy proposal and popular address rhetoric that have been used before him. Buchanan faced the threat of a Civil War within America's borders, yet he proposed fewer policies per 1000 words of the State of the Union Address than any other president in address lengths rivaling presidential history's longest (over 16,000 words). Taft was looking at a presidency on the heels of Roosevelt's that was largely devoid of conflict or trauma, yet he proposed the largest total numbers of policy in the State of the Union Address ever. Franklin

Roosevelt faced an unprecedented national depression as well as a conflict of global proportions that threatened to destroy freedom around the world in World War II. Yet, as a president faced with so many degrees of difficulty, his average number of policy proposals in any of the forms of address was one of the lowest of the eighteenth, nineteenth, or twentieth centuries. It is important that the presidents of old be examined along side contemporary presidents as "innovators" in their own right, for the standards that they may have set, the constraints they might have faced, as well as the incremental changes that they made to the ways that the president speaks to, interacts with, and proposes policy for the people.

Although this study takes the advantageous step of attempting to provide a more complete examination of different and consistently delivered forms of presidential addresses from the founding period until the present day, this is only the first of many necessary steps that must be taken in order to gain a richer understanding of the Presidency of the United States. Scholars of the presidency must break away from the tendency to begin study of the presidency in the twentieth century, as the data here have shown that much exists beyond the recent past. In addition, they must look at varied forms of presidential behavior and the history and backgrounds of the individual officeholders and their actions in and out of office, to give a fuller picture of what each president did in office and the motivations that they might have had.

Given seemingly scant attention in the constitution, the presidency has grown to the most powerful executive position in the world. As scholars of presidential study, it is important to realize that, like roll-call votes and other collectable data from our governmental institutions, there are personal motivations, considerations, and decisions that go into every stage of the political and policy making process. It is imperative that we apply the same rigor of examination to the areas of the presidency that might have been viewed as unprofitable or yielding few new findings in the past (such as the study of nineteenth century presidencies and their officeholders), and seek the same groundbreaking and enlightening findings that move our discipline and our understanding toward a more complete picture of our political world.

APPENDICES

Appendix A: Varying Words/Phrases Considered As Policy Proposal/Advocacy

The following excerpts from the State of the Union Addresses of each president represent different ways in which policies were proposed in that address. The cases below illustrate that some presidents of the 20th century proposed policy in ways very similar to those propositions of the founding and 19th century. In addition, these samples represent the guidelines that were followed with regard to counting policy proposals in the State of the Union Address. These guidelines are outlined in Chapter 1. If a president directly made a "recommendation" of any kind, it would be counted as a policy proposal. This includes statements such as "I recommend," or "it is recommended." Suggestions by the presidents were also counted as policy propositions. Statements such as "I suggest that," or "it is strongly suggested" were seen as very clear policy proposals originating from the Address. In addition, statements such as "it is important that," "you must," "we ought to," "it is desirable that," "I feel that," "it is necessary," "we cannot neglect," "it is essential that," "you need to," "you can," "the Congress should," or any use of the words must, will, should, could, would, have to, or shall were good indicators of places where policy proposal might be found.

After observing terminology that might suggest policy proposal, it was important to determine whether or not an actual policy was being proposed. If the statement contained recommendations to actions upon which Congress would specifically have to act or make legislative decisions, this was counted as a policy recommendation. Those items in the State of the Union that the president said he did as the result of the powers of his office (sending emissaries to foreign countries, head of state functions) were not treated as policy because they were things that the president, regardless of the desires of Congress, could enact by himself. In addition, abstract statements made by the president about the good of the people or the future of the nation such as "we must never give up," "we must always keep these things in mind," "we must continue our work for the people," were not counted because no specific policy was proposed.

Specific policies that were counted could be explicit requests or commands for Congressional action as well as abstract suggestions for Congressional legislation that would largely leave the details up to the Congress. Specifics such as "taxes should be lowered," or "the postal roads must be improved," were counted as single explicit policy proposals. Following the guidelines that a policy was defined as any proposal that would necessitate or require legislative action, sentences were sometimes made of more than one policy proposal. Indeed if a president, speaking of the economy, said that "we must lower taxes, raise the minimum wage, and provide a stable currency," this was counted as three separate policy proposals because each recommendation would necessitate separate changes of existent law, or separate considerations and hearings detailing specifics of each issue.

Abstract policies that pertained to specific subject matter were also counted as policy proposals. Statements such as "we must improve education," or "it is essential that our military remain strong," are counted as policy proposals. These statements speak directly to action that the president views as necessary to either alter or maintain existent law. In addition, these abstract recommendations are still policy proposals because they are the president's suggestion of policy that Congress has the duty to act upon and determine the changes regarding. Although, he "places the ball in Congress' court," in abstract proposals, the president is still bringing an issue to their attention upon which he would like to see action; it therefore must be considered a policy proposal.

Appendix B: Examples of Policy Proposal in the State of the Union Address from Washington to G.W. Bush
(emphasis added for highlight of policy proposal indicators)

"Under this view of our affairs, I should hold myself guilty of a neglect of duty if I forbore *to recommend* that *we should make* every exertion to protect our commerce and to place our country in a suitable posture of defense as the only sure means of preserving both." (Adams, 1797)

"It is my duty *to recommend to your serious consideration* those objects which by the Constitution are placed particularly within your sphere - the national debts and taxes." (Adams, 1797)

"But I can not refrain from again *pressing upon your deliberations* the plan which *I recommended* at the last session for the improvement of harmony with all the Indians within our limits by the fixing and conducting of trading houses upon the principles then expressed." (Washington, 1794)

"In this review *you will doubtless allow due weight to the considerations* that the questions between us and certain foreign powers are not yet finally adjusted, that the war in Europe is not yet terminated, and that our Western posts, when recovered, *will demand* provision for garrisoning and securing them. A statement of our present military force will be laid before you by the Department of War." (Washington, 1795)

"To accomplish this important object, a prudent foresight requires that systematic *measures be adopted* for procuring at all times the requisite timber and other supplies. In what manner this shall be done *I leave to your consideration.*" (Adams, 1798)

"*The Legislature will doubtless consider* whether, by authorizing measures of offense also, they will place our force on an equal footing with that of its adversaries." (Jefferson, 1801)

"We can not, indeed, but all feel an anxious solicitude for the difficulties under which our carrying trade will soon be placed. How far it can be relieved, otherwise than by time, *is a subject of important consideration.*" (Jefferson, 1801)

"I should fail in my duty in not *recommending to your serious attention* the importance of giving to our militia, the great bulwark of our security and resource of our power, an organization best adapted to eventual situations for which the United States ought to be prepared." (Madison, 1809)

"To be ready to meet with cordiality satisfactory proofs of such a change, and to proceed in the mean time in adapting our measures to the views which have been disclosed through that minister *will best consult our whole duty.*" (Madison, 1811)

"Judged, however, in candor by a general standard of positive merit, the Army Register will, it is believed, do honor to the establishment, while the case of those officers whose names are not included in *it devolves with the strongest interest upon the legislative authority* for such provisions as shall be deemed the best calculated to give support and solace to the veteran and the invalid, to display the beneficence as well as the justice of the Government, and to inspire a martial zeal for the public service upon every future emergency." (Madison, 1815)

"An improvement in the organization and discipline of the militia is one of the great objects which *claims the unremitted attention of Congress.*" (Monroe, 1817)

"The time seems now to have arrived when this subject *may be deemed worthy the attention of Congress* on a scale adequate to national purposes." (Monroe, 1817)

"The exigencies of the public service and its unavoidable deficiencies, as now in exercise, have added yearly cumulative weight to the considerations presented by him as persuasive to the measure, and *in recommending it to your deliberations* I am happy to have the influence of this high authority in aid of the undoubting convictions of my own experience." (John Quincy Adams, 1825)

"I have thought it more consistent with the spirit of our institutions *to refer to the subject again to the paramount authority of the Legislature to decide* what measure the emergency may require than abruptly by proclamation to carry into effect the minatory provisions of the act of 1824." (John Quincy Adams, 1826)

"The fortification of the coasts and the gradual increase and improvement of the Navy are parts of a great system of national defense which has been upward of 10 years in progress, and which for a series of years to come *will continue to claim the constant and persevering protection and superintendence of the legislative authority.*" (John Quincy Adams, 1827)

"The subject *is earnestly recommended to the consideration of Congress* in the hope that the combined wisdom of the representatives of the people *will devise* such means of effecting that salutary object as may remove those burthens which shall be found to fall unequally upon any and as may promote all the great interests of the community." (Jackson, 1832)

"Among the interests which *merit the consideration of Congress* after the payment of the public debt, one of the most important, in my view, is that of the public lands." (Jackson, 1832)

"In the meantime the existing laws have been and will continue to be faithfully executed, and every effort will be made to carry them out in their full extent. Whether they are sufficient or not to meet the actual state of things on the Canadian frontier *it is for Congress to decide.*" (Van Buren, 1838)

"*My conviction of the necessity of further legislative provisions* for the safekeeping and disbursement of the public moneys and my opinion in regard to the measures best adapted to the accomplishment of those objects have been already submitted to you." (Van Buren, 1838)

"Our laws *should* also follow them, so modified as the circumstances of the case may seem to require." (Tyler, 1843)

"*Should* a revision of the tariff with a view to revenue become necessary in the estimation of Congress, *I doubt not you will approach the subject with a just and enlightened regard to the interests of the whole Union.*" (Tyler, 1843)

"The reasons which *induced me to recommend the measure* at that time still exist, and I again *submit the subject for your consideration* and *suggest the importance of early action upon it.*" (Polk, 1846)

"*It may be proper to provide* for the security of these important conquests *by making* an adequate appropriation for the purpose of erecting fortifications." (Polk, 1846)

"From a policy so sacred to humanity and so salutary in its effects upon our political system *we should* never be induced voluntarily to depart." (Polk, 1846)

"No American ship *can be* allowed to be visited or searched for the purpose of ascertaining the character of individuals on board." (Fillmore, 1851)

"Your *attention is again invited* to the question of reciprocal trade between the United States and Canada and other British possessions near our frontier." (Fillmore, 1851)

"The report of the Secretary of the Navy, herewith submitted, exhibits in full the naval operations of the past year, together with the present condition of the service, and it makes suggestions of further legislation, *to which your attention is invited.*" (Pierce, 1855)

"The considerations which led me *to call the attention of Congress* to that convention and induced the Senate to adopt the resolution referred to still continue in full force." (Pierce, 1855)

"Establish the rule, and all will look forward to it and govern themselves accordingly. But justice to the people of the several States *requires that this rule should be established by Congress.*" (Buchanan, 1858)

"I entertain no doubt that indemnity is fairly due to these claimants under our treaty with Spain of October 27, 1795; and whilst demanding justice we ought to do justice. *An appropriation promptly made for this purpose could not fail* to exert a favorable influence on our negotiations with Spain." (Buchanan, 1858)

"The act passed at the last session for the encouragement of immigration has so far as was possible been put into operation. *It seems to need amendment* which will enable the officers of the Government to prevent the practice of frauds against the immigrants while on their way and on their arrival in the ports, so as to secure them here a free choice of avocations and places of settlement." (Lincoln, 1864)

"With this view *I suggest whether it might not be both competent and expedient for Congress to provide* that a limited amount of some future issue of public securities might be held by any bona fide purchaser exempt from taxation and from seizure for debt." (Lincoln, 1864)

"*It needs no argument* to show that legislation which has produced such baneful consequences should be abrogated." (Johnson, 1868)

"These startling facts clearly *illustrate the necessity* of retrenchment in all branches of the public service." (Johnson, 1868)

"In either event *it is your duty* to heed the lesson and *to provide* by wise and well-considered legislation, as far as it lies in your power, against its recurrence, and to take advantage of all benefits that may have accrued." (Grant, 1873)

"*I invite Congress now* to mark out and define when and how expatriation can be accomplished." (Grant, 1873)

"*It is desirable* to have these claims also examined and disposed of." (Grant, 1873)

"The reasons are *imperative for* the adoption of fixed rules for the regulation of appointments." (Hayes, 1880)

"*I trust the House of Representatives and the Senate*, which have the right to judge of the elections, returns, and qualifications of their own members, *will see to it* that every case of violation of the letter or spirit of the fifteenth amendment is thoroughly investigated." (Hayes, 1880)

"Its members have shown their public spirit by accepting their trust without pledge of compensation, but *I trust that Congress* will see in the national and international bearings of the matter a sufficient motive for providing at least for reimbursement of such expenses as they may necessarily incur." (Arthur, 1883)

"The convention for the resurvey of the boundary from the Rio Grande to the Pacific having been ratified and exchanged, the preliminary reconnaissance therein stipulated has been effected. *It now rests with Congress to make* provision for completing the survey." (Arthur, 1883)

"A just and sensible revision of our tariff laws *should be made* for the relief of those of our countrymen who suffer under present conditions." (Cleveland, 1888)

"The precise relocation of our boundary line *is needful*." (Cleveland, 1888)

"*I again urge* that national banks be authorized to organize with a capital of $25,000." (McKinley, 1899)

"Whatever power the Congress possesses over this most important subject *should be promptly ascertained and asserted*." (McKinley, 1899)

"*Let us* remove the only remaining cause by conferring the full and necessary power on the Secretary of the Treasury." (McKinley, 1899)

"*In my judgment the most important legislative act now needed* as regards the regulation of corporations is this act to confer on the Interstate Commerce Commission the power to revise rates and regulations." (Theodore Roosevelt, 1904)

"The ever-increasing casualty list upon our railroads is a matter of grave public concern, and *urgently calls for action by the Congress.*" (Teddy Roosevelt, 1904)

"The enlargement of scope of the functions of the National Government required by our development as a nation involves, of course, increase of expense; and the period of prosperity through which the country is passing *justifies expenditures* for permanent improvements far greater than would be wise in hard times." (Theodore Roosevelt, 1904)

"In completion of this work, the regulations agreed upon *require congressional legislation* to make them effective and for their enforcement in fulfillment of the treaty stipulations." (Taft, 1910)

"*I am strongly convinced that we need* in this Government just such an office, and that it can be secured by making the Tariff Board already appointed a permanent tariff commission." (Taft, 1910)

"Proper protection *necessitates*, as the Secretary points out, the expenditure of a good deal more money in the development of roads and trails in the forests." (Taft, 1910)

"*I take it for granted* that the Congress will carry out the naval programme which was undertaken before we entered the war." (Wilson, 1918)

"For the steadying, and facilitation of our own domestic business readjustments *nothing is more important* than the immediate determination of the taxes that are to be levied for 1918, 1919, and 1920." (Wilson, 1918)

"But the Congress *can make* available to the farmer the financial facilities which have been built up under Government aid." (Harding, 1922)

"*Special provision must be made* for live-stock production credits." (Harding, 1922)

"Let us pass for the moment the menace in the possible paralysis of such service as we have and *note the failure*, for whatever reason, *to expand* our transportation to meet the Nation's needs." (Harding, 1922)

"To meet these responsibilities *we need* a very substantial sea armament." (Coolidge, 1927)

"*We ought to* lend our encouragement in any way we can for more good roads to all the principal points in this hemisphere south of the Rio Grande." (Coolidge, 1927)

"*Legislation is desirable* for the construction of a dam at Boulder Canyon on the Colorado River, primarily as a method of flood control and irrigation." (Coolidge, 1927)

"The policy is well established that the Government *should* open public highways on land and on water, but for use of the public in their private capacity." (Coolidge, 1927)

"*It is my view* that the amount of taxation *should be* fixed so as to balance the Budget for 1933 except for the statutory debt retirement." (Hoover, 1931)

"Particular attention *should be given* to the industries rounded upon natural resources." (Hoover, 1931)

"To raise the purchasing power of the farmer is, however, not enough. It will not stay raised *if we do not also* raise the purchasing power of that third of the Nation which receives its income from industrial employment." (FDR, 1938)

"In regard to the relationship of government to certain processes of business, to which I have referred, it seems clear to me that existing laws *undoubtedly require* reconstruction." (FDR, 1938)

"On only one point do most of them have a suggestion. They think that relief for the unemployed by the giving of work is wasteful, and when I pin them down I discover that at heart they are actually in favor of substituting a dole in place of useful work. *To that neither I nor, I am confident, the Senators and Representatives in the Congress will ever consent.*" (FDR, 1938)

"Our minimum wages *are* far too low." (Truman, 1949)

"Moreover, *we need—and we must have without further delay*—a system of prepaid medical insurance which will enable every American to afford good medical care." (Truman, 1949)

"But it is particularly important to our planning that *we make* a candid estimate of the effect of long-range ballistic missiles on the present deterrent power I have described." (Eisenhower, 1958)

"While some increase in Government funds will be required, *it remains our objective* to encourage shifting to the use of private capital sources as rapidly as possible." (Eisenhower, 1958)

"Nearly three-fourths of our citizens live in urban areas, which occupy only 2 percent of our land-and if local transit is to survive and relieve the congestion of these cities, it *needs* Federal stimulation and assistance." (JFK, 1963)

"*I believe that* the abandonment of the mentally ill and the mentally retarded to the grim mercy of custodial institutions too often inflicts on them and on their families a needless cruelty which this Nation should not endure." (JFK, 1963)

"I have come tonight *to propose that we establish* a new department—a Department of Business and Labor." (LBJ, 1967)

"*I will ask that you* raise the minimum payments by 59 percent—from $44 to $70 a month." (LBJ, 1967)

"*It is vital* that the authorities contained in the trade bill I submitted to the Congress *be enacted* so that the United States can negotiate flexibly and vigorously on behalf of American interests." (Nixon, 1974)

"*We will establish* a new system that makes high-quality health care available to every American in a dignified manner and at a price he can afford." (Nixon, 1974)

"To supplement these proposals, *I ask that Congress* enact changes in Federal tax laws that will speed up plant expansion." (Ford, 1976)

"In the near future, I will take actions to reform and strengthen our intelligence community. *I ask for your positive cooperation.*" (Ford, 1976)

"And *I'm asking the Congress* specifically to reaffirm this agreement." (Carter, 1980)

"For this reason, *I have determined that* the Selective Service System must now be revitalized." (Carter, 1980)

"*We could focus* on some of the less contentious spending cuts that are still pending before the Congress." (Reagan, 1984)

"*I will continue to* press for tuition tax credits to expand opportunities for families and to soften the double payment for those paying public school taxes and private school tuition." (Reagan, 1984)

"And to help us support them *we need* a tough crime control legislation, and *we need* it now." (GHW Bush, 1991)

"So tonight *I am asking the Congressional leaders* and the Federal Reserve to cooperate with us in a study, led by Chairman Alan Greenspan, to sort out our technical differences so that we can avoid a return to unproductive partisan bickering." (GHW Bush, 1991)

"*Let us* pursue an S.D.I. program that can deal with any future threat to the United States, to our forces overseas and to our friends and allies." (GHW Bush, 1991)

"*I also ask this Congress to* support our efforts to enlist colleges and universities to reach out to disadvantaged children starting in the sixth grade so that they can get the guidance and hope they need so they can know that they, too, will be able to go on to college." (Clinton 1998)

"But whether the issue is tax cuts or spending, *I ask all of you* to meet this test: approve only those priorities that can actually be accomplished without adding a dime to the deficit." (Clinton, 1998)

"I also want to thank Congress for restoring some of the benefits to immigrants who are here legally and working hard. *And I hope you will finish that job this year.*" (Clinton, 1998)

"You and I serve our country in a time of great consequence. During this session of Congress, *we have the duty* to reform domestic programs vital to our country." (GW Bush, 2003)

"*Join me* in this important innovation *to make* our air significantly cleaner, and our country much less dependent on foreign sources of energy." (GW Bush, 2003)

Appendix C: Specific Words Counted/Variables Tested in Content Analysis

"we"
"our"
"you/r"
"us"
"America/n/s"
"American People"
"fellow"
"everyone"
"citizens"
"public"
"people"
"person"
"Community"
"senior/s"
"elderly"
"child/ren"
"parent/s"
"troop/s"
"soldier/s"
"taxpayer/s"
"tax/es"
"welfare"
"family"
"must"

BIBLIOGRAPHY

Andrews, James R. 2002. "Presidential Leadership and National Identity: Woodrow Wilson and the Meaning of America," In Leroy G. Dorsey, ed., *The Presidency and Rhetorical Leadership*. College Station, TX: Texas A&M University Press.

Aristotle. 1984. "The Rhetoric," In Edward Corbett (ed.) *The Rhetoric and The Poetics of Aristotle*. New York: The Modern Library.

Barber, James David. 1992. *The Presidential Character: Predicting Performance in the White House*. New Jersey: Prentice Hall.

Beasley, Vanessa B. 2001. (a) "Making Diversity Safe for America: American Pluralism and the Presidential Local Address, 1885-1992," In *The Quarterly Journal of Speech*. Vol. 87, No. 1, February, pp. 25-40.

Beasley, Vanessa B. 2001 (b) "The Rhetoric of Ideological Consensus in the United States: American Principles and American Pose in Presidential Inaugurals," In *Communication Monographs*. Vol. 68, No. 2, June 2001: pp. 169-183.

Beasley, Vanessa. 2004. *You the People: American National Identity in Presidential Rhetoric*. College Station, TX: Texas A&M University Press.

Benoit, William L. 1999. "Acclaiming, Attacking, and Defending in Presidential Nominating Acceptance Addresses, 1960-1996," In *The Quarterly Journal of Speech*. 85: 247-267.

Berman, Larry. 1987. *The New American Presidency*. Boston: Little, Brown, 1987: p 339.

Bimes, Terri and Quinn Mulroy. 2002. "Breaking Down the Modern/Traditional Divide: Presidential Rhetoric in the 19th Century," Paper delivered at the American Political Science Association Meeting, Boston, Aug 21-Sep 1.

Bimes, Terri and Stephen Skowronek. 1998. "Woodrow Wilson's Critique of Popular Leadership: Reassessing the Modern-Traditional Divide in Presidential History," in *Speaking to the People: The Rhetorical Presidency in Historical Perspective*, ed. Richard Ellis. Amherst: University of Massachusetts Press.

Bizzell, Patricia and Bruce Herzberg eds. 1990. *The Rhetorical Tradition: Readings from Classical Times to the Present*. Boston: Bedford Books.

Brace, Paul and Barbara Hinckley. 1991. "The Structure of Presidential Approval: Constraints Within and Across Presidencies," *Journal of Politics*. Vol. 53, No. 4, pp. 993-1017.

Caesar, James, Glen Thurow, Jeffrey Tulis, and Joseph Bessette. 1981. "The Rise of the Rhetorical Presidency," in *Presidential Studies Quarterly*. Spring, pp 158-171.

Campbell, Karlyn Kohrs, and Kathleen Hall Jamieson. 1985. "Inaugurating the Presidency," in *Presidential Studies Quarterly*. 15: 394-411.

Campbell, Karlyn Kohrs, and Kathleen Hall Jamieson. 1990. *Deeds Done in Words: Presidential Rhetoric and the Genres of Governance*. Chicago: University of Chicago Press.

Campbell, Karlyn Kohrs. 1996. "The Rhetorical Presidency: A Two-Person Career," In Martin J. Medhurst, ed., *Beyond the Rhetorical Presidency*. College Station, TX: Texas A&M University Press.

Carley, Kathleen. 1993. "Coding Choices for Textual Analysis: A Comparison of Content Analysis and Map Analysis," In *Sociological Methodology*. 23: 75-126.

Carney, Thomas F. 1972. *Content Analysis: A Technique for Systematic Inference from Communications*. Winnipeg: University of Manitoba Press.

Cohen, Jeffrey. 1995. "Presidential Rhetoric and the Public Agenda," *American Journal of Political Science*. 31: 87-107.

Corcoran, Paul E. 1979. *Political Language and Rhetoric*. St. Lucia, Queensland: University of Queensland Press.

Crigler, Ann N., ed. 1996. *The Psychology of Political Communication*. Ann Arbor: the University of Michigan Press.

Crockett, David A. 2002. *The Opposition Presidency: Leadership and the Constraints of History*. College Station: Texas A&M University Press.

Cunliffe, Marcus. 1971. "Elections of 1789 and 1792," in The History of American Presidential Elections. Arthur Schlesinger Jr. and Fred Israel, eds. New York: Chelsea House, pp. 3-32.

Dahl, Robert. 1990. "Myth of the Presidential Mandate," *Political Science Quarterly*. 105: 355-372.

Dayan, D. and E. Katz. 1992. *Media Events: The Live Broadcasting of History*. Cambridge: Harvard University Press.

Dolan, Frederick M., and Thomas L. Dumm, eds. 1993. *Rhetorical Republic: Governing Representations in American Politics*. Amherst: University of Massachusetts Press.

Bibliography 219

Dorsey, Leroy G. 2002. "Introduction," In Leroy G. Dorsey, ed., *The Presidency and Rhetorical Leadership*. College Station, TX: Texas A&M University Press.

Edwards III, George C. 1983. *The Public Presidency: The Pursuit of Popular Support*. New York: St. Martins Press.

Edwards III, George C. 1996. "Presidential Rhetoric: What Difference Does it Make?" In Martin J. Medhurst, ed., *Beyond the Rhetorical Presidency*. College Station, TX: Texas A&M University Press.

Edwards III, George C. 2003. *On Deaf Ears: The Limits of the Bully Pulpit*. New Haven: Yale University Press.

Edwards III, George C., and Stephen J. Wayne. 1983. *Studying the Presidency*. Knoxville: University of Tennessee Press.

Edwards III, George C., and Stephen J. Wayne. 1999. *Presidential Leadership*. New York: Worth Publishers.

Edwards III, George C., and Stephen J. Wayne. 1983. *Studying the Presidency*. Knoxville: University of Tennessee Press.

Edwards III, George C., John H. Kessel, and Bert A. Rockman eds. 1993. *Researching the Presidency : Vital Questions, New Approaches*. Pittsburgh : University of Pittsburgh Press.

Ellis, Richard and Stephen Kirk. 1998. "Jefferson, Jackson, and the Origins of the Political Mandate," In Richard Ellis, ed. *Speaking to the People: The Rhetorical Presidency in Historical Perspective*. Amherst: University of Massachusetts Press.

Ellis, Richard. 1998. "Accepting the Nomination: From Martin Van Buren to Franklin Delano Roosevelt," In Richard Ellis, ed. *Speaking to the People: The Rhetorical Presidency in Historical Perspective*. Amherst: University of Massachusetts Press.

Fields, Wayne. 1996. *Union of Words: A History of Presidential Eloquence*. New York: The Free Press.

Foster, James and Susan Leeson. 1998. *Constitutional Law: Cases In Context, Volume II: Civil Rights and Civil Liberties*. New Jersey: Prentice Hall, 1998: p. 1134.

Gamm, Gerald and Renee Smith. 1998. "Presidents, Parties, and the Public: Evolving Patterns of Interaction, 1877-1929." In Richard Ellis, ed. *Speaking to the People: The Rhetorical Presidency in Historical Perspective*. Amherst: University of Massachusetts Press.

Geis, Michael L. *The Language of Politics*. New York: Springer-Verlag, 1987.

Gelderman, Carol. 1997. *All the Presidents' Words: The Bully Pulpit and the Creation of the Virtual Presidency.* New York: Walker and Company.

Genovese, Michael A. 2001. *The Power of the American Presidency, 1789-2000.* New York: Oxford University Press.

Gleiber, Dennis and Steven Shull. 1999. "Justifying Presidential Decisions: The Scope of Veto Messages," in *Congress & the Presidency.* Washington: Spring, Vol. 26, Iss. 1, pp. 41-60.

Graber, Doris A. 1996. "Whither Research on the Psychology of Political Communication?" In Crigler, Ann N., ed. *The Psychology of Political Communication.* Ann Arbor: the University of Michigan Press.

Greenstein, Fred, Larry Berman, and Alvin S. Felzenberg. 1977. *Evolution of the Modern Presidency: A Bibliographical Survey.* Washington D.C.: American enterprise Institute.

Greenstein, Fred. 1978. "Change and Continuity in the Modern Presidency," In Anthony King, ed. *The New American Political System.* Washington D.C.: American Enterprise Institute.

Greenstein, Fred. 1982. *The Hidden Hand Presidency.* New York: Basic Books.

Greenstein, Fred. 1988. *Leadership in the Modern Presidency.* Cambridge: Harvard University Press.

Greenstein, Fred. 2000. *The Presidential Difference: Leadership Style from FDR to Bill Clinton.* New York: Martin Kessles Books/ Free Press.

Greenstein, Fred. 2006. "Presidential Difference in the Early Republic: The Highly Disparate Leadership Styles of Washington, Adams, and Jefferson," *Presidential Studies Quarterly.* 36: 373-388.

Gusfield, Joeseph R. and Jerry Michalowicz. 1984. "Secular Symbolism: Studies of Ritual, Ceremony, and the Symbolic Order in Modern Life," In *The Annual Review of Sociology.* 10: 417-435.

Hacker, Kenneth L. 1996. "Political Linguistic Discourse Analysis: Analyzing the Relationships of Power and Language," In Stuckey, Mary E., ed. *The Theory and Practice of Communications Research.* Albany: State University Press of New York, pp. 28-55.

Hart, Roderick P., Deborah Smith-Howell, and John Llewellyn. 1996. "News, Psychology, and Presidential Politics," In Crigler, Ann N., ed. *The Psychology of Political Communication.* Ann Arbor: the University of Michigan Press.

Hart, Roderick. 1987. *The Sound of Leadership.* Chicago: University of Chicago Press.

Hart, Roderick. 1984. *Verbal Style and the Presidency*. Orlando: Academic Press.

Henderson, Philip G. 2000. *The Presidency Then and Now*. New York: Rowman and Littlefield Publishers, Inc.

Hermanowicz, Joseph C. and Harriet P. Morgan. 1999 "Ritualizing the Routine: Collective Identity Affirmation," In *Sociological Forum*. 14: 197-214.

Hill, Kim Quaile. 1998. "The Policy Agendas of the President and the Mass Public: A Research Validation and Extension," *American Journal of Political Science*. Vol. 42, No. 4, Oct, pp. 1328-1334.

Hinckley, Barbara. 1990. *The Symbolic Presidency: How Presidents Portray Themselves*. New York: Routledge.

Hoffman, Donna R. and Alison D. Howard. 2006. *Addressing the State of the Union: The Evolution and Impact of the President's Big Speech*. Boulder: Lynne Rienner.

Houck, Davis W. 2001. *Rhetoric as Currency: Hoover, Roosevelt, and the Great Depression*. College Station, TX: Texas A&M University Press.

Howell, William G. 2003. *Power Without Persuasion: The Politics of Direct Presidential Action*. Princeton: Princeton University Press.

Kalb, Deborah, Gerthard Peters and John Woolley, eds. 2006. *State of the Union: Presidential Rhetoric from Woodrow Wilson to George W. Bush*. Washington D.C.: CQ Press.

Kelly, Alfred Hinsey. 1983. *The American Constitution: Its Origins and Development*. 6th ed. New York: Norton.

Kernell, Samuel. 1997. *Going Public: New Strategies of Presidential Leadership*, 3rd ed. Washington D.C.: Congressional Quarterly Inc.

King, Gary, Paul S. Hernson, Walter J. Stove. 1995. "Replication, Replication," In *PS, Political Science and Politics*. 28: 444-452.

King, Gary. 1993. "The Methodology of Presidential Research," In Edwards et al, eds. *Researching the Presidency: Vital Questions, New Approaches*. Pittsburgh: University of Pittsburgh Press.

Krause, George A. and David B. Cohen. 1997. "Presidential Use of Executive Orders, 1953-1994," In *American Politics Quarterly*. 25: 458-481.

Krippendorff, Klaus. 1980. *Content Analysis: An Introduction to its Methodology*. London: Sage Publications.

Kumar, Martha Joynt. 2001. "The Contemporary Presidency: The Pressures of White House Work Life: 'Naked in a Glass House,'" In *Presidential Studies Quarterly*. Vol. 31, No. 4, December, pp. 708-719.\

Landy, Marc, ed. 1985. *Modern Presidents and the Presidency*. Lexington, Massachusetts: Lexington Books.

Laracey, Mel. 2002. *Presidents and the People: The Partisan Story of Going Public*. College Station, TX: Texas A & M University Press.

Levy, Michael B. ed. 1988. *Political Thought in America*. Prospect Heights, Illinois: Waveland Press, Inc.

Liebovich, Louis W. 2001. *The Press and the Modern Presidency: Myths and Mindsets from Kennedy to Election 2000*. Westport, Connecticut: Praeger.

Light, Paul C. 1999. *The President's Agenda: Domestic Policy Choice from Kennedy to Clinton*. Baltimore: Johns Hopkins University Press.

Lim, Elvin T. 2002. "Five trends in presidential rhetoric: An analysis of rhetoric from George Washington to Bill Clinton," In *Presidential Studies Quarterly*. Washington. 32: 328-366.

Lorenzo, David. 1996. "Political Communication and the Study of Rhetoric: Persuasion from the Standpoint of Literary Theory and Anthropology," In Stuckey, Mary E., ed. *The Theory and Practice of Communications Research*. Albany: State University Press of New York, 1996; pp. 1-27.

Lowi, Theodore. 1985. *The Personal President: Power Invested, Promise Unfulfilled*. Ithaca: Cornell University Press.

Lucas, Stephen E. 2002. "George Washington and the Rhetoric of Presidential Leadership," In Leroy G. Dorsey, ed., *The Presidency and Rhetorical Leadership*. College Station, TX: Texas A&M University Press.

Malone, Dumas, Arthur Schlesinger Jr., Norman Graebner et al. 1987. *Rhetoric and the Founders*. New York: University Press of America.

Mayer, Kenneth R. 2001. *With the Stroke of a Pen: Executive Orders and Presidential Power*. Princeton: Princeton University Press.

McConnell, Grant. 1967. *The Modern Presidency*. New York: St. Martin's Press.

McGee, Michael Calvin. 1998. "Formal Discursive Theories," In Carol Corbin, ed. *Rhetoric in Postmodern America: Conversations with Michael Calvin McGee*. New York: The Guilford Press, pp. 27-62.

McGee, Michael Calvin. 1998. "The People," In Carol Corbin, ed., *Rhetoric in Postmodern America: Conversations with Michael Calvin McGee*. New York: The Guilford Press, pp. 115-136.

McNair, Brian. 1995. *An Introduction to Political Communication, Second edition*. New York: Routledge.

Medhurst, Martin J. 1996a. "A Tale of Two Constructs: The Rhetorical Presidency Versus Presidential Rhetoric," In Martin J. Medhurst, ed., *Beyond the Rhetorical Presidency*. College Station, TX: Texas A&M University Press.

Medhurst, Martin J. 1996b. "Afterword: The Ways of Rhetoric," In Martin J. Medhurst, ed., *Beyond the Rhetorical Presidency*. College Station, TX: Texas A&M University Press.

Medhurst, Martin J., ed. 1996. *Beyond the Rhetorical Presidency*. College Station, TX: Texas A&M University Press.

Milkis, Sidney. 1998. "Franklin D. Roosevelt, Progressivism and the Limits of Popular Leadership," In Richard Ellis, ed., *Speaking to the People: The Rhetorical Presidency in Historical Perspective*. Amherst: University of Massachusetts Press.

Negrine, Ralph. 1996. *The Communication of Politics*. Thousand Oaks, CA: Sage Publications.

Neuman, W. Russell, Marion R. Just, and Ann N. Crigler. 1992. *Common Knowledge: News and the Constructing of Political Meaning*. Chicago: The University of Chicago Press.

Neustadt, Richard. 1960. *Presidential Power: The Politics of Leadership*. New York: Wiley.

Nichols, David. 1994. *The Myth of the Modern Presidency*. University Park, Pennsylvania: The Pennsylvania State University Press.

Parry-Giles, Treveor and Shawn J. Parry-Giles. 2001. "Reassessing the State of Political Communication in the United States," In *Argumentation and Advocacy*. Vol. 37, No. 3, Winter, pp. 158-170.

Peabody, Bruce G. 2001. "George Washington, Presidential Term Limits, and the Problem of Reluctant Political Leadership," In *Presidential Studies Quarterly*. Vol. 31, No. 3, September, pp. 439-53.

Peterson, Mark A. 1990. *Legislating Together: The White House and Capitol Hill from Eisenhower to Reagan*. Cambridge: Harvard University Press.

Pfiffner, James P. 2000. *The Modern Presidency, third edition*. New York: Bedford/St. Martins.

Polsby, Nelson, ed. 1973. *The Modern Presidency*. New York: University Press of America.

Powell, Richard. 1999. "'Going Public' Revisited: Presidential Speechmaking and the Bargaining Setting in Congress," *Congress and the Presidency*. 26: 153-170.

Quaile Hill, Kim. 1998. "The Policy Agendas of the President and the Mass Public: A Research Validation and Extension," In *American Journal of Political Science*. 42: 1328-1335.

Ragsdale, Lyn. 1987. "Presidential Speechmaking and the Public Audience: Individual Presidents and Group Attitudes," *Journal of Politics*. Vol. 49, No. 3, Aug, pp. 704-736.

Reid, Ronald. 1995. *American Political Discourse*. 2nd edition. Prospect Heights, IL: Waveland Press.

Relyea, Harold C. 2007 *Presidential Directives: Background and Overview*. Washington: Congressional Research Service. www.fas.org/sgp/crs/misc/98-611.pdf

Remini, Robert. 1971. "The Election of 1828," in The History of American Presidential Elections. Arthur Schlesinger Jr. and Fred Israel, eds. New York: Chelsea House, p. 435.

Rodgers, Daniel. 1987. *Contested Truths: Keywords in American Politics and Independence*. Cambridge, MA: Harvard University Press.

Rozell, Mark J., and William D. Pederson, eds. 1997. *FDR and the Modern Presidency: Leadership and Legacy*. Westport, Connecticut: Praeger.

Ryan, Halford, ed. 1993. *The Inaugural Addresses of Twentieth-Century American Presidents*. Westport, CN: Praeger Publishers.

Ryan, Halford, ed. 1995. *U.S. Presidents as Orators: A Bio-Critical Sourcebook*. Westport, Connecticut: Greenwood Press.

Ryan, Halford. 1988. *Franklin D. Roosevelt's Rhetorical Presidency*. New York: Greenwood Press.

Ryfe, David Michael. 1999. "Franklin Roosevelt and the Fireside Chats," In *The Journal of Communication*. Vol. 49, No. 4, December: pp. 80-103.

Schlesinger, Arthur M., Jr. 1997. "Rating the Presidents: Washington to Clinton," in *Political Science Quarterly*. Summer: pp. 179-89.

Schlesinger, Arthur M., Jr. 1973. *The Imperial Presidency*. Boston: Houghton Mifflin Company.

Schlesinger, Arthur M., Jr. 1959. *The Coming of the New Deal*. Boston: Houghton-Mifflin.

Bibliography

Schlesinger, Arthur M., Jr., ed. 1971. *The History of American Presidential Elections, Volume 1, 1789-1844.* New York: Chelsea House.

Schmidt, Leigh Eric. 1991. "The Commercialization of the Calendar: American Holidays and the Culture of Consumption," In *The Journal of American History.* 28: 887-916.

Seymore-Use, Colin. 1982. *The American President: Power and Communication.* New York: St. Martin's Press.

Shaw, Malcom, ed. 1987. *The Modern Presidency: From Roosevelt to Reagan.* New York: Harper and Row Publishers.

Shogan, Colleen. 2003. "Rhetorical Moralism in the Plebiscitary Presidency: New Speech Forms and Their Ideological Entailments." *Studies in American Political Development.* 17: 149-167.

Skrownek, Stephen. 1997. *The Politics Presidents Make: Leadership from John Adams to Bill Clinton.* Cambridge, Massachusetts: The Belknap Press of Harvard University Press.

Smith, Craig Allen and Kathy B. Smith, eds. 1985. *The President and the Public: Rhetoric and National Leadership.* New York: The University Press of America.

Smith, Craig Allen and Kathy B. Smith. 1990. "The Rhetoric of Political Institutions," In David L. Swanson and Dan Nimmo, eds., *New Directions in Political Communication: A Resource Book.* Newbury Park, CA: Sage Publications.

Smith, Craig Allen and Kathy B. Smith. 1994. *The White House Speaks: Presidential Leadership as Persuasion.* Westport, CN: Praeger Publishers.

Stuckey, Mary E. 1996. "Introduction," In Stuckey, Mary E., ed. *The Theory and Practice of Communications Research.* Albany: State University Press of New York.

Stuckey, Mary E. 1997. *Strategic Failures in the Modern Presidency.* Cresskill, New Jersey: Hampton press, Inc.

Stuckey, Mary E. 1996. "Conclusion: Implications for the Future of Political Communication Research," In Stuckey, Mary E., ed. *The Theory and Practice of Communications Research.* Albany: State University Press of New York, pp. 224-229.

Stuckey, Mary E. 1996. "Presidential Rhetoric in Political Time," In Stuckey, Mary E., ed. *The Theory and Practice of Communications Research.* Albany: State University Press of New York, pp. 122-141.

Stuckey, Mary E., ed. 1996. *The Theory and Practice of Communications Research.* Albany: State University Press of New York.

Swanson, David L., and Dan Nimmo, eds. 1990. *New Directions in Political Communication: A Resource Book.* London: Sage Publications.

Teten, Ryan Lee. 2003. "Evolution of the Modern Rhetorical Presidency: Presidential Presentation and Development of the State of the Union Addresses," In *Presidential Studies Quarterly*. 33: 333-346.

Teten, Ryan Lee. 2007. " 'We the People:' The 'Modern' Rhetorical Popular Address of the Presidents during the Founding Period," In *Political Research Quarterly*. 60: 669-682.

Thompson, Kenneth W. 1987. *To Form or Preserve a Government: The Presidency, Congress, and Public Discourse*. New York: The University Press of America, 1987.

Thurow, Glen E. 1996. "Dimensions of Presidential Character," In Medhurst, Martin J., ed. *Beyond the Rhetorical Presidency*. College Station, TX: Texas A&M University Press.

Tulis, Jeffrey. 1987. *The Rhetorical Presidency*. Princeton: Princeton University Press.

Tulis, Jeffrey. 1996. "Revising the Rhetorical Presidency," In Martin J. Medhurst, ed., *Beyond the Rhetorical Presidency*. College Station, TX: Texas A&M University Press.

Tulis, Jeffrey. 1998. "Reflections on the Rhetorical Presidency in American Political Development," In Richard Ellis, ed., *Speaking to the People: The Rhetorical Presidency in Historical Perspective*. Amherst: University of Massachusetts Press.

Valls, Andrew. 2006. "Presidential Rhetoric: A Social Constructionist Approach," In Stuckey, Mary E., ed. *The Theory and Practice of Communications Research*. Albany: State University Press of New York, 1996; pp. 142-158.

Warber, Adam L. 2006. *Executive Orders and the Modern Presidency: Legislating from the Oval Office*. Boulder: Lynne Rienner.

Watts, Duncan. 1997. *Political Communication Today*. New York: Manchester University Press.

Wilson, John. 1990. *Politically Speaking: The Pragmatic Analysis of Political Language*. Oxford: Basil Blackwell.

Zarefsky, David. 2002. "The Presidency Has Always Been a Place for Rhetorical Leadership," In Leroy Dorsey, ed., *The Presidency and Rhetorical Leadership*. College Station, TX: Texas A&M University Press.

Zernicke, Paul Haskell. 1994. *Pitching the Presidency: How Presidents Depict the Office*. Westport Connecticut: Praeger.

INDEX

A

Adams, John · 16, 18, 48, 71, 73, 88, 116, 124, 125, 195
Adams, John Quincy · 23, 36, 107, 111, 116, 207
Aristotle · 20, 43
Arthur, Chester A. · 9, 36, 71, 73, 81, 87, 151, 160, 194, 196, 200, 210
authority rhetoric · 37, 38, 40, 41, 46, 70, 71-79, 81-87, 90, 102

B

Beasley, Vanessa · 7, 12, 14, 34, 38, 39, 40
Buchanan, James · 36, 84, 98-100, 103, 179, 200, 209
Bush, George H.W. · 10, 55, 56, 71-73, 88, 91-93, 131, 175, 177, 178, 214
Bush, George W. · 1, 2, 5, 7, 18, 23, 27, 28, 39, 41, 52, 56, 62-64, 68, 71, 79, 84, 88, 89, 91-95, 121, 127, 138, 146, 147, 161, 163, 164, 172, 175, 177, 178, 188, 192, 215

C

Campbell, Karlyn Kohrs and Jamieson, Kathleen Hall · 3, 17, 199
Carley, Kathleen · 25
Carter, Jimmy · 10, 11, 71, 91, 92, 113, 177, 178, 214
Clay, Henry · 84, 101, 108
Cleveland, Grover · 36, 55, 103, 105, 137, 146, 151, 175, 176, 179, 210
Clinton, Bill · 10, 18, 36, 52, 53, 56, 73, 78, 79, 81, 88-90, 175, 177, 178, 215
Cohen, Jeffrey · 8, 12, 19, 21
congressional address words · 35
Coolidge, Calvin · 16, 18, 55, 58, 59, 62, 71, 78, 84, 103, 157, 178, 181, 183, 195, 212
Cunliffe, Marcus · 3

D

Declaration of Independence · 42, 45, 46
directive rhetoric · 37, 38, 46, 87-95, 97-102
Dorsey, Leroy · 7, 13, 32, 40

E

Edwards, George C. and Wayne, Stephen J. · 9
Eisenhower, Dwight · 8, 36, 71, 78, 82, 83, 175, 213
ethos · 20, 42, 43, 45, 46
Executive Orders · 5, 7, 15, 18, 19, 23, 27, 84, 85, 103, 149, 163, 164, 184, 186, 188, 195

F

Fields, Wayne · 37, 38, 199
Fillmore, Millard · 59, 60, 73, 84, 87, 101, 103, 105, 208
Ford, Gerald · 36, 71-73, 88, 151, 178, 214

G

Gamm, Gerald and Smith, Renee · 8, 11
Garfield, James · 84, 101, 105
Gelderman, Carol · 6
Genovese, Martin · 104, 108, 109, 198
Grant, Ulysses S. · 71, 73, 75, 77, 135, 151, 177, 200, 209
Greenstein, Fred · 7, 8, 12, 14, 33, 103, 104, 109, 191, 193, 197, 198, 220

H

Hacker, Kenneth · 20, 21
Harding, Warren G. · 55, 58, 59, 62, 71, 87, 131, 134, 135, 151, 153, 154, 157, 172, 175-178, 181-183, 211, 212
Harrison, William Henry · 55, 81, 155
Hart, Roderick · 9, 21, 22, 31, 32, 40
Hayes, Rutherford B. · 36, 73, 84, 101, 175, 176, 185-187, 200, 210
Hermanowicz, Joseph · 69
Hoover, Herbert · 12, 55, 101, 103, 131-135, 151, 172, 194, 195, 212
Humphrey, Hubert · 31

I

identification rhetoric · 37-39, 42, 44-62, 69, 71, 74, 79, 86, 87, 90, 93, 102
Inaugural Address · 5, 7, 23, 27, 79, 86, 103, 171

J

Jackson, Andrew · 36, 60, 71, 73, 75, 76, 87, 98, 99, 101, 107, 108, 110- 112, 118, 160, 166, 178-181, 183, 207
Jefferson, Thomas · 16, 42-49, 65, 81, 88, 89, 91, 107, 115, 116, 123, 125, 126, 166, 171, 195-197, 205, 206
Johnson, Andrew · 101
Johnson, Lyndon · 36, 71-73, 88, 89, 108, 177, 195, 213

K

kairos · 45, 46
Kennedy, John F. · 36, 55, 71, 73, 91, 92, 108, 172, 175-177, 194, 213
Kernell, Samuel · 5, 8, 12, 14, 46
King, Gary · 15

L

Laracey, Mel · 7, 9, 13, 14, 17, 34, 103
Lim, Elvin · 7, 13
Lincoln, Abraham · 64, 68, 69, 73, 81, 87, 91, 101, 170, 175, 195, 209
logos · 20, 42, 43, 46
Lorenzo, David · 20

M

Machiavelli, Niccolo · 28
Madison, James · 49, 89, 115, 116, 179, 206
Massachusetts Spy · 17
McGee, Michael Calvin · 32, 39, 40
Milkis, Sidney · 8
Monroe, James · 47, 50, 111, 127-131, 174, 206

N

Neustadt, Richard · 5, 21
Nixon, Richard · 10, 36, 71, 73, 82, 83, 113, 178, 213, 214

O

Obama, Barack · 10

P

pathos · 20, 42-46
Pierce, Franklin · 18, 36, 59, 91-93, 140, 141, 148, 151, 175, 179, 208

Index

Polk, James · 9, 18, 36, 50, 59, 60, 61, 81, 101, 103, 105, 131, 140, 141, 148, 151, 153, 157, 160, 171-176, 181, 182, 194, 208
popular address · 2, 10, 26, 27, 33-38, 41, 42, 46, 47, 54, 56-58, 60, 61, 73, 76, 78-88, 90, 91, 95, 97, 100-105, 149, 160, 164, 184, 192, 194, 195, 199, 200
Presidential Proclamations · 5, 7, 15, 19, 23, 27, 102, 103, 136, 163, 177, 185, 188, 195

R

Reagan, Ronald · 36, 52, 53, 56, 71, 73, 81, 85, 86, 88, 89, 92, 108, 175, 177, 178, 214
Revolutionary War · 3, 189
Rodgers, Daniel · 31, 33, 38, 104
Roosevelt, Franklin Delano · 8, 12, 16, 36, 55, 71, 73, 81, 88, 108, 109, 122, 127, 133, 140, 141, 144, 148, 151, 155, 167, 169, 175, 176, 193, 194, 198, 200, 201, 212, 213
Roosevelt, Theodore · 8, 10-13, 24, 33, 54, 78, 81, 109, 119, 120-122, 125, 130, 161, 169, 194, 200

S

State of the Union Address · 1-3, 5, 7, 9, 14-21, 24, 25, 27, 33, 35, 36, 38, 39, 41, 47, 48-50, 52, 53, 58, 70-74, 79, 87-90, 94, 95, 104, 108, 110-128, 130, 132, 134, 158, 159, 163-171, 176, 182, 188, 194-196, 200, 203, 205
Stuckey, Mary · 8, 20-22

T

Taft, William Howard · 49, 50, 53, 58, 59, 62, 84, 112, 119-121, 125, 131, 134, 135, 140, 166, 169, 194, 200, 211
Taylor, Zachary · 36, 71, 73, 75, 77, 82, 151, 194, 200
terministic screen · 43

Thanksgiving · 58, 59, 61, 62, 64, 67-69, 83, 146, 179-183
Thurow, Glen · 21-23
"traditional/ modern" divide · 5, 17, 23, 26, 29, 33, 54, 59, 74, 75, 78, 79, 90, 97, 100, 101, 115, 123, 125, 139, 149, 155-159, 174-178, 187
Truman, Harry · 11, 16, 18, 36, 55, 71, 113, 172, 174, 175, 181, 213
Tulis, Jeffrey · 6, 8, 10-17, 21, 22, 26, 28, 32-34, 39, 40, 41, 50, 103, 109, 120, 126, 160, 164, 191, 193
Tyler, John · 59, 60, 87, 101, 140, 200, 208

V

Van Buren, Martin · 55, 75-77, 81, 87, 130, 131, 140, 171, 207
Virginia Dynasty · 116

W

Warber, Adam · 19
Washington, George · 2-5, 6, 7, 9, 13, 15-19, 22, 23, 27, 33, 37, 38, 47, 48, 58, 61-63, 65, 68, 71, 73, 74, 75, 79, 81, 88, 89, 90, 91, 92, 93, 102, 108, 111, 115, 125, 127, 135, 138, 147, 154, 160, 171, 175, 179, 189, 191, 192, 194, 195, 196, 205
Wilson, Woodrow · 6-8, 10-13, 16, 28, 31, 33, 34, 37, 48, 50-52, 62, 73, 81, 87, 103, 108, 112, 113, 121-125, 133, 140, 141, 148, 151, 168, 175-178, 181-183, 194, 195, 200, 211